Kenneth Cox

RHODODENDRONS
AND AZALEAS

a hamlyn care manual

HAMLYN

Publishing Director
Laura Bamford
Creative Director
Keith Martin
Executive Editor
Julian Brown
Executive Art Editor
Mark Winwood
Editor
Karen O'Grady
Designer
Ruth Hope
Production Controller
Julie Hadingham
Picture Researcher
Liz Fowler
Photography
Peter Myers
and Shaun Myers
Illustration
Fiona Fraser

First published in Great Britain
in 1998 by Hamlyn,
an imprint of Reed Consumer
Books Limited
Michelin House, 81 Fulham Road,
London SW3 6RB
and Auckland, Melbourne,
Singapore and Toronto

Produced by Toppan
Printed in China

Contents

Introduction

Left: The author's father Peter Cox on the Cangshan, Yunnan, China surrounded by the dwarf rhododendron species *R. cephalanthum* and *R. fastigiatum*

Right: The author in Pemako, S.E. Tibet holding a branch of the rare *R. cinnabarinum* ssp. *xanthocodon* 'Concatenans'

The word 'rhododendron' means different things to different people. Perhaps most familiar to inhabitants of the U.K. are the grand country houses with driveways lined with large old pink and purple flowered hybrid rhododendrons in late spring. In areas of Britain with a high rainfall in the south and west of the country, the word rhododendron produces the reaction 'weed' and 'pest'; here, getting rid of the invasive *Rhododendron ponticum* is a common task.

In North America, on both west and east coasts, wild rhododendrons and azaleas are found in forests and on mountains, as they are in the Alps of Europe. In Nepal and Tibet, the dried leaves of alpine varieties are used for incense in Buddhist temples. To the style gurus of gardening, rhododendrons are often frowned upon as an unfashionable plant, though of course they are planted and enjoyed by millions in gardens all over the world. And yet I am sure that a quick glance through the photographs in this book will reveal some surprises.

The genus *Rhododendron* includes an astounding variety of plant types with a range of flower shapes and colours that are second to none in the plant world. One of the things this book aims to do is to debunk the stereotypes associated with this enormous, astonishingly varied genus and, hopefully, to provide new ideas for enhancing the landscape with imaginative uses of this king of plants.

Rhododendrons come in all shapes and sizes and the genus includes all of the azaleas. Perhaps most familiar are the large, blowsy hybrids which are widely planted around country houses and stately homes.

In fact, these hardy hybrids form only a small proportion of the total picture. Many rhododendron species and hybrids have tiny leaves and only grow a few inches high. At the other end of the scale there are giants with leaves up to 1m (3ft) in length. Another part of the genus encompasses the tropical Vireya rhododendrons found in Indonesia and neighbouring areas. These need to be kept in greenhouses in all but the mildest climates.

My family has been long associated with rhododendron collecting and growing. My grandfather, Euan Cox, had his interest sparked off when he was invited to accompany the well-known plant hunter Reginald Farrer to Burma in 1919. Knowing virtually nothing about plants before he went on this expedition, he arrived back with considerable knowledge and spent the rest of his life in gardening related activities. He edited horticultural publications, wrote gardening columns and books on plants and gardening, in the process enthusing my father with whom he started a rhododendron nursery at Glendoick. My father, Peter Cox, V.M.H., is himself a nurseryman, plant-hunter, author and rhododendron hybridiser and I suppose that it was inevitable that I would follow in his footsteps.

Kenneth Cox

Where Do Rhododendrons Come From?

Rhododendrons belong to the family Ericaceae which also includes the heathers, *Kalmia*, *Enkianthus*, *Gaultheria*, blueberries and cranberries. What most of these plants have in common is their requirement for acid soil and a fair amount of moisture. Rhododendrons are found throughout much of the northern hemisphere and their distribution extends into the southern hemisphere through the Malay peninsula and the Indonesian islands, with a single species (some authorities claim two) on a mountain in northern Australia. The distribution of temperate rhododendrons, the kind commonly grown as garden plants in parts of the world with cold winters, centres on China and the Himalayas. There are several species native to Europe, while most of the deciduous azalea species come from North America. There are no species native to South America or Africa. The European species, such as the alpine *R. ferrugineum* and the sweetly scented pontic azalea *R. luteum*, have long been cultivated as garden plants and are referred to in both horticultural and medicinal literature of the sixteenth and seventeenth centuries. It was not until the introduction of species of azalea from America to Europe in the seventeenth and eighteenth century that rhododendrons began to be quite widely grown as garden plants. By 1800 there were around 12 species in cultivation in Europe, including the infamous *R. ponticum*. It

Right: Snow beds at 4000m (13,000ft) in the Th'Lonok valley, Sikkim, with rhododendrons in blossom (Kinchin-Junga in the distance) from Sir Joseph Hooker's Journal

Below: Joseph Hooker collecting plants for Kew Gardens in the Sikkim Himalaya, by Frank Stone, A.R.A.

was not long before hybidisers got to work on the raw material, trying to improve on nature. From 1810-1840 a range of hardy azalea hybrids known as the Ghents were developed, as well as the first so-called hardy hybrids such as 'Cunningham's White', raised at a nursery in Edinburgh and still one of the most popular hybrids today.

The next great breakthrough was the discovery and introduction of the first Himalayan rhododendrons. Joseph Hooker's expedition to Sikkim in 1850 collected 45 species, most newly described.

Many of these were soon recognised for their garden value and were in turn used to breed a huge range of hybrids. The Himalayan species included the blood-red *R. thomsonii* with rounded leaves and fine peeling bark, the tall and vigorous *R. griffithianum* with massive white flowers and the magnificent *R. falconeri* with large furry leaves and enormous trusses of creamy flowers. Suddenly, rhododendron species and hybrids were everywhere. No self-respecting country house was complete without beds of them incorporated into park landscapes. At the same time, and coinciding with the vogue for hothouses, tropical species

were introduced and many hybrids were raised. Alas, unlike their cold-hardy relatives, the tropical rhododendrons mostly met a sad end as heating was switched off during time of war and the great Victorian conservatories were abandoned. Recent years have seen a huge resurgence of interest in these tropical or Vireya rhododendrons, particularly in areas such as California, New Zealand and S.E. Australia where they can be grown outdoors.

The beginning of the twentieth century saw the introduction of evergreen azaleas from Japan to Europe and America and, more significantly, the opening up of China to foreign exploration. Following in the footsteps of French missionaries turned botanists, Ernest Wilson's first expedition to Hupeh province in 1899 introduced *R. auriculatum*, *R. maculiferum* and *R. sutchuenense*. He returned to China in 1903-4 and was followed by George Forrest in Yunnan in 1904, Frank Kingdon Ward in 1911 and Joseph Rock in 1920. These plant hunters sent back specimens and seeds of thousands of species of plants, including several hundred rhododendrons, which were duly described in herbaria at the British Museum or at botanic gardens such as the Arnold Arboretum, Edinburgh or Kew Gardens, London. Gardeners in Europe, the

United States and elsewhere grew the seeds on a huge scale. This was the era of the woodland garden, and great gardens such as Caerhays and Exbury in the UK were laid out, with their owners competing for awards at the exclusive gentleman's club that was The Rhododendron Society.

R. dalhousiae from the book Rhododendrons of the Sikkim Himalaya by Walter Fitch from field drawings in William Hooker's Journal, circa 1850

Some of the recently introduced species such as *R. griersonianum* and *R. wardii* soon proved to be excellent parents and many new hybrids of all shapes and sizes were produced. A number of the hybrids listed in the Plant Directory section, such as 'Loderi', 'Fabia', 'Vanessa', and 'Lady Chamberlain' were raised at this time.

The introduction of *R. yakushimanum*, a compact, hardy, easily grown species from Japan, in the early 1930s, proved to be another important breakthrough. This species became the most popular hybridising parent of all time, with many breeders

in the U.K., Germany and North America (and elsewhere) raising 'yak' hybrids, a range of low-growing, compact and hardy plants with showy flowers of many different shades. At Glendoick, Peter Cox began hybridising very dwarf varieties in the late 1950s and selections from this breeding programme, which continues today, are the well-known bird hybrids such as 'Curlew' and 'Ptarmigan'. China, and many of the other countries in the area, closed their doors to foreigners during the 1950s, 60s and 70s. Only a handful of new rhododendron species were introduced during this period. These included my parents' discovery *R. coxianum* from N.E. India, the wonderful *R. pachysanthum* from Taiwan and several species of Vireyas from Borneo and New Guinea.

China re-opened its borders in 1981 and my father, Peter Cox, who had waited 30 years for the chance, was on the first major expedition back into the stomping ground of his heroes from the early part of the century. The Sino-British Expedition to the Cangshan (in Yunnan) was the first of many

A magnificent mountain view in Pome, S.E. Tibet, taken on one of the author's expeditions, with the yellow R. wardii and the pinkish-purple R. calostrotum

which have explored and re-explored this extraordinarily plant-rich region of the world. Since 1981, many new plant species have been introduced, including several new species of rhododendron. Among the most important of these from the last few years are the giant *R. sinofalconeri* with yellow flowers and large leaves, the red species from the Yunnan/Sichuan border *R. ochraceum* and the neat, deep pink, dwarf species *R. dendrocharis.*

I have led several expeditions to South East Tibet during the last few years. We have managed to explore further than our predecessors and to introduce several species such as *R. bulu* and *R. dignabile* for the first time. 'Surely there aren't any more new species out there,' people often say to me. In fact these are being named all the time and there are several desirable species which we only know from photographs. Recent expeditions to Vietnam have revealed a wealth of interesting new species which should make fine garden plants in mild climates. There are still areas which have never been explored properly and there are certain to be more good plants out there about which we know nothing.

Rhododendrons in the Wild

There are few, if any, writers in the field of plant exploration to rival the plant hunter and prolific author, Frank Kingdon Ward. Here he describes the 'rhododendron fairyland' of the Doshong La in S.E. Tibet in his book *Riddle of the Tsangpo Gorges*:

'The Valley, flanked by grey cliffs, roofed by grey skies, with the white snowfields above, spouting water which splashed and gurgled in a dozen babbling becks; and everywhere the rocks swamped under a tidal wave of intense colours which gleam and glow in leagues of breaking light. The colours leap at you as you climb the moraine: Scarlet Runner dripping in blood red rivers from the ledges, choppy sulphur seas breaking from a long, low surf of pink.'

Few sights in the world can equal these plants in full flower in their native mountains. The greatest concentration of rhododendron species (around 300-400) is found in an area from Nepal, Bhutan and Burma, north and east through S.E. Tibet into Yunnan and Sichuan provinces in China. Here the mighty rivers, the Tsangpo, the Salween, the Mekong and the Yangtze flow though deep gorges at altitudes of up to 2,700-3000m (9,000-10,000ft) while on either side, mountain ranges climb to 7500m (25,000ft) or more. Wherever the rainfall is high enough for rich forest, there are usually rhododendrons growing from around the level of the river up to 4900m (16,000ft) or so. At the lower altitudes in deep, lush forest, epiphytic species can be found (which grow on other plants or mossy logs) and large-leaved species, such as the magnificent *R. sinogrande*, with leaves up to 1m (3ft) in length. A little higher up, rhododendrons often form the dominant forest: in Nepal the red *R. arboreum* paints the hillsides a dazzling shade in March and April.

Elsewhere, species such as *R. phaeochrysum*, *R. oreotrephes* and *R. uvariifolium* form a dense understory under the *Picea* and *Abies*, such that whole hillsides can burst into flower. A little higher still and the trees start to thin. Here shrubby species such as *R. campylocarpum* or *R. roxieanum* may be the dominant vegetation at and above the treeline. Nearer the top, the leaves get smaller and the species become lower growing. Here on the windswept moorland you might find Frank Kingdon Ward's 'Scarlet Runner', *R. forrestii*, with its bright red waxy flowers often opening up soon after the leaves emerge from the melting snow, or one of the small blue-purple Lapponica species such as *R. fastigiatum*. It is possible to find 20-30 species on a single mountainside in some of the richer areas, and the rhododendrons are usually accompanied by *Primula*, *Meconopsis*, *Diapensia*, *Clematis*, *Deutzia*, *Sorbus*, orchids and many other of our commonest garden plants.

If the flowers were not enough, the rhododendrons grow in some of the world's most dramatic scenery. Forget any photographs you have seen. Nothing prepares you for the vastness of the Himalayan and Chinese mountains until you are looking at 3-4,000m (10-13,000ft) of mountain towering above you when you are actually already standing at 3,000m (10,000ft) yourself. Short of breath but triumphant, you can sit at the top of a mountain pass, surrounded by snow-covered peaks, with the largest natural flower gardens you will ever see spread out around you. It is not at all hard to become hooked on rhododendrons, faced with such a feast!

A forest of *Abies delavayi* and *R. selense* var. *jucundum* on the Cangshan, Yunnan, China, taken on one of the author's plant hunting exhibitions

Site Preparation

Choosing a Site

Unless you are lucky enough to own a large estate, it is likely that you will have a limited number of possible sites in which to plant rhododendrons. Even within a small garden, however, aspect, wind shelter, shade and frost drainage can vary considerably, so choosing the best site is important. Situations facing away from the sun are colder with less light and warmth to ripen wood, but the advantages are that the plants require less watering, and growth and flowering will come later which is useful where spring frosts are a problem. In areas where hot summers cause high soil temperatures, such aspects may be the best option, both from a point of view of shade and keeping the soil temperature down. Strong winds can damage rhododendrons, especially those with large leaves, so it is important to be aware of the prevailing winds when selecting your planting sites. There are certain places where rhododendrons just will not grow. Alkaline soil, marshy and boggy ground with stagnant water or directly under mature beech trees are three examples.

Left: Japanese maples (*Acer palmatum*) make an excellent foil for evergreen azaleas flowering in the woodland garden at Exbury Gardens, Hampshire, England, in May and June.

Right: The fine apricot-pink and salmon American hybrid 'Virginia Richards' planted in a mixed border of perennials and rhododendrons

Shade

The advantage of good shade-cover from trees or artificial materials is the protection it offers from frost (especially in spring when flowers and growth are vulnerable), sunburn and heat. In very cold areas, such as northern Europe and N.E. North America, winter sun coupled with extreme cold can cause a great deal of damage, as the plant loses water to evaporation but cannot replace it because the ground is frozen. Shade can greatly reduce this risk. The disadvantages of shade can, however, be significant. Many shade trees are very demanding as regards moisture. Trees such as beech and sycamore are particularly greedy and rhododendrons growing under or near such trees invariably suffer from drought. Oak, larch, pines, spruce and fir are less greedy and let in more light. Heavy shade also causes spindly, straggly and sparse plants which are often shy-flowering.

How much shade rhododendrons require depends on the varieties you grow and where you live. In northern climates such as Scotland and Scandinavia where summer sun is not all that intense, most varieties grow and flower best with no overhead shade. Look up from where a plant is and you should be able to see sky. As you move south, foliage sunburn, flowers quickly wilting and high soil temperatures are all factors which indicate need for greater shade. In eastern U.S.A. and other areas with high summer temperatures, most varieties require a considerable amount of shade to avoid damage.

As a general maxim, I would say that people tend to garden in too much shade. This may not be through choice; often there are restrictions and difficulties in felling trees. It is worth bearing in mind, however, that it is always easier to fell trees before an area is planted rather than when the plants are already growing. Existing trees will get larger and larger, with their roots spreading further and further, so do consider doing some serious thinning before you plant up an

area. Think hard about which trees to remove. Often a group of trees shelter one another and, if you thin them out, the remaining ones may blow down. Another option is to leave most of the trees but to limb them up (remove all or most of the lower branches). It is sometimes an eye-opener how much better rhododendrons grow after trees making overhead shade are blown down in storms: initial despair often gives way a few years later to comments like, 'the best thing that ever happened to the garden'.

In the various rhododendron-growing regions of the world, different trees have been found to be particularly good for shading rhododendrons. We have found oak, Scot's pine, larch, *Sorbus, Malus, Prunus* and small-leaved maples to be particularly good. *Sorbus* are especially valuable as they bring colour into the garden in autumn when rhododendrons are at their least interesting. In North America, many of the native trees such as *Liquidamber, Nyssa*, dogwood, hemlock, redwood, pine, hickory and oak are all excellent subjects. Douglas fir is rather greedy and the constantly shedding branches tend to damage plants growing beneath them. In Australia, Eucalyptus species, such as *E. regnans*, and *Quercus coccinea* are successful while in New Zealand *Gleditsia* and alder are very good.

In semi-tropical areas, where Vireyas can be grown outdoors, wonderful combinations of palms, tree ferns, and other local vegetation can be made with the rhododendrons. If the rainfall is high enough, you may be able to plant them on mossy logs. Wherever you garden, the key is always to avoid hungry trees with shallow roots which will compete with those of the rhododendrons. Try to have the minimum canopy

High shade, provided by the native *Sequoia sempervirens*, provide excellent growing conditions for rhododendrons in northern California

which will give you the protection you require.

Some collectors (mostly in North America) have decided in favour of artificial shade and shelter for their species collections, constructing lathe houses with wooden or plastic strips. While not as ornamental as natural tree-cover, the fact that the shade is constant, and that there is no competition from tree roots, make this an attractive option to provide light or heavy shade with some heat and frost protection.

As plants of open moorland, alpine rhododendron varieties should ideally be grown in full exposure so that they maintain the compact, mounded shape that they would have in the wild. In shade, such varieties tend to be sparse and drawn and to be shy-flowering. Unfortunately, alpine varieties, with a few exceptions, are not heat-tolerant and particularly dislike having hot roots in summer, so shade is often the only option. In Scotland, the only reason for providing alpine varieties with a little shade would be to protect early-flowering varieties from spring frosts.

Wind Shelter

Shelter from the prevailing winds is very important for many varieties of rhododendrons. In the UK, for example, we get strong, rain-bearing, south-westerly winds and cold, sometimes snow-bearing, easterlies. Both can be severely damaging.

As a general rule, rhododendron varieties with the largest leaves need the most shelter as they can easily have their leaves broken at the petiole and even become completely defoliated. Many species have delicate new growth which is vulnerable to wind damage.

Buildings and walls do, of course, provide shelter, but as solid barriers they also funnel and lift the wind, redirecting it to strike as hard in other directions. The best protection is provided by permeable barriers, such as trees, shrubs or artificial materials, so that the velocity of the wind is reduced. Rhododendrons shelter one another very well and the tougher ones can always be planted as a barrier to protect less wind-tolerant vari-

The spectacular new growth of rhododendron species in the author's garden at Glendoick. The varied colour of the indumentum on the leaves is evident

eties. The shelter may take some time to establish and become effective, and in the meantime artificial material, such as plastic netting or plastic strips, may be used.

In coastal gardens, shelter is often absolutely crucial to the success of the garden; ferocious winds laden with salt spray can cause severe damage. In coastal gardens in the UK, such as Inverewe in Scotland, *Cupressus macrocarpa*, *Pinus muricata*, *Pinus radiata*, *Griselinia littoralis*, *Arbutus unedo*, *Escallonia*, *Olearia*, and many other trees and shrubs are used to create these essential, dense windbreaks.

In colder places, hardier trees and shrubs are required. In areas with harsh winters, strong winds when the ground is frozen can cause severe desiccation of foliage, defoliating and killing plants, while in warm areas, hot winds can cause similar damage. Low-growing and alpine rhododendrons usually require little or no wind-protection (as long as it is not laden with salt spray) since many of them grow in full exposure on mountainsides and passes in their natural environment.

Frost and Cold

Rhododendrons vary greatly in cold hardiness. The very hardiest (often known as ironclads) can withstand -32°C (-25°F) or colder, while in contrast, most of the tropical Vireya varieties can withstand little or no frost. Snow, which covers many of the rhododendron species in winter in their native habitats, is an excellent protection from extremes of cold (though its weight can cause breakage) but unfortunately snow does not necessarily coincide with the coldest weather. While it is common policy to select only varieties of certain hardiness for the area you live in, few gardeners can resist attempting to grow one or two which are of borderline hardiness. In this case, selection of site and clever use of shelter is very important.

Even within a small garden, there are microclimates. Walls facing the sun are amongst the warmest sites while hollows and the bottom of slopes, where frost settles, are usually amongst the coldest places. Overhead shade provides a few degrees of protection from late frosts for flowers and emerging young growth.

The leaves on this *R. wiltonii* show the tell-tale browning and distortion caused by late frost which has occurred after the growth buds have started to elongate.

Many people use forms of artificial protection for their more tender varieties. Beware of leaving such materials on when thawing occurs as it can cause rotting of foliage; all materials used must allow air to circulate. The purpose is as much to moderate temperature fluctuations as it is to protect the plant from extreme cold.

In the Pacific Northwest and even south into California, the most damaging weather is the occasional very sudden drop in temperature in autumn before plants have had time to harden off. Young plants of borderline hardiness are especially vulnerable to cold. A mature plant of the same variety may well be able to re-sprout from the trunk, even after severe damage, whereas a young plant might well be killed in those conditions.

At Glendoick, we use several materials to protect young plants from spring and early autumn frosts. Spun polypropylene (available in different widths and thicknesses) is lightweight but gives protection from a few degrees of frost. It is hard to anchor, gets heavy when wet and must be taken off if snow is forecast.

Better are sheets of opaque corrugated plastic – these are about 3-5mm (⅛-¼in) thick and act like double-glazing – which can be bent over to make miniature hoop or tunnel houses. These can be secured so they will withstand rain, snow and wind. The only problem is that plants dry out underneath them. Of course, this is simply an extension of the traditional cloche, which is expensive if made of glass, but which is also available in plastic.

Some people use wicker baskets which they place over individual plants overnight. These should come off in daylight hours unless it is still freezing. Others wrap stems or the whole plant in burlap or sacking, or use conifer branches (including the Christmas tree!). As is explained in the sections on shade (page 16) and shelter (page 19), plants in the open are much more vulnerable than ones in a sheltered site, so placing or moving borderline plants to the most favourable sites may reduce or eliminate the need for artificial protection.

Spring frosts (and to some extent early autumn frosts) are the bane of rhododendron gardeners in many parts of the world. Few rhododendrons have frost-resistant flowers or new growth and few rhododendron growers have not experienced the forlorn sight of a specimen in full flower one day, reduced the following morning to a mountain of limp, soggy, grey-brown mush after an overnight frost. Ideas mentioned above can all help prevent such disasters but with severe frost, there is very little that can be done.

Commercial growers in some parts of the world use their sprinkler systems to keep the air moving and prevent frost damage. This can cause flooding and even a garden full of icicle-covered plants but it does work. Start the watering before the pipes freeze up.

New growth damaged by frost can be cut off. This will usually be replaced by a flush from lateral buds further down the branches. Potentially most damaging of all is bark split. This is caused by the sap running

in the stem freezing and splitting a branch open. Often, it is not revealed immediately but the damaged plant, or part of the plant, can collapse later in the growing season. Young plants, even hardy varieties, can easily be killed in this way (see page 70).

To summarise: rhododendrons require varying degrees of shade and shelter. The amount depends both on the variety and the climatic conditions to be faced.

Dappled shade provided by birch, conifers and Japanese maples provides a perfect environment for azaleas at Exbury Gardens, Hampshire, England

Shade and shelter:
- provide protection from damaging winds.
- moderate the effects of sun on flowers and foliage.
- moderate/reduce soil temperature in summer.
- reduce the damaging effects of spring frosts on growth and flowers.
- reduce the combined stress of frozen ground and sun in winter.
- maintain humidity of atmosphere around plants.

Too much shade:
- encourages drawn and leggy plants.
- inhibits flowering.
- reduces moisture available to rhododendrons (due to tree roots).
- encourages disease such as powdery mildew.

Landscaping with Rhododendrons

Using Rhododendrons in the Landscape

Given the right soil conditions, acidity, drainage and moisture, rhododendrons are quite accommodating, easily grown, low-maintenance plants. They require no routine pruning, and little or no feeding. As most are evergreens, they can provide a year-round structure to the garden and their foliage can make a fine foil for other plants. Of course, in full flower few plants can equal rhododendrons for quantity of bloom (sometimes virtually hiding the leaves), variety of colours from white to pink, red, purple, yellow and orange and range of flower and truss shape, from rounded to hanging and tubular.

With careful selection of varieties you can have rhododendrons which flower around Christmas in milder climates, while at the end of the season, you can still have them in flower in August. Quite a number of rhododendrons have scent. These fall into two categories, those that can generally be cultivated outdoors except in the severest climates and those which, for most of us, need to be grown indoors. In both cases, the flowers are light in colour, mostly white or pink, or yellow in the case of *R. luteum*. The hardier (outdoor) ones include the species and hybrids of subsection Fortunea such as *R. decorum*, *R. fortunei* and the famous *R.* 'Loderi' hybrids; also many species azaleas such as *R. occidentale* and its hybrids like 'Irene Koster'.

There are several styles of gardening associated with rhododendrons, but they are seldom used in formal plantings. I have, once or twice, seen them trained as standards or clipped into hedges but generally they do not suit straight lines, order and regiment. Woodland gardening, rock gardens and peat gardens are all imitations of nature and are therefore essentially informal. The informality is also a boon in the amount of labour required for upkeep. Much of the weeding, pruning, clipping, edging and mowing that goes on in other sorts of gardens should be less necessary, especially in the woodland garden.

I leave the vexed question of colour co-ordination to others. The garden design guru Gertrude Jekyll only tolerated small-flowered white rhododendrons, while at the other end of the spectrum, many of the latest hybrids have massive multi-coloured flowers which some consider to be vulgar. There are varieties and planting combinations to suit every taste. The great thing about rhododendrons is that you can move them if you find a colour combination offensive. The depth of feeling inspired by this subject is extraordinary. The otherwise calm and reasonable rhododendron author David Leach, in his classic *Rhododendrons of the World*, takes exception to one of my favourite rhododendron species thus:

'I advise all readers to turn their eyes from *R. niveum* in its usual dull purple form, which is one of the most degraded, poisonously bilious colours to be found on earth. An axe, not a woodland, is the remedy for its appaling hue.'

The spectacular rhododendron walk which winds down to the river at Cotehele House and Garden, Cornwall, England

Foliage Effect

While most of the larger hybrids have fairly standard green leaves, many of the species and some of the smaller hybrids have foliage which gives year-round interest. The leaf under surface, and sometimes the upper surface too, may be covered in a layer of hairs known as indumentum, varying in colour from silver to white, fawn, rufous or dark brown. The indumentum is often particularly fine on the new growth as it unfurls. Species with this feature include *R. bureauvii*, with a thick reddish-brown layer on the leaf underside, and *R. pachysanthum* whose indumentum matures colour from white to fawn to deep reddish-brown.

Sometimes the foliage effect comes from the size of the leaf: those of *R. sinogrande* can be up to 1m (3ft) in length. In other cases it is the leaf shape: almost round in *R. williamsianum* and *R. orbiculare*, long and narrow in *R. roxieanum*; or the leaf colour, grey-blue in some forms of *R. cinnabarinum* and *R. lepidostylum* and red in

Right: The rare dwarf species *R. pronum* is prized by collectors for its blue leaves and compact habit, despite the fact that it hardly ever flowers

Below: The emerging new growth of the rare, red-flowered species *R. exasperatum* is a wonderful metallic purple colour. This species can be identified by its oval leaves and bristly stems

cultivars such as 'Elizabeth Lockhart'. The new growth of rhododendrons is very variable and often very showy, almost as good as a second flowering. Species with coloured new growth include forms of *R. keiskei*, *R. lutescens* (both red), *R. decorum* and *R. williamsianum* (bronzy). Other species have showy red leaf-buds scales (which protect the resting buds through the winter) and are displayed as the new leaves unfurl. Good examples are *R. fortunei* and *R. falconeri*. Many species have outstanding peeling or smooth, coloured bark. Some of the finest include *R. thomsonii* and *R. hodgsonii*.

How Far Apart Should I Plant?

Occasionally, one finds a wonderful old specimen plant growing out on its own, with no competition from other plants or trees. This has formed a perfect shape and is the envy of everyone who sees it. Such plants are the exception, not the rule. Individual specimens, planted on lawns, for instance, tend to be buffeted by wind, to dry out and to have weeds or grass growing at their roots.

Rhododendrons are sociable plants and unless you are prepared to put in the extra work required, do not dot them around too much. Conversely, planting too densely is also to be avoided: there are many once fine collections now reduced to a few spindly branches competing for light, with the handful of flowers high up and far out of reach. Planting close together for quick impact is fine if you are prepared to move them or thin them later but, in my experience, this is easier

said than done. A garden I visited recently was so over-planted that the paths had completely disappeared under the rhododendrons. In optimum conditions, rhododendrons live for a very long time: 100 years is quite common. Plant with one eye on posterity and you will not regret it.

The size dimensions given in the Plant Directory (see page 80) are very approximate and apply to plants aged 10-20 years. The rainfall, amount of fertiliser used, and length of growing season are all important factors. Often rhododendrons grow as wide as they are high, and there is a limit to the pruning you can do with many of them (see page 51). If you can spare the space, let the really large species grow into fully-clothed, rounded specimens. With the small-leaved and dwarf varieties, letting them grow into one another fairly quickly is the best plan.

Companion Planting

For the majority of gardeners who have limited space to work with, and a desire for year-round interest, rhododendrons will be used with all sorts of other plants for company. The golden rule here is to try to avoid too much competition for moisture. This can come either from below, in the case of greedy tree roots, or from above, in the case of ground cover. As rhododendrons are moisture-loving but shallow-rooted, they will tend to lose the battle and their health will suffer.

In choosing smaller trees, consider both the ultimate size and spread and the season of interest. As rhododendrons are predominantly plants of spring display, plants for autumn and winter are invaluable. In moderate climates such as the UK and the Pacific Northwest of North America, there is a huge range of choices for trees and shrubs. *Sorbus* species are particularly good, as they are not hungry feeders, provide filtered shade and have long-lasting berries of white, yellow, pink, orange or red. *Eucryphia* is another fine choice; these have very showy white flowers in late summer and early autumn. The hardiest forms are *E.* x *intermedia* 'Rostrevor', *E. glutinosa* and *E.* x *nymanensis*. They should be planted in full sun

Primulas often associate with rhododendrons in the wild as well as in cultivation. Here candelabra primulas are planted in front of *R. cerasinum*

and tend to flower on the sunny side of the tree only. Japanese maples (*Acer japonicum* and *A. palmatum* cultivars) act as a wonderful foil for the foliage of rhododendrons, and many have the bonus of autumn colour.

Winter colour can be provided by *Mahonia*, winter jasmine, *Viburnum* and *Hamamelis mollis*, as well as perennials and bulbs such as hellebores and snowdrops.

In severe climates, use a mixture of native and hardy exotics. There are many Japanese and North American natives such as *Styrax, Hamamelis, Cercis, Amelanchier, Halesia* and *Stewartia* which provide filtered shade, fine flowers and/or autumn colour and whose roots are not too greedy. Some of these thrive only in areas with hot summers. *Kalmia, Leucothoe, Vaccinium* and other Ericaceous plants enjoy similar soil conditions to rhododendrons and provide interest after the main period of rhododendron flowering.

Above: *R. kiusianum* is a fine plant for the rock garden, accompanying small perennials and other plants

Right: An undulating carpet of many species and hybrid dwarf rhododendrons in the author's garden at Glendoick, Scotland

The Woodland Garden

This style of gardening, developed as a naturalistic way of informal planting through woodland, often up a valley with a stream running through it or around a pond or lake, has become the most popular way to display rhododendrons on the larger scale.

Many of the great rhododendron collections of the south and west of England, such as Exbury and Leonardslee, and in Argyll, Scotland, such as Crarae, are examples of woodland gardens. The development of this gardening style coincided with, and indeed was largely inspired by, the flood of new rhododendron species from the Himalayas and China from 1850 onwards; it soon became apparent that many other plants from the Sino-Himalayan region also suited this method of cultivation.

The large foliage of *R. sinogrande* (in the fore-ground) contrasts well with the pink hybrid 'Atroflo' and the white *Prunus avium* in the back-ground

The essential character of the woodland garden is the informal nature of the winding paths through both native and exotic trees, underplanted with rhododendrons and other shrubs, often with a layer of wild flowers, bulbs and other smaller plants carpeting the ground underneath. Using contours and bridges to provide paths at different levels allows rhododendrons to be viewed from above and below. The steep slopes at Bodnant, North Wales, and the bridges over the burn at Crarae, Scotland are good examples.

Woodland conditions, with shelter and filtered shade, are essential for varieties of borderline hardiness; at Glendoick, the most favourable sites allow us to grow *R. lindleyi* and *R. sinogrande* which would not be hardy in the open. Woodland, especially if on a slope with frost drainage, will allow protection from several degrees of frost and often will make the difference between damage to flowers and foliage, and escaping from it.

Although predominantly a British development, this style of

woodland gardening has also been used in other areas with great effect, such as the University of British Columbia Botanic Garden's Asian garden. Exploit your native plants as part of the magic. Pukeiti in North Island, New Zealand is a good example of native woodland filled with indigenous trees and tree ferns, interplanted with rhododendron species. Particularly fine there are tender species, such as *R. elliottii* and *R. protistum*, which thrive in the luxuriant shelter growing in the high rainfall.

Obviously, few people are lucky enough to be able to garden on the grand scale which woodland gardening implies: many of these gardens cover acres and can take hours to walk round. However, the basic tenets of woodland gardening: informality, shade, shelter and plant associations apply equally well in smaller gardens. The most satisfactory displays of healthy rhododendrons in small and medium-sized gardens are often those which have adapted the principles of the woodland garden landscape.

In the UK, the dominant feature of most woodland

gardens is their rhododendrons, but certain other genera are commonly represented too. The best larger shade trees to associate with rhododendrons are discussed under shade and shelter on pages 16 and 19. The ideal is a mixture of conifers and hardwoods. In our west of Scotland garden, Baravalla, the natural woodland is oak, hazel and birch with a few mature fir trees which seed themselves.

At Glendoick, we have lost our dominant tree, the elm, from Dutch elm disease, leaving a mixture of larch, Douglas fir, sycamore and beech with an undergrowth of elder (*Sambucus nigra*) and other plants. In choosing trees, consider the bark as well as the flowers, foliage and berries. *Betula utilis* and *B. jacquemontii* have fine reddish-brown and white, peeling bark respectively. Other species with interesting bark include *Prunus serrula*, *Acer griseum*, *A. hersii* and other snake-bark maples.

Magnolias are another obvious choice. On the large scale in relatively mild climates, the massive-growing *Magnolia campbellii* and its relatives give a spectacular display in early spring. On a smaller scale you can use other species such as the summer-flowering *M. wilsonii* and hybrids such as 'Leonard Messel'.

In eastern North America, many of the new hybrid magnolias put on a

Attractive though the combination is between Dicentra and Rhododendron, the ground cover can very easily get out of control in a small garden

spectacular display in the few weeks before the main rhododendron blooming period. Magnolias are rather greedy feeders, so avoid planting rhododendrons directly underneath them in areas of low rainfall. Camellias are another mainstay companion plant, especially in the gardens of Cornwall. If you can obtain *Embothrium coccineum*, the fiery orange flowers of this South American native provide a fine contrast to the colours of the rhododendrons.

Pieris thrive in considerable shade and there are now many different forms with red, pink or white flowers, red or bronze

young growth and some have variegated leaves. These, and *Enkianthus*, are both members of the Ericaceae, the same family as rhododendrons, so they enjoy similar growing conditions. As well as their attractive hanging flowers, *Enkianthus* have amongst the most spectacular autumn colour with red, orange and yellow tones. Other plants with good autumn foliage are *Rhododendron luteum* (otherwise known as *Azalea pontica*), *Euonymous alatus*, Japanese maples and *Sassafras*.

Berries can be provided by trees and shrubs such as *Vaccinium*, *Gaultheria* (which now includes *Pernettya mucronata*), *Cotoneaster* and *Sorbus*. North American natives such as *Styrax* and *Halesia* have showy flowers and provide dappled shade. Bamboos are often found in association with rhododendrons in the wild and can be used effectively in cultivation. The best are the taller-growing, clump-forming types such as *Fargesia murieliae* (syn. *Arundinaria murieliae*).

Beware of the very rampant, spreading species such as the tall *Sasa palmata* and the low growing *Sasaella ramosa* (syn. *Arundinaria vagans*). These need lots of space, though they can be kept in bounds with artificial barriers in the soil. Most woodland gardens contain sites too dry for rhododendrons. These can be filled with shrubs such as *Ilex*, *Deutzia*, *Philadelphus*, *Viburnum*, *Ribes* and *Hypericum*. All of these associate with rhododendrons in the wild, as do climbers such as *Schisandra* and *Clematis montana*.

The best woodland gardens have extensive underplantings of bulbs and herbaceous plants.

The flowering cherry and other trees provide ideal dappled shade for the underplantings of azaleas and rhododendrons at Leonardslee Gardens in Surrey, England

Here the key is to use plants which are subtle rather than garish, to keep the 'natural' look of the garden. In the wild, rhododendrons are often associated with *Primula* and *Meconopsis* which make ideal companion plants in areas with fairly cool summers. The easiest primulas to establish and naturalise are the candelabra types such as *Primula japonica*, *P.helodoxa*, *P. bulleana* and *P. poissoni*. These tend to hybridise and produce seedlings of a huge range of colours. *Meconopsis*, particularly the blue poppies *M. betonicifolia*, *M. grandis* and their hybrid *M. x sheldonii*, prefer moist, cool woodland: they are a struggle to grow in areas with summer heat and low rainfall. Some of the monocarpic varieties such as the *M. napalensis* or *M. regia* hybrids are more suited to hotter and drier conditions. Other fine companion plants include *Trillium*, *Erythronium*, *Helleborus*, *Cardiocrinum* and *Lilium*.

Most woodland gardeners encourage wild flowers by avoiding mowing or scything until mid-summer, when most of the flowers are over. At Glendoick we have many native British plants which thrive among the rhododendrons; these include *Meconopsis cambrica* (the Welsh poppy), species of *Brunnera* and *Digitalis* (foxgloves), as well as several varieties of ferns.

The Rhododendron Border

Some may well argue that a border planted only with rhododendrons and azaleas is monotonous, particularly when they are out of flower. I would certainly agree that it can be, especially if you exclusively plant the larger hybrids, which look very similar to one another without blooms. With dwarf and medium-sized growers, if you garden in a moderate climate (winter minimum *c*. -18°C (0°F)), you can plant rhododendron borders which do remain interesting all year round. In such a border, I would tend to use plants with an ultimate height of up to 2m (6ft) in height at the back, gradually sloping down to low-growing varieties at the front. The great advantage of not mixing in other plants is that the conditions can be made to ideally to suit the rhododendrons in terms of soil, drainage, feeding and watering.

In nature, rhododendrons and azaleas are usually found in clumps and colonies, sheltering and shading each others' roots. In the garden, imitate this by allowing the rhododendrons to grow into one another, forming an undulating carpet. Before the individual plants start to join up, you can use pre-emergence herbicides to keep down the weeds. On a larger scale or for quick impact, plant three or more of each variety so that they can form large clumps. We often do this with dwarf varieties grown from wild seed, so that we can display the variation within a species.

Most people want as long and spectacular a flowering season as possible. With careful choice, the year can begin in winter with *R. lapponicum* and *R. dauricum* and end with late-flowering evergreen azaleas such as *R. naka-harae* in early and mid-summer, with a more or less continuous display in between.

Flower shape, size and colour should also be considered. The rounded trusses of the 'yak' hybrids are very different from the bells of the *R. william-sianum* hybrids, for instance. In frost pockets, choose early-flowering varieties such as 'Ptarmigan' and 'Christmas Cheer' which open their flowers over a long period. This ensures that if flowers are spoiled by frost, more will open later. Most 'yak' hybrids as well as evergreen and deciduous azaleas are late enough flowering to avoid spring frost danger. In milder gardens, you can have scent from some of the Maddenia species and hybrids. In colder climates some of the species and hybrids (mostly large-growing) and many of the deciduous azaleas, such as *R. luteum* can provide the perfume.

Always consider the importance of foliage when planning a rhodo-dendron border. After all, the flowers only last a few weeks while fine foliage is always on display. Choose a variety of leaf shapes, from the rounded and oval *R. williamsianum* and its hybrids such as 'Gartendirektor Rieger', 'Linda' and 'Osmar', to those with narrow or long leaves such as *R. roxieanum* and *R. elegantulum*. Leaf size is also important. The larger-leaved hybrids such as 'Unique' and some of the 'yak's' contrast well with those at the other end of the scale, such as the tiny *R. calostrotum ssp. keleticum* Radicans group which has some of the smallest and narrowest leaves of all. The texture of the leaf itself can provide interest. The hybrid 'Rubicon' has deeply ribbed, dark green leaves, while these of *R. thomsonii* are completely smooth and flat. Many dwarf and medium-sized species and a few hybrids have a magnificent indumentum. This is usually on the leaf underside but in some species, such as *R. pachysanthum*,

Japanese maples and Japanese azaleas produce a marvelous show in the Valley Gardens at Windsor Great Park, England

R. pseudochrysanthum,
R. yakushimanum and
several others, the silvery
dusting on the new growth
persists all summer, giving
a most attractive effect.
In many other varieties
the white, silver, fawn
or brown indumentum
on the upper leaf surface
is only temporary; good
examples are the 'yak'
hybrids such as 'Hydon
Dawn', 'Sleepy', and 'Ken
Janeck'.

Exploit the coloured
foliage of *R. lepidostylum,*
R. fastigiatum and
R. campanulatum ssp.
aeruginosum (glaucous-blue)
or 'Elizabeth Lockhart' and
'Elizabeth Red Foliage' (red-
dish-purple) or 'Ponticum
Variegatum' and
'Goldflimmer' (variegated).

Many species have very
showy new growth, giving
almost a 'second flower-
ing'. Some of the best
include the bronzy and
purplish new leaves of
R. williamsianum and its
hybrids and the red young
growth of forms of *R.
keiskei* and *R. lutescens.*

Good autumn colour
can be provided by deciduous azaleas such as *R.
luteum,* which can be
placed at the back of a
border, or *R. dauricum,*
R. mucronulatum and their
hybrids. Many varieties
have leaves which turn to
rich, deep reds, purples
and mahogany in winter.
Some of the best include
the 'P.J.M.' Group in its
various forms as well as
many of the evergreen or
Japanese azaleas.

The Mixed Border

In smaller gardens, where
space is at a premium, the
aim is usually for maxi-
mum impact and year-
round interest provided by
mixed borders. Usually a
structure of shrubs, both
deciduous and evergreen,
is interspaced and under-
planted with perennials
and even annuals.

As usual, the key is to
avoid greedy and invasive
plants. Roses and heathers
are two examples which
will dry out and impover-
ish the soil at the expense
of the rhododendrons.
Often a part of the garden,
or a particular bed, will be
selected for acid-loving
plants: other Ericaceous
plants, such as *Pieris,*
Kalmia latifolia, Leucothoe,
as well as shrubs such as
camellias, *Hydrangea* and
Japanese maples.

A lot of the choices
for mixed plantings are
questions of taste. I have
seen some bizarre and out-
rageous combinations
with bulbs such as tulips,
bedding plants and rhodo-
dendrons growing
together. Purists will be
appalled and others will

A riot of colour in a New Zealand garden with deciduous azaleas and rhododendrons in association annuals and perennials

love the effect. As most
rhododendrons are ever-
green, they provide much
of the permanent structure
of the mixed border, especially in winter when the
perennials have died down
and the deciduous shrubs
have only bare stems.
Because of this it is well
worth considering the
foliage and growth habit

of the varieties you choose
as much as the flower.
Planting the rhododen-
drons in clumps so that
they can grow into one
another, shading one
another's roots, cuts down
on the need for weeding
and watering. How close
you can plant to trees and
hedges depends on your
rainfall and whether or not
you can provide artificial
watering. Some of the subsection Triflora species
will withstand relatively
dry conditions once
established.

Peat Beds and Rock Gardens

The best way to display dwarf and alpine rhododendrons is in a peat bed or rock garden. Here, the alpine varieties are grown in an imitation of their wild state on moorland or rocky slopes. Such plantings should be out in the open, away from trees, allowing the dwarf plants to maintain their natural compact shape. Let the plants grow into one another, forming an undulating mat of foliage textures, leaving occasional patches of bare ground in which to plant bulbs and alpine perennials.

Peat gardening may be unfashionable due to the recent controversy over the extraction of peat. If people realised how live sphagnum peat can be grown and harvested as it is in Scandinavia, perhaps the furore would subside. Peat beds are constructed by using a soil mix, predominantly of peat, but often with added grit or other substances to ensure the drainage remains good. The best rock and peat gardens have natural or artificial contours, imitating the mountain slopes where the plants grow wild. Often, levels are created using peat blocks which themselves become an excellent medium for spreading plants to root into. As well as dwarf rhododendrons, peat beds are ideal for other low-growing Ericaceae such as *Phyllodoce* with pink or creamy-white bells, *Cassiope* with tiny white bells, *Kalmiopsis* and its hybrid x *Phylliopsis* with pink flowers, and dwarf *Gaultheria*, *Andromeda*, *Gaylussacia* and *Vaccinium*. Dwarf bulbs and alpines such as *Rhodohypoxis*, *Primula*, *Corydalis*, *Nomocharis*, *Fritillaria* and smaller ground orchids are all excellent choices.

At Glendoick we have found by bitter experience that certain bulbs and perennials are too invasive and soon get out of control. For us, these included *Muscari*, *Chionodoxa*, *Crocus* and bluebells, all of which are almost impossible to eradicate. In different climates, other plants will probably be equally troublesome. In rock gardens, rhododendrons and dwarf azaleas can form a dominant part, or just be scattered through a mixed planting of assorted alpines.

Natural rock gardens on windswept Himalayan mountains give plenty of ideas on how to garden with such plants as are found there. Those which require excellent drainage grow on scree, others which require more moisture grow in snowmelt. Some species prefer full exposure while others grow in the lee of rocks which provide wind shelter and help to retain moisture. Imitate these habitats in gardens, using scree beds, planting species next to rocks to protect new growth from prevailing winds and making use of moisture-retaining crevices to keep roots damp and cool.

This peat border contains a fine choice of plants to associate with dwarf rhododendrons and azaleas. The bright red azalea is 'Vuyk's Scarlet' is surrounded by *Pieris*, *Phyllodoce*, *Lilium* and *Trillium*

Growing in Containers

Rhododendrons in containers, whether outside or indoors, need a fairly free-draining and open, but at the same time moisture-retentive, compost. This is not a contradiction and is essential for healthy plants. Rhododendrons cannot survive for long with dry roots but, equally, if the compost is too soggy and the water in the pot becomes stagnant, then chlorotic foliage and poor growth, or even death through root-rot (*Phytophthora*), may result. A mixture of fairly coarse bark and fibrous peat, sometimes with added perlite, needles or woodchips, is the ideal combination for container rhododendrons inside or out.

The first two substances, either singly or together, are used by most commercial growers of rhododendrons in containers. The easiest option for feeding in containers is the slow-release granules, lasting up to 18 months. These can be either incorporated into the compost or clusters can be pushed into the soil of already containerised plants. Otherwise, granular or liquid feeding can be applied from late spring to mid-summer. Do not go on feeding longer or growth will continue at the expense of flower buds.

Rhododendrons should not be over-potted. If anything, they grow and flower better if slightly pot-bound, as long as they are well fed and watered. Be ware of shallow, pan shaped pots due to the physical properties of water in containers: all pots tend to have a soggy layer at the bottom and this layer should not come into contact with the roots. All containers need adequate drainage holes and

you may have to make extra ones, especially for Vireyas and Maddenia. I have seen excellent results, indoors and out, of rhododendrons growing in slices of tree-fern logs, which may be available in places such as Australia, New Zealand and similar mild climates. Many rhododendrons are epiphytic in the wild and this method imitates that habitat. Beware of the fungal disease Phytophthora in containers which is caused by a combination of poor drainage and high soil temperatures and is lethal (see page 68)

Outdoors

Many of the saddest-looking rhododendrons I have ever seen were in containers outside town houses. These straggly, yellow and brown-leaved sentinels were expending the last months of their short lives pushing out the odd feeble flower, before expiring, unloved and abandoned.

It is certainly possible to grow fine rhododendrons in containers but only if you are prepared to maintain them properly. They require more attention than those in the ground; they need re-potting every few years together with regular feeding and watering. There are several

The heavily scented hybrid 'Fragrantissimum' is commonly grown in a container which can be taken into the house when in flower. Here, on a patio, the clay pot is raised off the ground to ensure free drainage

reasons why containers may be the best or only option for growing rhododendrons. Many people have no garden but have perhaps some hard space suitable for pots. Others have gardens with alkaline or heavy clay soil. The fine foliage and compact habit of 'yak' hybrids are amongst the best choices as they look good for 12 months of the year and their, often silvery, new growth adds interest when flowering is past.

By all means put other plants in your containers with the rhododendrons, but avoid those such as ground covers with greedy root systems, which will compete for moisture and nutrients. Bulbs, non-invasive alpines and bedding plants can all be used successfully.

Rhododendrons (especially evergreen azaleas) are one of the most popular subjects for bonsai. There are thousands of varieties of Satsuki and other azaleas bred in Japan for this purpose, but they need winter protection in colder and more northern climates.

As with many other plants, the foliage of rhododendrons will tolerate much colder temperatures than the roots. The roots are usually killed at a temperature 5-10°C (10-20°F) less cold than would damage or kill the foliage. In the ground, the snow can actually creates a layer of insulation, preventing the soil from getting as cold as the air above. Plants in containers do not have this insulation and the roots, usually pressed against the inside of the pot, are very vulnerable to being hard frozen which can kill an otherwise hardy plant. If you can not bring your containers indoors in the severest weather, then it is worth taking other precautions. Insulation with polystyrene, bubble-plastic, straw or similar materials will help. Placing your containers 'pot thick' so they are all touching and then insulating the outside of the block, is a practice followed by nurserymen. Alternatively, dig the container into the ground so that the surrounding soil insulates it, which also stops the container blowing over.

The many varieties of Japanese or evergreen azaleas make ideal subjects for bonsai

Indoors

Unless you live in the milder areas where rhododendrons are cultivated, for example, western Britain, France, California, Australia or New Zealand, the more tender rhododendrons need to be grown indoors, at least during the winter. Indica, or tender azaleas, are the only part of the genus rhododendron which make good 'house' plants, as they can put up with the low light levels coupled with warm winter temperatures and dry air of the home. Maddenia and

Vireyas really need a greenhouse or conservatory with plenty of light, cool winter temperatures and a fairly high humidity. Maddenia species and hybrid plants can be brought into the house in flower and can stay in for a week or two, as long as they are kept fairly cool, but Vireyas can only stand a day or two.

The new greenhouse at Windsor Great Park, England, where the whole front can be opened in summer, gives the best of both worlds as it allows cool summer temperatures and frost protection in winter.

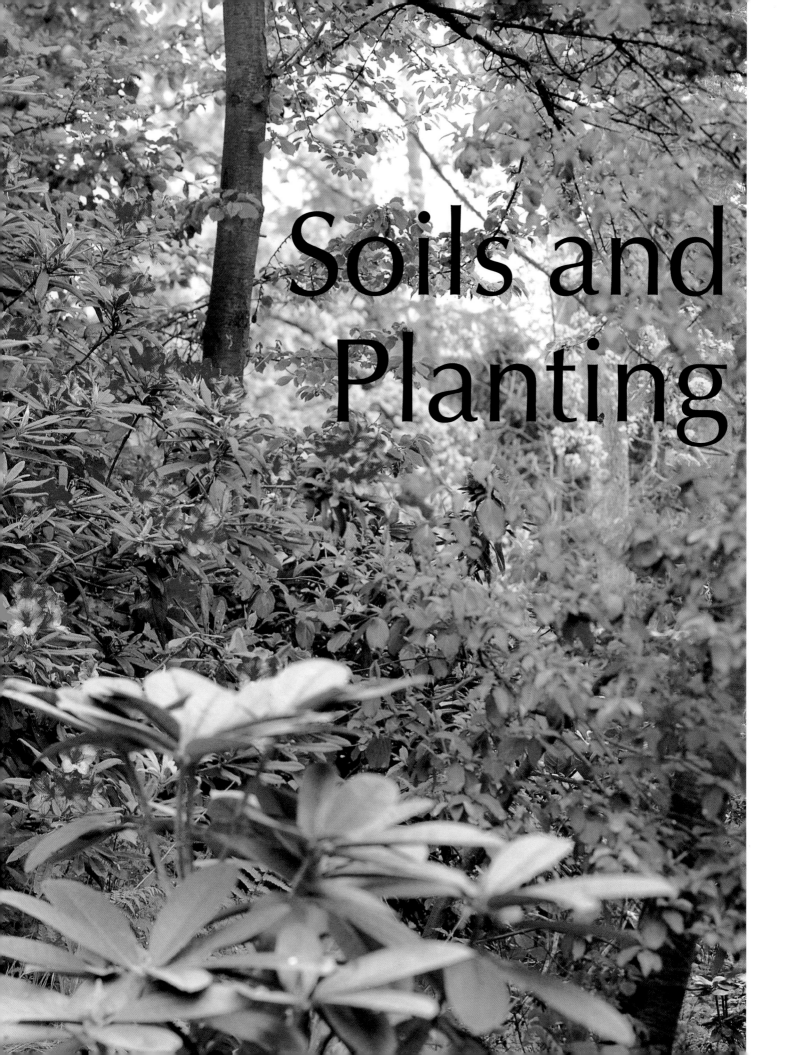

Soils and Planting

Soils: Acid or Alkaline?

Rhododendrons have several basic requirements:
1 Acid soil.
2 A loose/coarse organic planting medium which allows air circulation around the roots. Compacted and heavy clay soils are very poor for rhododendron culture.
3 Sufficient moisture at the roots during the growing season.
4 Many early-flowering, larger leaved tender varieties benefit from a certain amount of shelter, especially from wind. In more southerly locations, where summer sun is strong, for instance in North America, many rhododendrons require considerable shade for best results.

Acidity in soil is measured in terms of its pH. pH 7 is neutral. Lower numbers are acid and higher numbers are alkaline. Most rhododendrons enjoy a pH of between 4 and 6, and ideally between 4.5 and 5.5. On chalky, limy or alkaline soils, where water is very hard, rhododendrons grow poorly or not at all. The reasons for this are complex, but essentially soil pH causes a toxic intake of calcium, and affects the availability of nutrients and the health of essential micro-organisms, the lack of which hinders photosynthesis.

Some rhododendrons do actually grow on limestone in the wild but this is usually in areas of high rainfall and the limestone is dolomitic (contains magnesium). This apparently accounts for the fact that the plants are not 'poisoned by' taking up too much calcium, though the exact mechanisms are still not completely understood. There are various ways of determining the pH of soil. It can be analysed professionally, or with a soil test kit or pH meter purchased from a garden centre. Ensure that soil samples are taken from several sites in the garden as pH can vary considerably even within a small area. The important thing to ascertain if you have alkaline soil, is whether it is artificially (and therefore temporarily) so, or whether the area you live in is genuinely alkaline. In areas with naturally acid soil, the pH may have been raised by artificial means. Both farmers and vegetable gardeners often lime their soil routinely to increase yield. In this case, the lime will be washed out over several years, so the high pH is not a great worry. Sometimes the materials of house

The bold colours of evergreen azaleas brighten up a large-scale rock garden, filled with an enormous variety of plant material

Raised Beds

Raised beds are used to isolate the growing medium of the rhododendrons and other acid lovers from the natural garden soil. Beds are usually lined with heavy polythene or similar material, and filled with acidic topsoil from elsewhere, or a compost made up from peat, bark and other acidic organic matter. It is most important to ensure good drainage. A flat, polythene-lined bed can all too easily become a muddy swimming pool in wet weather, conditions which rhododendrons will not tolerate! Where possible, the lining should be sloped so that excess water can drain out from the front, back or sides. Where this is not possible, fill the bottom layer of the bed with coarse, free-draining material such as crushed rock or gravel, or even build small drains or soakaways.

The bed should be 30cm (12in) or more in depth so that the roots are not in contact with the lining. The sides of the bed can be of any suitable materials: wood, bricks, peat blocks or, parts of walls. The bed must be watered with rainwater or artificially acidified water. Many people collect rainwater which drains off their roofs into waterbutts for this purpose. To cut down on evaporation, it is well worth applying a mulch to the surface of a raised bed.

There are several varieties of rhododendron which can tolerate more or less neutral soil. Some such as *R. hirsutum* grows only on limestone in its native European Alps and dislikes very acid soil.

Varieties for near neutral soil:
Species. *R. augustinii,*
R. rubiginosum, R.
decorum, R. hirsutum,
R. sanguineum ssp.
didymum, R. vernico-
sum.
Hybrids:
'Cunningham's
White', 'Puncta'.

An important breakthrough for alkaline or neutral soil-tolerant rhododendrons has been developed recently in Germany and has been launched on the market. German growers have long known that benefits such as easier culture can be obtained by grafting rhododendrons onto selected rootstocks. A rootstock called INKARHO® which grows well in pH 5.5-7 has been bred and popular hybrids are now being grafted onto it and which should gradually become available. As yet it has only been tested in northern Europe, where apparently it is very promising.

building and hard landscaping such as rubble, cement and mortar will result in pockets of soil having a high pH. Chlorotic leaves are a good indicator. Usually the easiest and quickest way to ascertain the natural soil pH of an area is to look for tell-tale plants. Rhododendrons (including azaleas) and other members of the family Ericaceae, such as heathers, are a good indicator, as are blue Hortensia hydrangeas. Conversely, a lack of acid-loving plants in the area and hard water (which does not lather) in the taps are two very obvious clues to alkalinity. A few words over the fence to anyone with a good garden will soon give you all the information you need.

What to do if you have neutral or alkaline soil?

Neutral soil or artificially limed soil can be acidified by mixing in a percentage of peat. Alternatively, flowers of sulphur or iron sulphate can be applied. To reduce an area of soil of 20m^2 (216ft^2) by one pH unit (from pH7 to pH6 for instance) requires approximately 1.5kg (3½lb) of iron sulphate. These substances are best applied in later winter. They should only be used in moderation around established plants.

Iron chelates (sequestrols) can be used to treat plants with an iron deficiency chlorosis caused by too high a pH. This is quite an expensive and temporary way to solve the problem. All too often, even gardening experts prescribe sequestrols to cure any yellow-leaved rhododendron. In 19 times out of 20, I am convinced that the yellow leaves will be caused by lack of fertiliser, poor drainage, over-deep planting or drought rather than a soil pH/iron problem. Of course if the water in your area is hard, the acidified soil will gradually return to an alkaline state. In this case, growing in raised beds or containers (see page 34) is probably a better option.

In areas with alkaline soil (and water), it is possible to grow rhododendrons in a raised bed. Such beds must be watered with rainwater rather than tapwater to maintain acidity

Types of Soil

Soil types are usually defined by the particle size that they contain. Soils with the largest particle size are sands. These have excellent drainage but poor retention of water and nutrients. At the other end of the scale are clays, which have microscopically small particles and very good water and mineral retentive properties but are often slow-draining and compacted, preventing aeration for the roots. Loams are made up of a combination of these particle sizes and are the ideal basis for a growing medium for rhododendrons, being well aerated but moisture-retentive and able to hold nutrients. The type of soil can be ascertained both by the appearance and feel, the weight of it and by digging a hole and filling it with water. Clay soils tend to have very slow drainage while in sandy soils, the water drains too quickly.

Almost all soils are best improved artificially for optimum growing conditions; for rhododendrons heavy clay or very sandy soils will normally require the most work. Clay soils should be improved by the addition of inert materials such as grit or perlite or, better, the use of organic matter such as leafmould and composted bark (see opposite). The soil should be worked in fairly dry conditions and compacted clay can be broken up by exposure to frost. Soils with poor drainage encourage the potentially lethal fungal disease *Phytophthora*. Certain varieties are particularly sensitive to this (many species and most yellows hybrids for instance) and it is very prevalent in areas with hot summers (see page 68).

Sandy soils also benefit from the addition of organic matter and in this case peat can be added to the list as it has excellent moisture retention. A thick mulch to cut down evaporation is also useful on light or sandy soils.

Top: Well-rotted leaf-mould is one of the finest organic materials, especially that from oak and beech trees

Centre: Conifer needles are an excellent organic material as they help prevent soil compaction, allowing plenty of air to the roots

Bottom: Composted bark is one of the finest organic materials for soil improvement, propagation and as an ingredient for container composts

Organic Matter

There is no doubt that thorough soil preparation pays dividends when trying to establish newly planted rhododendrons. It is astonishing how many people are prepared to invest a lot of money in plants but who are reluctant to spend anything on soil improvement with organic matter.

Partially rotted leaf mould from the previous years leaf fall is an excellent medium which may well be available for nothing. Composted bark can be bought by the bag or by the lorry load. We make very good organic matter at Glendoick by chipping conifer trimmings (from *Cupressocyparis leylandii* hedges for instance) and letting them compost for a year. We more or less coppice our leylands and this may well prove a long-term solution for the many out-of-control Leyland hedges, a particularly common sight in the U.K.

General garden compost or, on a larger scale, composted straw, green waste, sawdust, wood chippings, newspaper and other substances have been used successfully. All these contribute to soil aeration and moisture retention as well as providing nutrients as they rot down. There have been some disasters – I do not recommend using large quantities of a new source of organic matter until it has been tested on a small scale, especially if you are not sure what the source or exact ingredients and age of the material is. In the case of bark, sawdust and wood-chips, extra nitrogen is required as these substances use large amounts in the breaking down process and the soil soon becomes nitrogen-starved. All are best left to compost for several months or longer, before being used.

Sawdust can be a good medium but it can also be a curse. In the Pacific Northwest of North America, the sawdust from the Douglas Fir seems to be of a consistent standard and is commonly and successfully used in huge quantities by nurserymen to raise field-grown rhododendrons. The downside of sawdust is that over the years it can rot down to a fine sludge with very poor drainage. It also seems to be a substance which encourages the dreaded *Phytophthora cinnamoni*. Outside the Pacific Northwest, I would only add a small percentage of sawdust to your soil mix as the due to the variability both

Top: Peat is an acid, moisture-retentive material which is much used in cultivation

Above: Needles, composted bark and leaf mould provide the ideal combination of organic matter to mix with garden soil for rhododendrons

of tree source and degree of composting (and therefore fertiliser requirement).

The one substance definitely to avoid is lawn-mowings; the ferocious heat and chemical by-products of composting grass have killed whole collections!

We find that the ideal growing medium is a combination of garden soil with a generous mixture of several of the above sub-stances mixed into the planting area. Think about preparing an area large enough for the rootball of the future rather than just a small hole large enough for the root at time of purchase. Individually prepared holes are fine for large growing varieties but smaller ones may well benefit from having a whole bed made up for them.

Planting Procedures

Rhododendrons are shallow rooted plants and must not be planted too deeply. The top of the rootball should be just below the soil surface. The roots which feed the plant are usually just near the top, and rarely more than 30cm (1ft) below the surface. If roots are buried deeper, they tend to die off. In heavier soils, loosen the soil up to a considerable depth below where the rootball will be, to ensure that it is not left sitting on a hard pan.

The advice given when planting most shrubs, to put fertiliser at the bottom of the hole (e.g. bonemeal) will not do any harm, but is largely a waste of time because there are few feeding roots on the underside of the rootball. When planting any rhododendron, remove weeds and improve the soil in an area considerably larger than the existing rootball, so that there is ample surrounding soil for the new roots easily to grow into. As they are so shallowly rooted, it is advisable to keep the area over the roots free of weeds and other competition for moisture. For the same reason, it is usually not a good idea to plant rhododendrons singly in holes cut into lawns, where they will be competing with the grass.

When planting on steep slopes, especially in areas of low rainfall and on very well-drained soils, it may be necessary to plant in a saucer-like depression so that rainwater and artificial irrigation is allowed to collect and soak into the ground around the rootball. Conversely, in mild climates, where rainfall is very high or the ground is heavy clay, considerable success can be had by planting the rhododendrons on the soil surface itself and mounding up a compost high in organic matter around the plant for the roots to grow into. It may take a while to establish plants in these conditions.

When to Plant

Rhododendrons have compact, fibrous and shallow rootballs allowing them to be planted and moved at any time of year. I have heard of American gardeners (admittedly with good irrigation systems) moving their plants around in full flower to ensure the best colour combinations. Having said this, there is no doubt that autumn planting allows the best establishment of plants, especially for large plantings. The warmth of the soil will allow a little root growth before the onset of the severest weather and the winter rains will wash soil well into contact with the rootball. These conditions allow the plant to develop new roots in early spring, which penetrate the surrounding soil before growth starts above ground. This provides a degree of drought resistance and ensures the

PLANTING SEQUENCE

1: After the organic matter has been mixed into the soil (see page 44), a hole larger and deeper than the rootball should be dug out and then backfilled. This ensures good drainage. Make sure that the rootball is moist right through. If it is dry, soak it for a while

2: Make sure the top of the rootball is more or less level with the soil surface. Do not plant too deep. Soil should be firmed up well around the rootball, but do not press down much on the rootball itself, as this compacts the soil underneath and impedes drainage

3: Unless the soil is already soaking wet (which would indicate less-than-ideal planting conditions), water the newly planted rhododendron in thoroughly

1

best possible growth in the first growing season (usually leading to the best flowering too). The exception to this is in very severe climates, such as N.E. U.S.A. and E. Canada and parts of N. Europe. Here, it is probably preferable to plant in late spring so that the plant has a full growing season *in situ* before having to brave the winter.

Prepare the planting area in summer or early autumn when weeds respond to weedkillers and the ground is dry enough to work easily without compacting the soil. If you are not yet ready to plant, you can cover the prepared area with polythene to keep heavy rain and weed seeds out.

Planting stages
- Remove weeds, with weedkillers if necessary (see page 50), from the planting area.
- Prepare the soil. This normally requires the addition of organic matter, as discussed previously over an area wider and deeper than the rootball.
- Make sure the rootball of the plant is moist right through. Soaking it in a bucket of water is necessary. A dry rootball will repel water once it has been planted and the plant will languish or die.
- Do not plant the rhododendron too deep. Just cover the rootball and no more. Firm up the soil thoroughly around the roots but do not compress the rootball itself. This just compacts the soil under the plant and impairs the drainage.
- Unless the soil is very wet, water in thoroughly. This helps settle the soil around the rootball.
- It is often useful to mulch the area over the rootball (see over).

Mulching

Mulching involves putting a layer or barrier of suitable material on top of the rootball of a plant or plants. A mulch can be of many different substances: chipped bark, woodchips, compost, grit, old newspaper or old carpets.

This can have several benefits: it can cut down evaporation (lessening the need for watering), keep the roots cool in hot weather and insulated from frost in cold weather, and to discourage weeds from growing over the rootball. There can be disadvantages too: It can prevent the rain penetrating the soil and it can tend to provide a hiding place for insects such as vine weevil.

Different mulches have different attributes. In our woodland garden we mulch in midwinter with the leaf litter left around after leaf fall, coupled with general prunings, compost, twigs from storm damage and so on. Beech and oak leafmoulds are particularly good, while sycamore, lime and horse chestnut are less suitable as the resulting leafmould is slimy at first and powdery later, and can even be alkaline. Leaves from these trees should be mixed with oak and beech.

There are many other materials which work. Old carpets are a favourite of the organic gardening fraternity but they are hardly something which comes readily to hand most of the time, they look dreadful and they do not allow water to penetrate. Bark and woodchips are excellent for keeping down weeds but they take nitrogen out of the soil as they break down, so you may need to apply extra fertiliser. I recommend not using these substances fresh as they heat up as they compost and may also release undesirable chemicals.

We have recently started using sheets of old newspaper for mulching around small and fussy plants. Several layers can be laid on the surface of the soil. Water it until it becomes soggy and plant through the paper. Then cover with a thin layer of bark or woodchips to improve the appearance. This is especially good for keeping down weeds for the first year when plants are very small, and it cuts down on watering.

I should put in a word here about using peat as a mulch. Many garden centre labels give the advice 'mulch with peat once a year' when you buy a rhododendron. This is pretty useless advice and I cannot think of any good reason to do it. Peat has no nutrients, repels water and tends to dry to a fine powder which is liable to blow away. And weeds love it!

Finally, avoid the worst mulch of all. Fresh grass clippings are deadly. Whole collections have been killed by mulching with clippings which heat up and kill the surface roots. If you use grass, make sure it is well composted and mixed with other things. Whichever mulch you choose, keep the layer thin. If you pile mulch on rhododendrons in thick layers, or layer upon layer, you bury the feeder roots and the plant will suffer.

2

3

Moving Rhododendrons

Because of their compact, fibrous rootballs, mature rhododendrons can generally be moved, even when they are very large, provided you can find the physical means to lift and move them. The British national rhododendron collection at Windsor Great Park was established by moving the huge collection from Tower Court. The majority of the plants, some of which were enormous, survived the move; many are still living quite happily.

We find that larger leaved species and hybrids are the easiest to move as large plants, dwarf rhododendrons move less well and both evergreen and deciduous azaleas are often very slow to re-establish if moved as mature plants. The best time of year for such moving is generally in autumn, when rootballs are moist and the plants will have time to re-establish and then send out roots into the surrounding soil in spring before the heat of the summer. The exception to this is in very cold areas such as east North America where wind and frozen ground can easily desiccate newly planted specimens. Spring may be a better choice in such areas.

There are many reasons why a mature plant may need to be moved: the area may be crowded with too many plants close together, competing for light. The plant may be expanding to block a path. It may just look out of place with its surroundings. Often, as a rhododendron collector moves from hybrids to species, the massive colourful hybrids are given away to friends to be replaced with a connoisseur's selection of species.

Left: The garden soil is improved by the addition of organic matter such as conifer needles, leaf mould and bark. These should be well mixed in

Below: The famous peat beds at the Royal Botanic Garden, Edinburgh, constructed with peat blocks, are filled with dwarf rhododendrons, other dwarf Ericaceae, dwarf bulbs and acid-loving perennials and alpines such as gentians

When moving a rhododendron, try to keep as much width of rootball as possible since the most recent and most vigorous roots are usually at the outermost part of the rootball. Investigate with a spade until you find the healthy, new roots and dig round just outside this circle. The depth of rootball required is seldom much more than 30cm (1ft) and usually considerably less. Beware of trying to keep too much root as the weight of it (particularly when wet) may break the stem of the plant, or cause the whole root to drop off. If the rootball you end up with looks to be too small, because a bit breaks off for instance, or the foliage is sparse and straggly, it may be necessary to prune quite hard (see page 51).

One of the easiest ways to move large plants is by making a sledge out of heavy-duty polythene or similar material and simply dragging the plant along on this. Good soil preparation for the new hole, careful planting (see page 42) and diligent watering in the first growing season, are all crucial to good establishment.

Plants may need staking and artificial wind protection to prevent rocking and to allow quick anchoring from fresh roots put out into the surrounding soil.

Labelling

Many a fine collection has been reduced in value by inadequate labelling. While species can usually be identified, hybrids and azaleas are often very difficult and once the labels or records are lost, there is seldom a way back.

Over the years we have tried many different methods. Embossed labels, such as those found in botanical gardens, are clear, large and last well but are very expensive. Probably the best cheap option we have tried are aluminium labels, written on in pencil. These are small and rather hard to find and they must be periodically loosened or relocated to avoid strangling the branch they are tied to. Plastic labels only last a few years and then become brittle. The writing of so-called indelible pens only seems to last for a year or two.

Whatever method you use, it is well worth keeping some sort of records of when and where things are planted. Such lists, and maps, have been invaluable to new owners of good collections. Do not forget to record collector's numbers on labels and in records (see page 79).

Maintenance

Fertilisers and Feeding

Rhododendrons are not greedy plants when it comes to fertilisers; indeed, if you follow the correct procedures in soil preparation, with well-drained, moisture-retentive soil without competition from other plants, rhododendrons may need no feeding at all. Many fine collections, not to mention the plants in their wild state, get by without any application.

Vigour, good leaf retention and deep green foliage are the signs of a healthy plant which needs no added help. Short growth, a sparse appearance and pale or yellowish leaves all indicate an unhappy plant which may well require feeding, though the symptoms may also point to poor drainage or drought. The golden rule with rhododendrons is 'little and often' rather than a single large dose. Most evergreen and deciduous azaleas and most larger hybrids can take considerable amounts of fertiliser without any ill effects and some, such as 'Lem's Cameo' and some of its hybrids, seem to require extra large doses to maintain healthy foliage. Conversely, some dwarf varieties and many species are extremely sensitive and will suffer leaf tip burn or worse if you over do it. Young plants can be particularly sensitive.

Compound fertilisers contain three main ingredients: nitrogen, phosphorus and potassium. These have an NPK rating giving the ratio of the three ingredients. For example 5N:5P:5K signifies equal amounts of each. Nitrogen is essential for growth and foliage formation and is quickly leached out of the soil, so needs to be replenished. It is this ingredient in excess which causes leaf scorch so it is important to be very careful with high-nitrogen fertilisers such as those used on vegetables. Phosphorus promotes root growth and the ripening of wood at the end of the season so the plant can withstand the winter. Potassium induces flower buds, hardiness and disease resistance.

At Glendoick, we use a general fertiliser with a ratio 12N:6P:6K and sometimes add extra nitrogen using ammonium sulphate. Many fertilisers also contain trace elements which include calcium, sulphur, magnesium, iron and other substances essential for healthy plant development. These minerals are required in minute quantities; too much of some of them can be as harmful as too little. The trace elements usually occur naturally in garden soils in sufficient quantity, and rarely need replenishing artificially, but they are useful for making potting composts for plants growing indoors and/or in containers.

Both organic and inorganic fertilisers can be used. Beware of farmyard manures; they can be extremely high in nitrogen if too fresh and can therefore cause severe leaf burn. This is especially true of poultry manure. Well-rotted cow manure is fine. Some of the substances used as mulches in parts of the world, such as pea straw and oilseed rape straw, are naturally high in nitrogen and will feed as they break down. Some of the traditional organic fertilisers such as bone meal are not particularly recommended for rhododendrons, though they are unlikely to do any harm.

Of the inorganic fertilisers, ammonium sulphate is undoubtedly the cheapest and most effective way to increase nitrogen in the soil. Yellow-leaved plants, if they are suffering from nitrogen deficiency due to the breakdown of organic materials in the compost, respond very quickly and soon green up. Use small doses at first and ensure that the powdery fertiliser is not left on the foliage, as it tends to burn. It can be washed off with water if it sticks to the leaves. Chlorosis (when leaves turn yellow with just the veins remaining green) can be caused by drainage problems, soil pH or drought as well as by mineral deficiency. Iron chelates or sequestrols are often recommended as the cure-all for chlorotic foliage. This will only be of benefit if the problem is one of a lack of available iron. As the iron chelates are relatively expensive, try a small amount on a few plants during the growing season to see if there is any improvement. If lack of iron is the cause it should take no more than a month to green up the leaves.

How and when to feed

As the main feeder roots of a rhododendron are near the soil surface and tend to be at the perimeter of the rootball it is not usually worth putting fertiliser at the bottom of the hole (as recommended for many other plants). Nor is it worth scattering it around the trunks of older plants, as the feeder roots are further out. How much to put on depends on the strength of the fertiliser

Weeds

The shallow roots of rhododendrons are not good at competing with vigorous weeds for moisture. Hand weeding, hoeing and weedkillers can be used but it is also worth looking at planting strategies which will reduce the need for weeding. In the wild, rhododendrons usually grow in colonies, growing into one another, providing shelter from wind and sun and preventing enough light reaching the ground for vigorous weeds to thrive. Often it is only moss that is found growing under dense canopies of rhododendrons in their native habitat. Particularly with dwarf and alpine rhododendrons, it is best to plant them in groups which will mat together and carpet the ground. Once this state begins to be achieved, the weeding required is minimal. Mulching is another method of reducing weed growth (see page 43). When hand-pulling weeds and hoeing, bear in mind that the shallow roots of rhododendrons are vulnerable to being exposed if soil is removed with the weed roots, or to being cut by careless hoeing.

and the composition and temperature of the soil. A soil whose organic content is mainly added bark or sawdust requires much more fertiliser than one which is predominantly peat or leafmould.

Although some authorities recommend applying phosphate and potash outside the growing season, our own trials have shown no benefit from this. Wait until growth starts in spring and then feed with two to three small doses in the growing season. By midsummer, growth may be slowing down and flower buds are starting to be set. If you continue fertilising beyond this time, it tends to encourage leaves at the expense of flowering

and makes the resultant soft growth vulnerable to early autumn frosts. This is especially important in severe climates, where new growth must have the maximum length of time to harden up before the onset of coldest midwinter temperatures.

For young plants, such as recently propagated material, as well as plants grown in pots or other containers, slow-release granules or liquid feeding

Slow release fertiliser pellets are incorporated into the compost of container-grown plants and provide nutrients and trace elements for up to 18 months

to the roots or foliage are often the safest and most convenient methods. Slow-release granules can last up to 18 months and can be incorporated into the potting mix. These usually contain all three major ingredients as well as trace elements. Liquid foliar feeding is another excellent method, as the little and often philosophy allows careful monitoring of any signs of leaf tip burn caused by too much nitrogen. Liquid feeding mature plants outdoors is also possible.

Herbicides and Weedkillers

Weedkillers are either total or selective (that is they will kill everything or only specific plants). Their action is contact (surface only) or systemic (penetrate the plant itself) or pre-emergence (kills germinating seedlings). All have their place in rhododendron growing but environmental concerns should always be borne in mind before using them. Legislation concerning their use by professional growers and amateurs varies greatly from country to country and rules are constantly changing, so I have not been specific here.

All weedkillers are, of course, potentially dangerous, harmful to humans and wildlife and they can pollute water. Many should be used with protective clothing and some have very unpleasant fumes. Spray must be fine to coat leaves effectively, which means that spraying should be done on fairly calm days. Wetting agents can be added to some chemicals to increase their effectiveness. Some herbicides, such as glyphosate require a minimum dry period to work well. Some of the pre-emergence weedkillers are relatively safe to apply as they come in granular form and can be applied with a 'pepper-pot' type shaker, which ensures even distribution.

Total weedkillers are used to clean up an area before planting. Glyphosate is now the most common total weedkiller used by professionals and amateurs, replacing the much more dangerous sodium-chlorate. Effective by systemic action on most herbaceous weeds and some woody ones, including *R. ponticum*, it should be used when weeds are in full growth. The foliage of stubborn weeds with a waxy leaf surface, such as ivy, may need to be bruised before application. Planting of the area can commence seven days after application as it is not residual in the soil. The hormone weedkiller 2,4,D is effective on hard-to-eradicate weeds such as creeping thistle. Triclopyr can be used in grassland, but is not safe to use around cultivated rhododendrons. It is very effective for stubborn woody weeds such as tree saplings, brambles (*Rubus*), *R. ponticum*, broom and others such as nettles.

Selective weedkillers. Developed for use against difficult-to-eradicate weeds, destroying one plant growing amongst other sorts e.g. broadleaved weeds in grass. One of the best is cycloxydim which kills grass (including couch) but which is virtually harmless to most other cultivated plants, so may be sprayed among them. Asulam is invaluable for killing bracken and docks (Rumex) and we have used it successfully around mature plants in our Argyll garden without adverse effects.

Contact Weedkillers such as Paraquat and Diquat. These quickly kill the top growth of most weeds but are inactivated in the soil. These chemicals are usually harmless on woody trunks so can be used right up to old, established rhododendrons. Damage occurs to anything green, including leaves and any stems and trunks which remain green from chlorophyll. Maples are an example. Drift causes unsightly black spotting on rhododendron foliage. Both can even be applied during light rain. They encourage the growth of moss and are sometimes used deliberately for this purpose. These very useful products may be removed from the market due to environmental concerns. An alternative is the gas flame-gun which, rather than actually burning the weeds, causes fatal damage to plant cells. Obviously extreme care should be taken to avoid damaging precious plants.

Pre-emergence weedkillers are applied to clean soil and prevent germination of seed. They can be watered or applied as granules around growing plants. They generally have little effect on established weeds, so they are best applied after an area has been cleaned by other means. Some of them have been proven to cause damage to rhododendrons rhododendrons but we have found that propachlor, oxadiazon and propyzamide seldom cause damage, even to very young plants. Simazine is best on mature plants only; we have found it can damage young stock. (This chemical now has very restricted use in Europe.) There are some rhododendron varieties which are sensitive to them, especially as young plants. We have found that specific weeds, such as nettles and cleavers (*Galium*) are resistant to most pre-emergence herbicides. It is advisable to wash the foliage of rhododendrons after applying, in case there are any adverse effects.

Pinching and Pruning

It is another of the old myths about rhododendron cultivation that you cannot, or should not, pinch and prune them to improve their shape. Despite the fact that many of the books on the subject say pruning is not necessary, nurserymen do it routinely to produce those symmetrical bushes which garden centres like to stock

and their customers like to buy. As far as improving the shape of rhododendrons, pinching is preventative while pruning is a cure. Pinching means removing the terminal or central growth bud of a rhododendron shoot as it elongates, in order to encourage multiple branching lower down. Pruning involves cutting a shoot or branch so that buds break further down, hopefully improving the shape.

I am not claiming that rhododendrons require pruning in the same way that a rose, for instance, does on an annual basis. It is just a tool that can be used from time to time to improve the shape of your

Pinching. Removing the central growth bud (right) encourages branching below as can be seen on the left where three growth buds are starting to swell. Each will produce a new shoot, encouraging bushiness

plants. Many of the alpine and dwarf varieties such as 'yak' hybrids need little or no pruning to maintain a good shape, as long as they are grown in plenty of light. As soon as rhododendrons start to flower freely, most growth comes from lateral shoots below the flower buds and therefore nature does its own pinching.

When plants are young and before they start to flower freely, the simplest way to ensure a plant of good habit is to pinch out all the single, terminal buds as they elongate in the spring. Wait until this becomes easy to do: if you have to dig out the bud, it is too early. I recommend this for vigorous dwarfs, subsection Triflora species and most larger hybrids.

With species, many of the largest ones are, in essence, trees and they should be left to form a single trunk until they reach a good height. Others, such as the very vigorous *R. decorum*, are better pinched as a small plant to encourage bushiness. Spring frosts do a lot of natural pinching, with the central bud being frosted and leaving the later growth to come from below as multiple shoots. This usually gives good results, though I have seen some large-leaved species which were frosted so often that their growth became unnaturally congested.

There are several reasons why you may want to prune a bush. It may have become crowded out by other plants and have

become straggly. It may have been severely damaged by cold or wind, or had its first flush of growth frosted, causing unsightly, brown, distorted foliage. You may want to reduce it in size because it has got too big or because you want to move it. Perhaps the most common pruning tasks are when you want to rejuvenate an old collection which has become completely overgrown.

Scaly-leaved rhododendrons and all azaleas can be pruned to any point on a branch or shoot and new growth will come from buds lower down. With larger-leaved non-scaly varieties, you must cut back to a whorl of leaves (see photo). New growth will only come from a bud, or buds, within these leaves.

Although it is possible to prune at any time of year, perhaps the most satisfactory time is straight after flowering (except for varieties flowering later than early summer). This gives time for production of new growth and, hopefully, formation of flower buds for the following year. Alternatively, prune in early spring, before new growth is starting to elongate.

Scaly-leaved rhododendrons and almost all azaleas can be pruned with success. Azaleas and species from subsection Triflora such as *R. yunnanense* and *R. augustinii* can be hard pruned and, provided the roots are healthy, they soon send out plenty of new growth. Most small-leaved dwarfs can be pruned into shape but it is best to leave a fair amount of leaves: cutting back into too much old wood is risky. Maddenia and Vireyas grown indoors tend to get straggly if not hard pruned every few years. Among larger species and hybrids, there is considerable variation in how well they respond. If you can cut back to a healthy whorl of leaves, one or some of the buds above each leaf stalk will almost certainly grow.

It is when a more severe pruning is required, cutting back to a bare trunk, that results vary considerably. As a general rule, those with a smooth bark such as *R. thomsonii*, *R. barbatum* and some of the large-leaved species such as *R. sinogrande* are reluctant to respond to this. Of the large-leaved species, *R. macabeanum* can produce plenty of shoots out from the base if cut back deliberately or by severe weather.

Amongst the best responders are *R. arboreum* and the ubiquitous *R. ponticum*. The latter's ability to regenerate is one of the reasons it is so hard to eradicate in areas where it has become a pest. This species was traditionally used as a rootstock for grafting cultivars and its extreme propensity to throw suckers has in many cases meant that the rootstock has overwhelmed whatever was grafted on top of it. This is important to bear in mind when try-

When pruning larger-leaved varieties, cut back to just above a circle of leaves (known as a whorl). Even if the old leaves have dropped off, it should be possible to see where a whorl of leaves was and cut back to this point

ing to rejuvenate bushes which date back to the 1950s or earlier. The characteristic dark green, shiny, narrow leaves of *R. ponticum* should make it possible to identify, even outside flowering time, which the suckers are. These should be broken off at the base of the stem. If you prune them off, they will just produce a whole cluster of shoots from the below the cut.

Since the 1950s, cuttings, and more recently, micro-propagation have been the major production techniques for rhododendrons (except in northern Europe where most cultivars are grafted on 'Cunningham's White' which fortunately is far less prone to suckering).

Dead-heading

Rhododendrons are not perpetual-flowering so dead-heading does not prolong the flowering season as it does with some rose varieties, for instance. There are, however, sound arguments for doing at least some deadheading. Rhododendrons are a rather promiscuous lot and they are very often cross-pollinated by insects. The resulting seed set can be large and unsightly but, more importantly, it waste energy in ripening seed, discouraging vigorous new growth and, therefore, a good flowering season the following year. If you only have a few rhododen-

DEAD-HEADING

1. Firmly grasp the base of the truss (after the flowers have fallen off)

2. Snap the flower stem off at the base as cleanly as possible, being careful not to damage the emerging buds below

1

2

drons, deadhead them if you have time. If you have a large collection, then concentrate on those which will benefit the most. Young plants, especially those bought and planted in flower, will definitely benefit. So will most larger-growing species which produce enormous, multiple-flowered trusses. Anything with a mass of swelling seed heads is best deadheaded.

Most popular hardy hybrids, 'yak' hybrids, dwarfs and deciduous and evergreen azaleas seldom need it and will flower well every year whether deadheaded or not. One or two dwarfs such as *R. campylogynum* tend to produce large, unsightly seed heads held above the foliage which are most easily removed with a pair of scissors. The technique when removing spent flower heads from larger species and hybrids is to break the truss off at the base above the whorl of leaves below it. Be careful not to break off the emerging growth buds underneath. Take your time until you get the knack; it does not take long before you can do it very quickly.

Irrigation and Watering

On the mountains of the Himalayas and China, there is typically a relatively dry period in spring when flowering occurs and this is followed by heavy monsoon rains during the main part of the growing season. Few of us are fortunate (or unfortunate!) enough to live in areas with such reliable summer rains and so we are forced to supplement our rainfall with artificial watering.

Rhododendron root systems are shallow and compact, so if the soil dries out, they are one of the first plants to wilt. None will withstand sustained periods of drought but small-leaved species and evergreen azaleas plus one or two larger-leaved species, such as *R. macrophyllum* and *R. decorum*, are able to tolerate fairly dry conditions. Ample moisture throughout the growing season is required to see the spectacular large leaves on species such as *R. sinogrande*. Rhododendrons wilt and curl up their leaves very demonstratively when they are suffering from lack of water. Most varieties can withstand this for a few days without ill effects but if it happens when there is new growth unfurling this tends to stunt its size.

Watering systems varies hugely, from a single can or hose for a small garden, to sophisticated and computer-controlled sprinkler systems with pipes buried underground. Seep-hose and trickle irrigation, which slowly leak water from numerous holes or small pipes laid in or on the planting beds, are an excellent way of directing moisture to exactly where it is needed, and cut down on waste. As a general rule it is better to give plants an occa-sional good soaking than a series of inadequate doses. Rhododendrons with good root systems can survive a surprising amount of drought, though the stress this incurs may make them vulnerable to other problems such as honey fungus. In very hot weather it is best to water in early morning or late at night to avoid burning of foliage and evaporation. Excess water coupled with poor drainage and high temperature is a sure recipe for the lethal *Phytophthora* root rot. Watering plants in flower in warm climates encourages petal blight which can soon ruin the flowers completely.

With recent changes in weather patterns, as well as huge increases in demand, water is becoming a precious commodity and the threat of hosepipe bans hangs over many gardens. There are various things that can be done to cut down on the amount of watering required. Autumn planting with plenty of moisture retaining organic matter and good mulching are well worth considering.

In our experience, tree roots rather than evaporation are the most common cause of dry soil. If greedy trees cannot be removed or are required for shade and shelter, it may be worth trying to isolate the rhododendron roots from the tree roots with barriers such as thick polythene. We have found that beds lined with polythene (ensuring good drainage) with a good mulch almost never require watering, even in our sunny garden with long periods of inadequate rain. In areas with alkaline soil, this method may be essential, as all watering will have to be done with collected rainwater. The fact that seep-hoses and trickle hoses can be buried means they are much less wasteful and, they should be encouraged in any case.

There are several advantages to cutting down watering in late summer, even to the extent of causing some stress to the plants. In very severe climates, where fully ripened wood is essential to withstand extreme lows of temperature, plants which go on growing into the autumn are very vulnerable to damage. Those whose roots are a little dry from late summer onwards are much better prepared for winter. It is, however, important to water the plants thoroughly in autumn, if conditions are dry, before the onset of winter.

In all climates, cutting down on watering in late summer encourages the setting of flower buds for next season; nurserymen do this as a matter of course. Larger species flower at a younger age in dry eastern Scotland than they do in the much wetter west, where they grow more lushly and vigorously.

Propagation

POLLINATING A
FLOWER

Fig. 1

Flower bud

Pollen

Stamen

Fig. 2

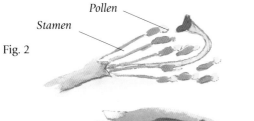

The corolla
removed

Stamen

Fig. 3

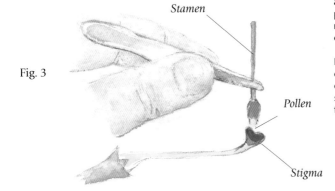

Pollen

Stigma

Fig. 1: The unopened flower bud, a day or two before opening

Fig. 2: The unopened corolla is removed, revealing the stigma and and stamens. The stamens should be removed at this point

Fig. 3: Several days later, the stigma becomes ripe (sticky) and the pollen of the male parent can applied

Below: A cross-section of a flower, showing the floral parts

Rhododendrons and azaleas are not one of the easier plant groups to propagate; seedlings are slow-growing and cuttings generally take several months to root. With a little care and attention, however, it is possible to have very successful results.

Propagation falls into two main categories, sexual (from seed) or asexual (cuttings, layers, grafts etc.). The crucial difference is that from sexual reproduction, the offspring are all different and are NOT identical to the parent, while the asexual, or vegetative, methods produce plants which are an exact replica of the parent. All named varieties and selected clones must be produced by vegetative means.

Seed

This method can be used to raise species from wild or garden seed and for creating new hybrids. It cannot be used to reproduce a named hybrid. Seeds grown from 'Pink Pearl' are not 'Pink Pearl'.

Rhododendrons are notoriously promiscuous; this means that in a garden they will be cross-pollinated by insects flying from one plant to another and the seed-grown offspring will almost always be hybridised, unless there is no compatible plant flowering at the same time in the vicinity.

If you want to grow species or make hybrids from garden seed, you have to make deliberately controlled pollinations. This involves removing the corolla (petals)

PARTS OF A FLOWER

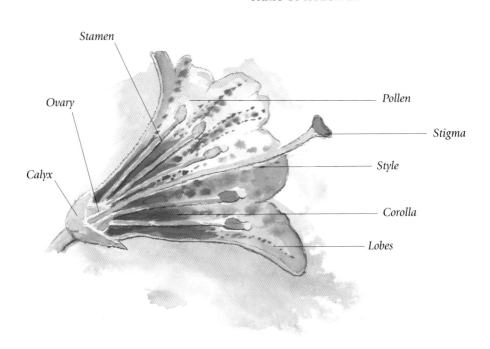

Stamen

Ovary

Calyx

Pollen

Stigma

Style

Corolla

Lobes

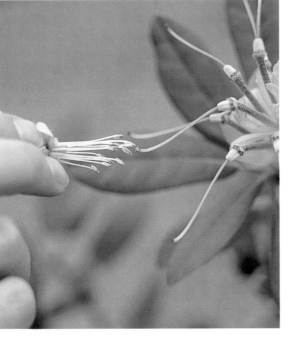

and stamens from the flower on the female parent before it opens, waiting for the stigma to ripen (it becomes sticky), and then applying pollen from the stamens of the other (male) parent to the ripened stigma. Pollen can be stored in a fridge for several weeks, it can be frozen and thawed and be sent through the mail, so the male parent does not have to be flowering near by or at the same time.

Do not forget to label the pollinated flower and record it so you can find the right seed capsules in the autumn. Seed of both hybrids and species is available from Rhododendron Society seed exchanges. The most exiting seed to grow is that collected in the wild. Such seed often has a collector's number recording by whom, when and where the seed was collected.

Rhododendron seed takes three to seven months to ripen and is therefore harvested in the autumn or winter following pollination. The seed capsules will be swollen and turning brown. Try to collect them just before they split. If capsules are collected green, place them in a dry place such as a window sill and they will dry and split within a few days or weeks.

HYBRIDISATION

1. The pollen from the stamens of the male parent is applied to the stigmas of the emasculated female parent. The stigma is ready for pollination when it is sticky

2. The ovary starting to swell after a successful pollination. The smaller ovaries have not been successfully pollinated

The seed is fairly small. Try to separate from the chaff and debris to avoid the seed going mouldy. Once dried, it can be stored in envelopes in the fridge until you are ready to sow. Seed should be sown in pans or trays containing moist (but not soaking) peat or clean, live sphagnum moss. Sow seed thinly onto the surface and do not cover with compost. We find covering pans with perforated polythene keeps the humidity up but lets air circulate.

Germination usually takes two to three weeks if the temperature is 59-70°C (15-20°F) in a propagator or heated frame.

In a cold frame, germination will probably not take place until the spring. All watering of seed pans should be done by soaking from below to avoid encouraging mould on the foliage. Once seed has germinated it needs sufficient light (but not direct

sunlight) to keep plants strong and compact. Inadequate light causes weak etiolated (drawn) seedlings.

When large enough to handle, prick out the seedlings into trays in a peat-based compost. Be very careful with feeding at this stage as seedlings, especially dwarfs and species, are very sensitive to fertiliser. Use slow-release or dilute liquid feed. Usually, seedlings are best over-wintered under cover, in a coldframe, greenhouse or similar. Small seedlings are vulnerable to botrytis (mould) and other pests and diseases (see page 66).

Asexual/ Clonal Methods

LAYERING

This is a good method to obtain a few new plants. It involves bending side branches of the chosen plant into the surrounding soil so that they make roots. In moist climates, it often happens naturally. After one to three years (depending on the variety, soil penetration and rainfall), the rooted, layered shoot can be cut from the mother plant and moved elsewhere.

Above: Ripened and splitting seed capsules collected in the autumn, showing the chambers filled with seeds. The seeds are relatively large, indicating a larger-growing variety

Right: Seedlings in a seed pan. These are becoming rather crowded and will soon need to be pricked out

Left: Sowing seeds on the surface of a seed pan. Try to sow the seeds fairly thinly to avoid over-crowding when the seedlings germinate

Right: Seedlings pricked out into a seed tray in a peat-based compost

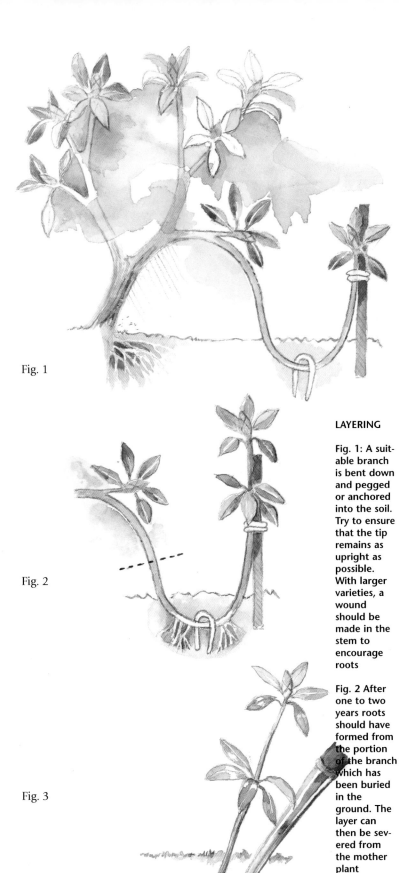

Fig. 1

Fig. 2

Fig. 3

Varieties which are very upright in habit are unlikely to have suitable branches to layer. It is usually advisable to improve the soil where the layers will be made, by adding organic matter. In moist climates, you can layer into pots or trays placed around the growing plant. which avoids root disturbance when the layers are cut.With dwarf varieties, shoots can be anchored using rocks and stones. With larger varieties, layers are usually held in place with stakes, or wire. Bend the branch or shoot into the surrounding (prepared if necessary) soil and anchor it so that the end of the shoot is as near upright as possible. Many layers can be made from a single specimen, we have sometimes layered the entire plant.

To encourage root-production in larger varieties it is advisable to cut a thin layer of bark off the underside of the branch or shoot where it is to be anchored into the ground. Once a good root system has formed, the plant can be severed from the mother and transplanted. Ensure the layers are well watered before moving them. The disadvantage of layered plants is that they usually have a rather obvious bend in the stem. Judicious pruning can usually result in an acceptable specimen.

LAYERING

Fig. 1: A suitable branch is bent down and pegged or anchored into the soil. Try to ensure that the tip remains as upright as possible. With larger varieties, a wound should be made in the stem to encourage roots

Fig. 2 After one to two years roots should have formed from the portion of the branch which has been buried in the ground. The layer can then be severed from the mother plant

Fig. 3: The layer is now ready for transplanting

CUTTINGS

Rhododendrons and azaleas vary greatly in the ease with which they root from cuttings. Evergreen azaleas and most dwarf rhododendrons are relatively easy, while many species, deciduous azaleas and larger hybrids, are rather slow and tricky to root. One or two varieties refuse point blank to root at all and these have to be grafted.

The easiest way to root rhododendrons is under polythene in a box, tray, pots or modules, or in a propagator; ensure these are all well cleaned before use. Some people have small mist systems which can give excellent results, but which require more looking after. Bottom heat is advisable but not essential; without it, cuttings put in during late summer or autumn will take twice or three times as long to root. Cuttings should be taken when they are sufficiently hardened up to be flexible and springy when subjected to a bit of bending. This tends to be from late summer onwards.

Dwarfs and evergreen azaleas should be cut to 2.5-5cm (1-2in) or so, larger varieties can be up to 10cm (4in) long. Remove leaves to form a single circle of four to seven leaves at the top of a cutting. Shaded leaves tend to rot in the rooting bed. With longer-leaved varieties, you can reduce the leaf length by 30-40 per cent to save space. The most satisfactory rooting media tend to be 50-60 per cent peat and 40-50 per cent composted bark, perlite, grit or other substance to keep the compost open. Rooting hormones are useful to speed up the process.

With larger varieties it also helps to cut a thin slice off the lower stem. Compost should be moist but not wet as this causes rotting. Cuttings can be sprayed with a general fungicide to discourage disease. Cover them with a propagator lid, polythene sheet, or a polythene bag, making it more or less airtight so that the humidity is maintained.

Keeping the atmosphere humid is most important. If the leaves dry out, the cuttings wilt and will not root. They need plenty of light but must be shaded from direct sunlight. Cuttings root best with bottom heat of 15-20°C (59-70°F). In mid-winter we reduce heat to about 10°C (50°F), as Scottish light levels are very low. Further south this may not be necessary.

Check over the cuttings regularly and remove any dead material to avoid the spread of disease. Once roots have formed which are roughly the same size as the foliage on the cutting, it should be removed from the heat and hardened off by covering it with slit polythene, or shading material.

Rooted cuttings can be transplanted into a peat-based compost which will usually also contain some composted bark, perlite, leaf-mould or needles and often some slow-release fertiliser. Some protection will be needed for most of their first growing season. Beware of vine weevil in pots and trays (see page 64). We plant out our cuttings near the end of their first growing season.

The other propagation methods, grafting and tissue culture, tend to be for professionals and keenest amateurs only. Consult the further reading list for sources of information on these methods (see page 124).

Top left: In preparing cuttings, remove large flower buds, trim the leaves if they are long. With thicker-stemmed varieties, make a thin cut or 'wound' on the lower portion of the stem

Centre left: The clearly labelled cuttings are covered with thin transparent polythene, placed directly on, or held up just above the cuttings

Opposite: Place cuttings in a tray, spacing them so that leaves do not overlap too much. Overcrowding encourages rotting

Bottom left: Cuttings showing root development. The roots are just starting to grow on the cutting on the right. The cutting on the left has a root-ball large enough to remove from the rooting tray or bench and it will now be hardened off

Pests and
Diseases

Pests and Diseases

Although the list of pests and diseases in this section is quite daunting, you will be relieved to know that each area where rhododendrons are grown suffers only some of them. Indeed it is possible to say that in areas with a moderate climate, the most likely-to-be-encountered pest will be vine weevil, the most damaging disease powdery mildew and the most irksome climatic problem spring frosts. Many of the other problems are unlikely to be encountered. On the other hand, where temperatures are more extreme, such as in eastern North America and parts of continental Europe, the problems are more likely to include stem and root rots, and others associated with these climates such as winter cold damage. More plants are killed or maimed by poor soil preparation and lack of care in the first growing season than most of the other problems put together.

Pests

WARM-BLOODED PESTS

Rhododendrons are poisonous to many animals which usually know not to eat them, but there are cases of sheep and cattle poisoning from time to time. Horses and cattle are more likely to cause breakage than to graze your plants, but this and the soil compaction that they can cause means that is advisable to keep farm animals fenced from your rhododendrons. Birds can cause considerable damage, both in dust bathing and in looking for food, especially around small, newly planted stock. Indoors and in frames, mice and voles can be troublesome, especially in cold and snowy winters.

The two most common animal pests in the U.K. are deer and rabbits. Both tend to be rather particular as to which varieties or groups of varieties they prefer to eat. Azaleas, both deciduous and evergreen, seem to be especially palatable and certain species such as *R. canadense* always seem to be the first to be attacked. When grazing is lush and there is plenty to eat, rhododendrons are often left well alone. The problems usually occur when there is snow on the ground, especially when the earth is frozen solid. Often, rhododendrons are one of the few evergreen plants which the deer and rabbits can easily reach and so considerable damage, such as the loss of leaf tips, branch tips or, more seriously, the stripping of the bark, may occur.

Right: A plant which has had the bark eaten off around the base by vine weevil larvae, completely girdling the stem. This is almost always fatal, though collapse may take several months

Bark eaten away

Vine Weevil (adult)

Larvae

Above left: The adult vine weevil (x2 life size) is usually around 1cm (½in) long and cuts notches out of rhododendron leaves at night

Above right: The very destructive vine weevil grubs eat the roots and bark of rhododendrons and many other plants and this can often be fatal. They are quite hard to control

Ideally, fencing is the perfect option but this is expensive, especially where deer are concerned. To fence effectively against rabbits, use netting at least 1m (3ft) wide and bury 10-15cm (4-6in) in the ground to prevent them from digging underneath. In really severe infestations, it may be necessary to poison rabbit warrens using sodium cyanide or similar gasses. Such chemicals are potentially very dangerous and countries have strict regulations as to who is allowed to use them. An effective deer fence needs to be 2m (6ft) high for Roe deer (the most common deer species in the U.K.) but may need to be higher for larger species.

The alternative is to attempt to protect vulnerable plants with substances whose smell will discourage the deer. Some people swear by bundles of human hair (try your local hairdresser), while others obtain dung of predatory animals such as lions from their local zoo! Several commercial animal repellents have been developed over the years. The most common is aluminium ammonium sulphate (sold under the name 'scoot', 'stay off', etc). A substance called Bitrex is now available in North America. This is taken up by the plant, making its leaves unpalatable to all animals.

caterpillars which usually eat away whole portions of the leaf or make holes in it). This damage is seldom more than cosmetic and it often tends to occur in shady conditions where the insects can shelter in the undergrowth or leaf litter during the day. A plant moved out into more light will often not be attacked. Alternatively, a plant can be sprayed with a contact insecticide.

Adults tend to hatch out from late spring onwards and need to feed for several weeks before egg-laying can begin; the main reason to kill adults is to prevent them from laying the eggs which produce the much more damaging larvae. Each adult can lay several hundreds of eggs and one larva can kill a young plant on its own, especially if it is in a con-

tainer. Spray the foliage of plants as soon as the characteristic notching is seen on the new growth of the rhododendron.

The vine weevil larvae are white, 'C' or crescent shaped, 1-1.2cm ($\frac{1}{2}$in) long at maturity with a brownish head. They hatch out from eggs laid around the stem of plants (usually in summer or autumn) and eat either the bark or the roots of the plant through late summer, autumn and winter. The girdling of the bark all round the stem at soil level, or above and below it, usually results in death, the plant collapsing quite quickly during the growing season but more slowly during the winter. This is the most common damage in containers. In the open ground, the larvae tend to graze the fresh roots. On

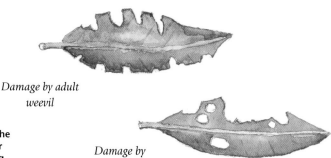

Damage by adult weevil

Damage by caterpillar

Right: The irregular notching typical of adult vine weevil (top) on a rhododendron leaf in contrast to the more general damage done by caterpillars (bottom)

Below: Irregular notching on the leaf margins is usually caused by adult vine weevils which feed at night

an older plant, this is often more debilitating than fatal unless there are large numbers of larvae, but in small and young plants, the root eating can cause death.

Many plants are very vulnerable to vine weevil. Some of their favourites include young yew, strawberries and primulas. Some people use such plants as indicators to show when weevils are active. For amateurs, apart from targeting adults with insecticides, the main weapons available are biological controls against larvae. These include eelworm species *Steinernema* and *Heterorhabditis*. These products are available by mail order and arrive in a packet the contents of which are mixed with lukewarm water in a watering can and watered on. Nematodes (eelworms) require a minimum temperature to breed and attack the weevil larvae and so are only effective in warm weather outdoors. They are most useful in greenhouses and in containers, where the worst problems occur. Compost must be moist in order that the nematode solution can soak well into the soil. The best time to apply is mid to late summer

when soil temperatures are high and before larvae have had a chance to do too much damage. The fact that weevils are flightless means that infestations usually start in localised areas and, provided these can be dealt with, the spread may be halted.

Aphids
Whitefly and greenfly can suddenly appear in large number on the underside of young leaves and on the stems, particularly in dry weather, sucking out the sap and causing puckered or wrinkled leaves. Vireyas seem particularly prone to attack.

Spray with a systemic insecticide but if you dislike using chemicals, soap concentrates can be used. It may take several doses to clear the infestation. With both chemicals and soap sprays, it is important to target the insects on the leaf undersides. This requires a fine spray to allow the water droplets to adhere. There are also a number of biological controls which are most effective under glass. These include *Aphidoletes* (midge) and *Aphidius* (predatory wasp).

containers, where the worst problems occur. Compost must be moist in order that the nematode solution can soak well into the soil. The best time to apply is mid to late summer when soil temperatures are high and before larvae have had a chance to do too much damage. The fact that weevils are flightless means that infestations usually start in localised areas and, provided these can be dealt with, the spread may be halted. A promising recent development is the insecticide imidacloprid which is now available to amateurs. It is incorporated into compost and protects the roots and leaves from vine weevil and other insects, including aphids, for up to one year

Aphids

Whitefly and greenfly can suddenly appear in large number on the underside of young leaves and on the stems, particularly in dry weather, sucking out the sap and causing puckered or wrinkled leaves. Vireyas seem particularly prone to attack.

Spray with a systemic insecticide but if you dislike using chemicals, soap concentrates can be used. It may take several doses to clear the infestation. With both chemicals and soap sprays, it is important to target the insects on the leaf undersides. This requires a fine spray to allow the water droplets to adhere. There are also a number of biological controls which are most effective under glass. These include *Aphidoletes* (midge) and *Aphidius* (predatory wasp).

Other Insect Pests

Caterpillars (from several species of moth, depending on the part of the world) can be troublesome and we find that they do most damage to certain plants where the caterpillars drop from surrounding trees and shrubs. Sometimes they destroy expanding buds, leaving shredded new growth which usually has to be removed. If you cannot pick off and squash the offenders by hand, then use a suitable chemical control. Other insect pests can be very troublesome locally or regionally, but are not widespread.

Scale is a small insect which sucks sap and leaves an unsightly black residue of sooty mould. Spray with insecticide and use a winter tar or paraffin oil wash when dormant to prevent re-infection.

Thrips is a problem in warm and dry climates such as California and parts of New Zealand. It is characterised by a silvery discoloration on the leaf upper surface. Most of the standard insecticides and insecticidal soaps can be used. Locally, biological controls may also be available.

Other pests such as red spider mites, capsid bugs, rhododendron borer, lacewing and leaf miners can cause damage locally. All can be treated with suitable chemicals if necessary.

Diseases

POWDERY MILDEW

Mildews occur on many plant genera with new strains and mutations occurring from time to time. There are three different powdery mildews which attack the genus *Rhododendron*. The three types appear to be mutually exclusive as regards the parts of the genus they affect. One mildew occurs on deciduous azaleas, one on Vireyas and the most troublesome occurs on temperate rhododendron (as opposed to azalea) species and hybrids.

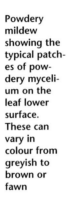

Powdery mildew showing the typical patches of powdery mycelium on the leaf lower surface. These can vary in colour from greyish to brown or fawn

Deciduous Azalea Mildew

Characterised by a silvery mycelium which develops on the upper and sometimes lower surface of the leaf from midsummer onwards. It occurs on wild populations of *R. occidentale* in western North America and on cultivated azaleas, particularly varieties containing *R. occidentale* and *R. luteum*, which includes many of the paler-flowered and scented ones. Most azalea species and hybrids with orange and red flowers seem to be resistant. Apart from being unsightly, the disease, if unchecked, can cause early leaf fall and therefore a general loss of vigour and decrease in flowering. Breeding for mildew resistance has been quite suc-

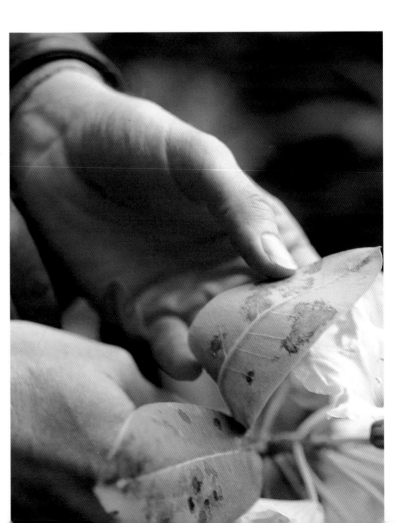

Powdery
mildew
showing
typical discol-
oration on
the upper
surface of
the leaf

Mildew-Susceptible Plants

Species: *R. cinnabarinum*, *R. thomsonii*, and their relatives, *R. calostrotum* ssp. *riparioides*.

Hybrids: most *R. cinnabarinum* hybrids such as 'Lady Chamberlain' and 'Lady Rosebery', *R. thomsonii* hybrids e.g. 'Cornish Cross', 'Naomi, *R. griersonianum* hybrids such as 'Vanessa Pastel', 'Anna Rose Whitney', 'Elizabeth' and yellow hybrids containing *R. wardii* such as 'Virginia Richards', ' Lila Pedigo', 'Golden Star' etc. Semi-dwarfs such as 'Seta'.

The only sure way to control this disease is to spray with suitable systemic fungicides but this only works as a preventative and only for as long as you spray. Fungicides which have proven reliable include bupirimate and triforine, propiconazole and myclobutanil (sold under the names Nimrod T, Tumbleblite, Systhane etc). These are available for amateurs in the U.K. Benomyl and triadimefon (Bayleton) are used in North America by the horticultural industry while Funginex and Fungaway are available to amateurs (these last two control both mildew and rust and unlike most of the other products, do not smell too unpleasant). I know of no effective non-chemical or organic controls, though several avenues are being pursued.

Only recently developed growth is susceptible to the disease. It will not

cessful and many disease-resistant cultivars are available. For susceptible cultivars, spray with a suitable fungicide containing benomyl (benlate), bupirimate and triforine, propiconazole or myclobutanil. This strain of mildew has recently spread to Europe.

Vireya Mildew

This is apparently a mildew which also affects other parts of the family Ericaceae such as *Gaultheria*. It is characterised by white patches on the young leaves which often become under-sized or distorted. It can be controlled using the same fungicides as are used to treat rhododendron mildew.

Rhododendron Powdery Mildew

Although said to have been first reported in the 1960s, this disease did not start to cause problems until the early 1980s. Since then, it has become one of the major problems for rhododendron growers in moderate climates such as the British Isles, western North America, Australia and New Zealand. In places with high summer temperatures and/or cold winters, such as most of Germany, Sweden and Eastern North America (except the most favourable coastal areas), it has not become widespread.

The symptoms are light, usually yellowish rings, circles or blotches on the upper leaf which correspond on the leaf's lower surface with brown or grey patches of mycelium. These may spread and cover the whole surface or just remain as patches. Severe infections cause premature leaf-drop and a plant can be defoliated. Unless the subsequent new growth is kept clear of the disease, the plant cannot photosynthesise effectively and may die. Thankfully, only some species and cultivars are susceptible, though, if the infection is allowed to increase unchecked, most varieties can be affected to some extent.

spread onto old leaves. New growth should therefore be sprayed as soon as it is fully extended. This will probably be from late spring to mid-summer in the northern hemisphere. The problem is that many smaller-leaved plants produce new growth more or less continuously through the growing season, and this requires a spraying program every 3-4 weeks from late spring to autumn. The disease spreads most quickly in dry, mild weather and in conditions of shade and of poor air circulation. Overplanted or mature, dense gardens are therefore often the worst affected and, of course, large plants are the hardest and most time-consuming to spray.

There are several possible strategies to follow in dealing with this disease:

Option 1 Spray all your plants several times a year. Using large amounts of fungicide is a dangerous, unpleasant, time-consuming and expensive business. It is possible, however, to keep everything disease-free.

Option 2 Identify and spray only the most susceptible plants. This should prevent obvious sources of infection building up in the garden and it may well cut down infection to other plants. Those plants which can live happily with moderate levels of infection can be left to fend for themselves.

Option 3 Let nature take its course. You will probably lose the most susceptible plants such as 'Lady Chamberlain' and 'Elizabeth' and badly

infected plants are always a source of infection. Some will look semi-permanently under-clothed and sparse with unsightly disease. It may well be worth eliminating these as a preventative measure and avoiding susceptible ones when planting. Although some plants have been lost, the effect of the disease on the majority is largely cosmetic and most flower and grow freely.

Rust

Like the mildews, rusts are a group of constantly evolving fungi which attack many genera of plants. In wild populations, rusts are most commonly found on natural hybrids. There are several species of rust (up to 13 have been reported) which attack rhododendrons in different parts of the world and which have differing alternative hosts. (Most rusts have two hosts and the rust moves from one host to the other as part of its life cycle, though apparently it can live for several years on one host.)

Rhododendron rusts have alternative hosts which include *Picea* and *Tsuga*. Rust usually appears on the leaf underside and is characterised by the spores which form an orange powdery covering. If left untreated, it will cause black spotting on the upper surface of the leaf and infected leaves will usually drop off. As with mildew, a severe attack can defoliate and kill a plant, though this is rare except in the most susceptible varieties. Many of the

mildew fungicides are also effective on rusts.

Rust-susceptible plants: Few are very susceptible.

Hybrids: *R cinnabarinum* hybrids such as 'Trewithen Orange', *R. edgeworthii* hybrids such as 'Fragrantissimum'.

Azaleodendrons such as 'Martha Isaacson'.

Dwarf hybrids such as 'Anna Baldsiefen' and 'Arctic Tern'.

Rusts seem to be affecting more varieties and cultivars from year to year.

Root Rot and Stem Dieback

In hot climates, these diseases are undoubtedly the greatest causes of rhododendron death and have wiped out whole collections and thousands of plants of nursery stock. In climates with regular 32°C (90°F) heat in summer, many varieties will be so susceptible to these diseases that they are not worth attempting, and considerable effort in soil and soil temperature moderation is required.

Above: Rust on rhododendrons is characterised by black or dark brown spotting on the upper leaf surface which, at certain times of year, is matched by orange spores on the lower leaf surface

Right: The healthy white roots of the left hand plant contrast with the dark brown dead ones of a plant killed by root rot

Root Rot/Wilt (*Phytophthora*)

Phytophthora cinnamoni is a root disease which is usually fatal and often kills a plant extremely quickly. The symptoms are (usually) a sudden collapse during the growing season, of the whole plant, or several plants in one area of the garden. Check the roots and cut into the stem of the plant. The disease is characterised by the roots turning a deep brown colour (rather than white as healthy growing roots should be). If you scrape away the bark at ground level, you will find the cambium layer below the bark has been stained a dark reddish-brown.

The disease is caused by inadequate drainage and high soil temperatures. The combination of these is very often fatal to rhododendrons. It is most common in areas with hot summers but can occur anywhere if poor drainage in allowed to occur. Plants in containers are particularly susceptible (see page 34).

To avoid the disease, ensure that the planting area is well prepared with coarse organic matter which will allow improved drainage and aeration. Freshly composted bark has been shown to have some root-rot resistant properties and is the most popular medium for container growing in North America. Ensure that the soil where the rhododendrons are growing is not allowed to become compacted by people or animals walking over it. In warmer climates, growing in shade and mulching (see page 43) will help to keep the soil temperature down. In Germany, most varieties of rhododendron are grafted as this seems to increase the tolerance to poorly-drained soils. In areas with heavy clay soils, the best practice is often to plant above soil level, either in raised beds or by mounding up the soil around the root of the plant.

Susceptible varieties: Most members of subsections Taliensia (e.g. *R. phaeochrysum*), subsection Neriiflora (e.g. *R. dichroanthum*), and many other species such as *R. souliei* and *R. lanatum*. Most larger yellow hybrids (which are almost all derived from *R. wardii*), such as 'Hotei' and 'Goldkrone', are also susceptible, as are many of the smaller leaved or alpine species and hybrids. Most larger-growing hybrids (other than in yellow shades) and most azaleas are more heat tolerant and less susceptible. One or two cultivars such as 'Roseum Elegans' and 'Cadis' are known to be particularly resistant to *Phytophthora*.

If you remove a plant which has died of this disease, dispose of the whole plant including all of the rootball. There is little point replacing with the same or a similar variety without doing something to improve the drainage or decrease the soil temperature. It is also prudent to remove the soil which surrounded the dead plant's rootball as it will have many fungal spores in it. There are several chemicals on the market, mostly not available to amateurs, which can be used as a drench to suppress Phytophthora. Good hygiene and optimum planting conditions should be used as none of these fungicides will eradicate the fungus, just control it temporarily.

Stem Dieback (*Botryosphaeria, Phytophthora cactorum* and Other Species)

These are serious diseases of rhododendrons in regions with considerable summer heat such as eastern North America. Both are characterised by the sudden wilting and death of a branch or part of a plant and they tend to attack where plants have been physically damaged in some way (including pruning).

With both diseases, the inside of the wilted stem will have turned brown. The dead stem must be cut out well into green wood in the healthy part of the plant and the dead branch should be removed or burnt (not composted). Ensure secateurs are sterilised using bleach or alcohol, to avoid spreading the disease. Good hygiene, adequate air circulation and moderate use of fertiliser all help prevent the diseases. *Botryosphaeria* can begin as leaf spot and soon cause stem dieback. Benomyl (with maneb) gives control and can be used after pruning to prevent fungal entry. For Phytophthora, fungicides such as mancozeb, metalaxyl and fosetyl-aluminium can be used.

Honey Fungus (*Armillaria*)

There are many species of honey fungus or *Armillaria* which occur in different parts of the world, most of which feed exclusively on decaying matter. Several species unfortunately are also able to colonise and weaken or kill living plants, and rhododendrons are particularly susceptible.

Sometimes sending up conspicuous fruiting bodies, the main part of the fungus lives underground, sending out vigorous rhizomorphs (commonly known as bootlaces) which colonise both dead and living tree and plant roots. Apparently the world's largest living thing is a species of honey fungus in North America!

Almost exclusively, gardens with a honey fungus problem are those with lots of old tree-stumps in the ground. Of course, one can glibly recommend that all tree roots are removed, but when the extent of the root system of a mature broad leaf such as elm, beech or sycamore is appreciated, it becomes apparent that this is often impossible.

Digging out a dead plant killed by honey fungus will usually reveal the tell-tale black bootlaces which have run through the rootball and into the stem, virtually strangling it in severe cases. Symptoms vary from yellowing of leaves, poor leaf retention, poor growth length, partial dieback of branches on the plant, or sudden total collapse. Often a 'last gasp' attempt to flower heavily will be made. There is little doubt that stressed plants (by waterlogging, drought, etc) are more susceptible to the fungus. Certain species such as *R. lacteum*, most of subsection Taliensia and many in subsection Neriiflora are particularly at risk, while many hybrids seem to be able to withstand having

the fungus engulfing their roots, though it usually reduces their vigour.

To prevent the fungus occurring, it is advisable to remove the roots of trees wherever possible. Apart from this, there is very little you can do, other than using barriers to keep it from spreading. The fungus usually remains close to the surface, seldom deeper than 30-45cm (12-18in) in lighter soils, though it is said to go deeper in clay soils, so heavy-duty plastic and other materials can be used to make impermeable barriers rather like underground walls. Alternatively, plants can have an underground wall made in a circle around the rootball.

Raised beds with a solid lining are another

solution, but ensure there is adequate drainage: try to construct them on a slope if possible. We have tried using permeable membranes but the fungus appears to be able to penetrate these. There are various phenolic compounds which may help to control honey fungus. These are expensive and they can only be safely used around mature plants. The fungus will usually return if there is infection nearby.

Petal Blight (*Ovulinia*)

This fungal disease is one of the most upsetting as it ruins the flowers you have waited so long to enjoy. It has long been associated mainly with warmer parts of the rhododendron growing world such as S.E. U.S.A. but is has begun to be a problem in much of North America, parts of Europe and Australasia.

Infected flowers first exhibit small spots which appear water-soaked. These rapidly enlarge, turning the petals into a slimy grey mass with sinks limply onto the leaves below. It can even strike before the flowers open.

It takes 2-3 days for the flowers to be completely ruined and a whole bush or group of plants can quickly be affected. The destroyed petals when dry stick to the foliage and white patches which turn to black fruiting bodies are produced which will infect the following year's flowers. The disease usually occurs during moist weather at flowering time, especially if accompanied

by warmth and poor air circulation. Watering overhead which it wets the flowers is to be avoided if possible.

The disease is particularly devastating on plants in greenhouses and tunnel-houses and it seems to cause the most widespread damage on evergreen azaleas. If you have an infected plant brought in from another source, it is well worth removing and destroying all blooms immediately so that the spores cannot be spread. If you have a large amount of infection, it may be necessary to spray with a fungicide when buds start to show colour and at weekly intervals until the flowers go over. Keeping the foliage, and especially the flowers, as dry as possible is the best way to avoid the disease. *Botrytis* can cause similar, less devastating symptoms, especially on plants indoors which are watered overhead. It differs in the lack of black fruiting bodies.

Leaf Gall

This bacterial disease is found on wild populations of some species and also found in gardens on some species, hybrids, and especially on evergreen/Japanese azaleas and *R. ferrugineum* and its hybrids. It is an unsightly disease characterised by green, pink or red swellings on the leaves, shoots or occasionally flowers. They should be picked off and destroyed and the problem often arises only once a season.

Leaf galls on *R. ferrugineum*. This problem is very commonly observed on evergreen azalea varieties. Picking the galls off is the most common solution

Weather-related and Physical Problems

Sunburn

Rhododendron and azalea varieties vary greatly in their ability to withstand hot sun. In Scotland, sunburn is rarely a problem, while in the south of England a hot summer can cause considerable foliage damage. In south-eastern North America and California, most rhododendrons need shade to avoid sunburn.

The key here is to use the minimum shade required to protect the foliage. Too much shade means drawn and leggy plants which seldom flower. The problem with shade is that as your trees grow, the shade increases (until you get a great storm). Mild sunburn turns leaves bright yellow while a more severe attack will burn the leaves to a crisp. There is not much you can do once it has happened apart from providing extra shade, to avoid the problem occurring in future. There are many varieties which are known for their sun-tolerant qualities, such as 'Gomer Waterer', 'Purple Gem' and 'Jean Marie de Montague'.

Above: Sunburnt new growth is characterised by yellowing of the leaves and burnt patches. This variety requires more shade

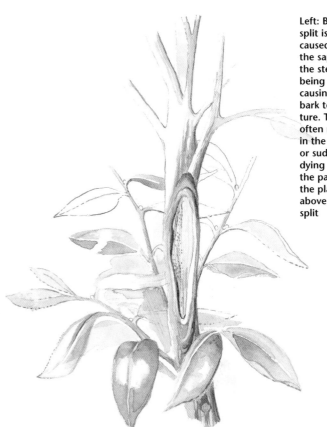

Left: Bark split is caused by the sap in the stem being frozen causing the bark to rupture. This often results in the slow or sudden dying back of the part of the plant above the split

Spring Frost

Spring frosts are undoubtedly the single most frustrating thing that rhododendron growers have to put up with in many areas. Few rhododendrons have frost-resistant flowers or growth and all too often those long-admired buds are open or are just about to open when a few degrees of frost turns everything brown. This problem is perhaps most extreme in the maritime climate of the British Isles, where mild winters can bring plants into flower as early as late winter and early spring and then see the return of frost in mid-or late spring. A sharp frost in late April 1997 destroyed flowers and growth over much of the U.K. The Valley Gardens in Windsor Great park in early May had virtually every single flower on thousands of bushes turned to brown mush, while new growth on rhododendrons and magnolias was literally smashed and left hanging, limp and brown from the previous year's branches.

Thankfully this sort of devastation does not occur very often; it is such things that make gardeners so philosophical!

Early varieties are always going to be vulnerable to damage, especially if you garden inland or in a frost pocket. Frost flows downwards and so hollows such as river beds will be particularly vulnerable, while surrounding higher ground may escape the worst effects, so site plants with care. Overhead shade from trees will also moderate the temperature a degree or two, which can often make the difference between damage and escaping virtually unscathed. A few early-flowering varieties such as *R. lapponicum* and *R. hippophaeoides* have frost resistant flowers while one or two others including the very popular 'Ptarmigan' and 'Christmas Cheer' open flowers in batches over a long period so if one flush is frosted, another one soon opens.

You can, of course, put artificial protection over early flowering plants at night. The problem is that the best protection is afforded by covering but not touching the plants and this is often hard to achieve. Use textiles rather than sheet polythene or plastic if possible: old sacks and bedsheets, bubble plastic or spun polypropylene (sold specifically for this purpose) are all effective. Try to keep the material dry as the weight of damp cloth is often a problem, and wet material is less effective in keeping frost off. Covers are often blown away and we expend much energy at Glendoick trying to attach covers which will stay put. A rather drastic method which does work is to leave sprinklers on your plants during frosty nights.

Having the flowers frosted does no long-term damage to the plant. Even when growth is badly damaged and looks distorted and unsightly, the plant will usually recover well and put on new growth or it can be pruned off and will be replaced from lateral buds.

Long-term damage can be caused by bark split when sap running in the stem is frozen, busting the outer layer of bark. Often the plant looks healthy for a few months and then the split branch will die off. In the case of young plants, they can easily be killed outright. Species such as *R. yunnanense* and certain forms of *R. augustinii* are particularly vulnerable as small plants. They usually get tougher and more resistant with age. Sometimes the wound will heal over time, but if not, you may have to prune back to

below where the split occurred. Bark split is usually caused by spring frosts but can also occur in autumn in late growing varieties such as those with *R. griersonianum* and *R. auriculatum* parentage. ('Vanessa Pastel' and 'Polar Bear' for instance).

Wind Damage

Leaves broken at the petiole and ragged or brown-edged leaves are a sure sign of wind damage. See page 19 for a discussion of shelter.

Cold

As well as spring frosts, midwinter cold can be very damaging. This is usually seen in browned, brittle foliage, not to mention brown and dead flower buds. Even the hardiest varieties can be severely damaged by a combination of frozen ground with sun and/or wind. This causes foliage desiccation and can defoliate a plant. Prudent use of shade and shelter is the way to alleviate this (see page 16).

Everyone likes to grow plants of borderline hardiness, making use of the most favourable, sheltered sites in the garden. If a variety is on the tender side for your area, then extreme winters will cause substantial problems or

Below: Frost damage on the flowers of *R. wardii* after a mild frost. In a harder frost, the flowers would have been completely browned

even death. At Glendoick, we like to grow species such as *R. lindleyi* and *R. sinograndei* outside. In our severest winters, which occur every 10-15, years these are severely damaged or even killed. In colder

Right: Late frosts have damaged the already emerging new growth of *R. wiltonii*. If such damage is severe, it is often best to prune it off, encouraging new growth to come from below

parts of continental Europe and much of the eastern states of the U.S.A. and Canada, the majority of rhododendron hybrids, and especially species, simply are not hardy enough to survive the winter temperatures so the choice of which varieties to grow is crucial.

The ironclads are increasingly large group bred to withstand -32°C (-25°F). The early crosses in this group were made in Europe, especially by Waterers in England, but there are many hybridisers, such as D. Leach in Eastern North America, who have greatly increased the range.

Yellow Leaves

Yellow leaves are simply a sign that the plant is not happy, and this can be caused by many different factors (or a combination of them). If the whole leaf is yellow, the cause is usually sunburn or starvation. If yellowing is more pronounced on the blade of the leaf, with greener veins (chlorosis) the cause is more likely to be mineral (too much or too little) or pH. The following can cause yellow leaves:
• Poor drainage from heavy or compacted soil.
• Drought through lack of rain or watering, or competition from tree roots.
• Planting too deeply. The top of the rootball should be just below the surface of the soil.
• Nitrogen deficiency. The plant is starving. This can be easily remedied by applying feeding.
• pH is too high (or occasionally too low). Test your soil pH.
• Mineral deficiency. This is fairly rare and it requires a soil analysis to prove. If you have ruled out the other possibilities in the above list, it may be worth applying trace elements which are available on their own or in combination with fertilisers. Sequestered or chelated iron is often recommended as a catch-all cure for yellow leaves. Unless you have an iron deficiency, this is an expensive remedy which may do little more than provide a little fertiliser.

Lichen

This often forms on old, straggly specimens, particularly when they have few leaves and are lacking in vigour. Evergreen azaleas and deciduous azaleas seem particularly prone. You can scrub it off but, really, it is a sign of poor soil conditions, lack of fertiliser or old age. It can best be dealt with by rejuvenating the plants by pruning and fertilising or by throwing them out and starting again. Lichen grows on weak plants rather than causing the weakness.

Left: Lichen often forms on older varieties, especially in damp climates. Soil improvement, pruning and fertiliser are all possible solutions

No Flowers – Buds Do Not Open

This is most likely to be caused by frost, either in mid-winter by the hardest frosts of the year, or in spring when the buds are swelling and about to open. Certain varieties such as *R. pemakoense* have very frost-vulnerable swelling buds, while many species in subsection Maddenia have buds which are easily destroyed even by quite mild winter frosts. A variety which always has its buds frosted, unless it has fine foliage, may not be worth space in your garden. If the dead buds are covered with spore-laden black bristles, you have bud blast, a disease which affects a few species and hybrids such as *R. maximum* and 'Cunningham's White'. It is usually not serious enough to warrant spraying, but you can use a suitable fungicide if necessary.

No Flowers – No Flower Buds

There are several possibilities why rhododendrons may not flower freely:
• Too much shade. This is very common in North America where, in order to regulate sun and soil temperature, plants are placed in deep shade making healthy, if straggly growth but not flowering. The more light you can give a plant, the more likely it is to flower, so there is a subtle trade-off between the need for shade and the need for light.

• The variety takes many years to flower. Some hybrids and many species need to be quite old before they start flowering. This particularly applies to the large-leaved species such as *R. sinogrande* and some of the species in subsection Taliensia. Some species such as the infamous *R. pronum* hardy ever flower in cultivation at all. Thankfully, this species is mainly grown for its foliage! Many species do not flower well every year and, especially after a heavy flowering year, they will take a rest.
• Kindness. Rhododendrons flower in order to reproduce. A contented, well fed, well, watered, well-shaded plant may not feel any need to reproduce, as it perceives no threat to its survival. Do not feed after mid-summer as this encourages growth at the expense of flowers. Nurserymen cut down watering in late summer to stress plants into flowering the following year. If all else, including threats fail, then try a bit of root pruning. You can even lift a plant and replace it in its hole.

Buying and Collecting

Obtaining the Best Plants

Rhododendrons are one of the more tricky genera to grow well commercially and, due to the sheer number of varieties available, it may take some searching to find what you are looking for. If you want to buy species and more unusual hybrids you will have to go to one of the many specialist nurseries, some of which offer between 500-1,000 different varieties or more. Many have a mail order service.

Traditionally, rhododendrons have been purchased bare-rooted from nurseries when dormant in autumn, winter and early spring to be planted before the onset of new growth in the spring. Buying from specialist nurseries is usually cheaper than buying from garden centres and, most importantly, you are more likely to get correctly named stock.

Rhododendrons are hard to identify, partly because there are so many of them, and the naming of species is particularly poor. Species should be grown from hand-pollinated seed, wild-collected seed (preferably with a collector's number), cuttings or grafts. Never accept plants that have been dug up from the wild; they will almost certainly fail, and it is totally unethical.

These days, most rhododendrons are probably bought from garden centres and are container-grown; the largest range is usually held in spring, as it is the flowering season. While there is no reason why a well looked-after, container-grown rhododendron should not thrive once planted in the garden, it pays to know what to avoid. Modern nursery practice involves forcing containerised plants as fast as possible to a saleable size using fertiliser, heat and artificial protection to ensure good budding and healthy foliage. This treatment can result in a plant which takes a considerable time to recover when planted in the garden. This is especially true if a plant is becoming root-bound in its pot. Rhododendron roots are shallow and spreading, while the pots they grow in are narrow and deep.

I have often seen pot-bound rhododendrons planted in gardens where, several years later, the pot shape is still visible when roots are inspected. Very little in the way of new roots have been put out into the surrounding soil, resulting in a corresponding lack of healthy new growth and flower buds. Such 'plants-to-avoid' are usually found in garden centres in late summer or early autumn, looking forlorn and lonely, vainly hoping someone will take pity on them. The rootball will invariably have dried out and there may be roots coming out the drainage holes. Look out for signs of powdery mildew (see page 66). Do not buy such plants unless they are irresistibly cheap!

Left: Evergreen azaleas associated with heathers and conifers at Rosemoor Garden, Devon

Opposite: A fine display of azaleas sold as houseplants at a garden centre. The tall azalea is grown as a half standard

Grafted Plants

For some people, grafted plants have a bad reputation. This is largely due to the use of *R. ponticum* as an understock. This species is so vigorous that it constantly sends up suckers which, if not removed, gradually take all the sap from the plant, eventually causing the grafted variety to die off. This is incorrectly referred to as 'reverting'. Few nurseries graft onto *R. ponticum* these days, but it is always worth enquiring what the rootstock was. If you do not get an answer, do not buy. Most now use 'Cunningham's White', 'County of York' and other rootstocks which throw far fewer suckers.

Do not buy grafts less than two years old as it takes this long to know whether the graft has taken or not. Avoid plants with an unnatural bulge where the union is, as this indicates incompatibility: in the long term, these usually fail. In Germany and Holland, almost all larger hybrids are grafted. This makes them expensive, but it does allow tolerance of poorer growing conditions.

78

Right: 'Crest' is one of the finest yellow hybrids. Unfortunately several years ago many plants of 'Crest' were produced by tissue culture turned out to have smaller-than-normal leaves and small, poor flowers. This problem has, thankfully, been rectified

Left: When buying a grafted plant, try to ensure that a strong union has been formed between rootstock and the variety grafted on top, and that there is no exaggerated bulge at the union

Tissue Culture

Most larger hybrids these days are produced by tissue-culture. As long as correct procedures have been followed, there is nothing against this technique, but unfortunately, things can go wrong. Avoid unnaturally bushy plants with thin stems and smaller-than-normal leaves. These plants are in suspended juvenility, which they never grow out of, caused by high rates of hormones. There were thousands of 'Crest' like this sold several years ago.

Collecting Rhododendrons

There are many rhododendron societies worldwide, from North America to Europe, Japan, Australia, New Zealand and elsewhere. These reflect the serious addiction to collecting rhododendrons many people have. It certainly keeps nurseries such as our own in business.

Most people start growing some of the widely available, readily grown hybrids and gradually start to notice the qualities of other choice varieties when they visit some of the great collections. As people's knowledge and enthusiasm increases, they tend to get more and more hooked on species. There are several reasons for this; the most obvious is that they often have more interesting foliage. There is admittedly also a degree of snobbery involved.

One of the most interesting facets of species collecting is collectors' numbers. Most of the great early collectors, as well as many contemporary ones, collect seed in the wild under a collector's number. This means that the collector assigns a number to the seed packet and keeps notes on when and where the plant was collected, how large it was and what grew with it. Often a specimen of the plant is pressed and sent back to a botanic garden.

For example: *R. macabeanum* KW 7724 was collected by Frank Kingdon Ward on his 1927-28 expedition to India, Tibet and Burma. In his field notes, he records it as: 'a forest tree with handsome foliage, truss with 12-18 flowers … it goes right to the summit where it forms forests … it should be hardy'. He records the location as Mt. Javpo, Naga Hills, Assam, occurring from 2.5-3,000m (8-10,000ft), and he collected the seed on 1 December 1927. The seed from this collection was distributed far and wide but wherever the plants have ended up, as long the collection number was retained, the plant's origin can be traced. It turns out that KW 7724 was the first introduction of the species *R. macabeanum*, discovered by Sir George Watt 40 years earlier.

Above: *R. macabeanum* is one of the finest of the large-leaved species with spectacular yellow flowers and handsome foliage. It requires wind shelter and a favourable climate

Rhododendron species are quite widely available with collector's numbers, either propagated from selected clones in collections, or as seedlings grown from recent expeditions to the wild. The latter are perhaps the most exciting, as each seedling is unique and you may be lucky enough to have one of the best. If you buy species with collector's numbers, or grow them from seed, keep the collector's number on the label, so that the plant always carries its own coded identity card. The number can later be decoded, with a bit of research, allowing each plant to tell its own story. This makes a collection more interesting, more complete and more fun. It is very exciting as a collector to find plants with your numbers on them growing well in far-flung corners of the globe.

Plant Directory

There are about 900 species of rhododendron and azalea and around 15,000 named hybrids so, in a book this size, it is only possible to survey a small percentage of what is available. Many new hybrids are named every year. A few of them become successful and perhaps one a year joins the list as a nurseryman's standard.

There are specialist nurseries all over the rhododendron-growing world which offer several hundred varieties; many provide a mail order service. I have tried to cover a selection of the best of the widely available varieties for all of the diverse climates of the rhododendron-growing world. Some of the most promising of the newer varieties are also included.

Contents

Dwarf and Low-growing Varieties

Larger Species

Larger Hybrids

Deciduous Azaleas

Evergreen Azaleas

Tender Rhododendrons (H0-H2 varieties)

Hardiness

Hardiness is difficult to quantify precisely, as it depends on the timing of the cold weather. Many plants which are mid-winter-hardy are more vulnerable to damage in early autumn or late spring. The combination of high summer temperatures and cold winters cannot be tolerated by many varieties. The ratings here are an extension and adaptation of those used by the Royal Horticultural Society for rhododendrons.

H0   0°C (32°F) minimum. USDA 10-(9b) +/- frost free
Greenhouse culture, except in mildest areas such as parts of California, Hawaii, Australia and north New Zealand.

H1   -10°C to -8°C (15°F to 20°F) USDA 8b-9a
Greenhouse culture, except for milder areas such as those above and also mildest western U.K. gardens.

H2   -12°C (10°F) minimum USDA 8a
Hardy outdoors in milder parts of U.K. (such as Cornwall, Argyll), southern Ireland, most of California, also west Vancouver Island, Canada, most of New Zealand, Tasmania.

H3   -15°C (5°F) minimum   USDA 7b
Hardy in a sheltered site in most U.K., Coastal France and northern Italy and Pacific Northwest gardens, but may be damaged in severest winters. Often early into flower and growth.

H4   -18°C (0°F) minimum   USDA 7a
Hardy in all but coldest parts of Pacific Northwest and U.K., France and northern Italy, around Bergen (Norway) and mildest parts of N.E. U.S.A. such as Cape Cod and parts of Long Island.

H5   -23°C (-10°F) minimum   USDA 6
Hardy anywhere in the U.K. and moderate parts of Europe such as Holland, southern Sweden, coastal Denmark, favourable parts of Germany etc, moderate parts of N.E. U.S.A. and eastern Canada.

H6   -29°C (-20°F) minimum   USDA 5
Hardy in colder parts of Germany and Scandinavia, New York, Nova Scotia etc.

H7   Colder than -29°C(-20°F)   USDA 4b(-a)
Ironclads. These are the hardiest varieties suitable for the coldest areas suitable for growing rhododendrons, including parts of eastern Europe and much of inland eastern U.S.A. and Canada. Most are heat-tolerant.

Height

Heights given are those attainable as a plant after 10-15 years. Most will eventually grow much bigger under ideal conditions, and reach a considerable age. Plants in dry and cold climates grow more slowly than those in mild and wet climates which have long growing seasons.

Dwarf To 40cm (16in) usually spreading, wider than high.

Semi-dwarf 40-80cm (16in-2½ft), often spreading wider than high.

Low 80-135cm (2½-4½ft), sometimes spreading wider than high

Medium 35-190cm (4½ft-6ft), considerably more with time.

Tall 190cm (6ft) and more; much larger over time.

FLOWERING TIME

In mild and maritime climates, the flowering season can cover seven months or more, while in severe climates, the flowering season is compressed into a three month period. We find with the vagaries of the British climate, there is considerable variation from year to year, especially with early-flowering varieties.

		Northern hemi moderate	Northern hemisphere severe	Southern hemisphere
VE	*Very Early*	Dec-February	April	July
E	*Early*	March	Early May	August-September
EM	*Early-Mid*	April	Mid May	September
M	*Mid*	May 1st-15th	Late May	Early October
ML	*Late Mid*	May15th-31st	Early June	Late October
L	*Late*	June	June	November
VL	*Very Late*	July-August	July	December

R. degroni-anum is a very tough Japanese species, with the hardiest forms suitable for severe climates

Dwarf and Low-Growing Varieties

This section includes varieties most suitable for the smaller garden. Although many of them can tolerate cold winters, most small-leaved alpine types are not suitable for areas with hot summers. This group includes the very popular 'yak' hybrids bred from the species *R. yakushimanum*. These are useful for their full, rounded trusses, their relatively late-flowering and their fine foliage and compact habit. Many are very hardy and their only drawback is that a large number of them have flowers which fade. Most of the varieties listed are widely available from Garden Centres.

'Arctic Tern' is a most unusual low growing hybrid with masses of tiny white flowers in late May

'April' Hybrids
H7 Low *E-M*

This is a range of double-flowered, very hardy hybrids bred for severe northern climates. The flowers are very showy but the plants tend to be semi-deciduous and need pruning, and some are susceptible to root rot. 'April Snow', 'April Gem' and 'April White' have double white flowers. 'April Mist' and 'April Rose'. 'Weston's Pink Diamond' and 'Staccato' have double pink flowers. There are several others.

'Arctic Tern'
H4-5 Low *ML-L*

A useful late-flowered, small leaved dwarf. Rounded trusses of a mass of tiny white flowers. Its habit its rather rangy, requiring pruning, and it is susceptible to rust.

'Blue Diamond'
H4-5 Low *EM-M*

Masses of bluish-purple flowers. Small leaves. Tends to suffer from leaf spot. 'Blue Tit' is very similar, with paler flowers and a similar tendency to leaf spot. Many similar hybrids have been raised, many of which have better foliage.

'Bow Bells'
H4-5 Low *EM-M*

Light pink, bell-shaped flowers in loose trusses on a tidy plant with oval leaves and bronzy new growth. Very popular in areas of moderate climate.

calostrotum
H4-5 Dwarf-Low *EM-L*

This is a variable small-leaved species. Ssp. calostrotum has purple or pink flowers. 'Gigha' is a bright pink, large-flowered selection with grey-blue foliage. Can be hard to please. **Ssp. *keleticum*** has pointed leaves, a dense habit and flat-faced purple flowers, relatively late for a dwarf. The slowest-growing and most compact forms are known as Radicans Group.

'Caroline Albrook'
H5 Low M-ML

Frilly lavender-pink flowers in full trusses which fade to pale lavender. A tough, compact 'yak' hybrid which is free-flowering. 'Hoppy' is taller growing and 'Centennial Celebration' is a popular American hybrid of similar colour.

campylogynum
H4 Dwarf/Semi-dwarf M

One of the most captivating of the dwarf species, with its little thimbles of red, purple, pink or white flowers held above the foliage on long stalks. Best in moderate climates with cool summers.

'Carmen'
H4 Dwarf EM-M

Deep red, waxy flowers on a neat grower which likes cool roots in summer.

'Cilipense'
H3-4 Semi-dwarf E

Pink buds open to pale pink flowers which fade to white. Small leaves on a fairly compact and tidy plant. Magnificent at its best but its buds and flowers are so subject to frost damage, it is only worth growing in mild areas. 'Snow Lady' and 'Lucy Lou' are equally early flowering with pure white flowers and hairy, oval leaves. 'Lucy Lou' has the more compact habit.

'Curlew'
H4 Dwarf EM-M

The best-known of the Glendoick 'bird' hybrids. A compact spreader with relatively large yellow flowers, spotted red. Flowers vulnerable to frost damage. Dislikes hot summers. 'Chikor' has smaller leaves and flowers, 'Princess Anne' and 'Shamrock' have smaller and paler flowers.

dendrocharis
H4-5 Dwarf E-EM

One of the most exciting new species introductions of recent years. Small deep green, hairy leaves on a neat, compact plant. Relatively large deep pink flowers. Needs good drainage.

'Egret', raised by the author's father, is a fine, compact dwarf hybrid with masses of tiny, white bell-shaped flowers

'Dopey'
H4 Low ML

One of the 'seven dwarf' series of 'yak' hybrids, this has amongst the best, unfading, red flowers of this group. Pale green foliage, somewhat subject to mildew. 'Titian Beauty' is slower growing with small flowers, of an equally good red, and more handsome foliage with indumentum on the leaf lower surface. 'Skookum' (H6) is a much hardier alternative for severe climates. Fairly compact, with full rounded trusses of strong red.

'Dora Amateis'
H5-6 Semi-dwarf EM-M

One of the best dwarf hybrids for colder areas. Masses of pure white flowers with green markings. A rather spreading habit. Sometimes has yellowish foliage.

'Egret'
H4 Dwarf/Semi-dwarf M

Masses of tiny white bells on a compact plant with very small deep green leaves. Very distinctive.

'Elisabeth Hobbie'
H5 **Low** *EM-M*

One of the best selling low-growing red hybrids. Very easy to please and reliable. Loose trusses of bright red flowers on a dense and compact grower. There are many very similar hybrids such as '**Scarlet Wonder**', '**Baden Baden**' (which has a twist in the leaf) and '**Bengal**'.

'Elizabeth Lockhart'
H4 **Low** *EM-M*

Mainly grown for its deep reddish-purple leaves. Flowers deep red. Oval leaves on a compact bush. Needs to be grown in shade to retain leaf colour. '**Elizabeth Red Foliage**' (H4) has red flowers and bronzy-red new growth which remains this colour for several months.

The 'yak' hybrid 'Fantastica' has become one of the most popular of the many hybrids of the species *R. yakushimanum*. The inside of the corolla fades quicker than the outside, giving a very attractive, two-toned effect

'Fantastica'
H5-6 **Low** *M-ML*

One of the most spectacular 'yak' hybrids. Full, rounded trusses open bright pink and fade to off-white. The rim of each flower remains deeper than the centre, giving a most attractive effect. There are many other pink 'yak' hybrids of similar colouring: some of the most popular include '**Morgenrot**' (H5) Reddish flowers, fading to deep pink, and '**Surrey Heath**' (H4) with a very dense habit and pink flowers.

fastigiatum
H5-6 **Dwarf** *EM-M*

This popular, compact and dwarf species has masses of small purplish-blue flowers and tiny bluish-green leaves. Very good in cooler areas and very hardy, but this species and its relatives dislike hot summers. *R. impeditum* is very similar species and most of what is sold under this name is in fact *R. fastigiatum*. *R. russatum* is taller-growing with very deep purple flowers in the best forms.

'Golden Torch'
H4 Low *ML*

The name is a misnomer as this is a cream-coloured 'yak' hybrid, severely over-rated in my opinion, but popular in moderate areas. Foliage tends to be yellow-ish. Needs good drainage.

'Grumpy'
H4 Low *EM-M*

Cream-coloured flowers, with pink flushing in flat-topped trusses on a fairly tidy 'yak' hybrid with dark green leaves and indumen-tum on the lower surface. Very similar are its sister seedlings **'Dusty Miller'** with pale pink flowers and the cream and apricot **'Molly Miller'**. All these have insipid flowers but some find them attractive.

ferrugineum
H5-6 Semi-dwarf-Low *L-VL*

The 'Alpenrose' is a useful late-flowering species with small pink flowers on a small-leaved, compact grower. Very hardy but needs good drainage. Its close relative, *R. hirsutum*, will tolerate near neutral soil.

forrestii
H4 Dwarf *E-EM*

Fine, waxy-red flowers on a mounding or prostrate plant with small oval leaves. Needs cool condi-tions for both foliage and roots.

'Gartendirektor Rieger'
H5 Low-Medium *M*

A fine, vigorous and easy hybrid with large cream flowers, spotted red in an open-topped truss. Leaves are deep-green and somewhat rounded. Less hardy and smaller leaved hybrids with creamy, bell-shaped flowers include 'Moonstone' and 'Cowslip'.

R. haematodes is a very low-growing species with waxy red flowers and small dark green leaves with thick indumentum on the lower surface

'Ginny Gee'
H5-6 Dwarf *EM*

This award-winning hybrid is one of the most popular dwarf hybrids. Masses of pale pink and white flow-ers virtually hide the foliage. Easy and vigorous but compact. Two newly introduced similar hybrids are **'Crane'** (raised by the author) and **'June Bee'**. Both have masses of creamy-white flowers.

haematodes
H4-5 Low *M-L*

This is a fine compact foliage plant with deep green leaves and thick woolly indumentum on the underside. The very fine red flowers may take a few years to appear. Needs good drainage.

'Hummingbird'
H3-4 Low *EM-M*

There are several clones
of this hybrid in com-
merce. Cherry to rose red
bells hang down over the
foliage on long stalks. Fine
foliage on a dense, com-
pact grower.

hypoleuceum
(formerly *Ledum*)
H5 Semi-dwarf *M-ML*

The ledums have recently
been reclassified as part of
the genus *Rhododendron*.
All have rounded trusses of
a mass of tiny white flowers. They have aromatic
leaves which tend to curl
up, turn brown and look
dead in Winter. Species
include *R. groenlandicum*
and *R. neoglandulosum*
from North America,
and *R. tomentosum* and
R. hypoleucum from Europe
and Asia.

keiskei
**H5-6 Dwarf/Semi-dwarf
*EM-M***

One of the hardiest dwarf
species. Pale yellow flowers, usually spotted red.
The most dwarf form, usu-
ally grown as 'Yaku Fairy' is
one of the slowest-growing
of all dwarfs with a near
prostrate habit and fine
pale yellow flowers.

'Ken Janeck'
H6 Low *M*

One of the finest 'yak'
hybrids for foliage, with
the underside of the leaf
and the upper surface on
the young growth covered
with indumentum.
Compact and dense grow-
ing with fine pale pink
flowers which fade to
white. **'Mist Maiden'** is
very similar. **'Crete'** (H6-7)
is hardier but has less
impressive flowers. **'Yaku
Princess'** (H5-6) is taller
growing with similar
flowers.

lepidostylum
H4-5 Semi-dwarf *L*

This species is mainly
grown for its very showy,
glaucous-blue young
growth on a spreading
plant. The small, yellow
flowers tend to be hidden
in the foliage.

*R. hypoleucum
(Ledum
hypoleucum)
with its tiny
white flowers
and aromatic
foliage. Until
recently, con-
sidered a sep-
arate genus,
the Ledums
have recently
been classi-
fied within
the genus
Rhodod-
endron*

'Linda'
H5-6 Low *M*

One of the many hybrids
of *R. williamsianum* (see
below). Egg-shaped, pale
green leaves and frilly,
bright pink flowers in
showy trusses. Good habit
and one of the latest of
this group in flower and
growth. Other similar
hybrids include **'Osmar'**
(H5) and **'Oudijk's
Sensation'** (H5). All these
have pendulous bell-
shaped pink flowers and
bronzy young leaves.

'Mary Fleming'
**H6 Semi-dwarf-Low
*E-EM***

This is one of the best
hybrids of this type for
Eastern North America as
it is sun and heat tolerant
as well as very tough.
Clusters of yellowish-
cream flowers, shaded
pink.

minus
H3-7 Low *EM-ML*

This American east coast
native is one of the hardiest lepidote (scaly-leaved)
rhododendrons and has
been much used as a par-
ent. Pink flowers (occa-
sionally white) on a fairly
tidy bush. Carolinianum

P.J.M. Group
H7 Low *E-EM*

P.J.M. in its various forms is probably the world's best selling hybrid. Rosy-purple flowers on a fairly compact plant with mahogany-purple foliage in winter. The commercial standard low growing hybrid in N.E. U.S.A. and Eastern Canada. Not very successful in southeastern U.S.A. as it is subject to root rot there. There are several clones. 'Peter John Mezitt' selected in the U.K. is rather shy flowering. Much better are 'P.J.M. Regal', 'P.J.M. Victor' and 'P.J.M. Elite'. These vary slightly in their flowering time and vigour. 'Checkmate' is a fine dwarf clone which we have found very free-flowering.

includes hardiest (H7) forms while var. *chapmanii* (H3) is not cold-hardy but, as it comes from Florida, is very heat-tolerant.

'Patty Bee'
H5 Dwarf *EM*

One of the most popular of the dwarf yellow hybrids and one of the hardier ones. Masses of pale yellow flowers on a very compact plant. A winner of several awards.

'Penheale Blue'
H4-5 Low *EM*

One of the finest of the low growing, small-leaved purple-blue hybrids. Fine, deep blue-purple flowers on a fairly compact plant with deep green, healthy foliage. Other similar varieties include 'Gristede', 'Night Sky' and 'Gletschernacht' ('Starry Night').

'Percy Wiseman'
H5 Low *ML-L*

One of the most popular 'yak' hybrids, this extremely free-flowering plant has peachy-pink to cream flowers and rather pale green leaves. Proving to be hardier than first thought.

'Linda' is one of the finest of the many *R. william-sianum* hybrids, most of which have bell-shaped pink flowers and bronzy-coloured young leaves

'Praecox'
H4-5 Low-Medium *E*

One of the earliest dwarf hybrids ever raised, but still popular in moderate climates. Masses of pink-ish-purple flowers in early spring. We find it best hard pruned every few years to keep the habit dense. 'Tessa Rosa' with fine pink flowers and 'Tessa Bianca' with white flowers are equally early and very fine.

primuliflorum 'Doker LA'
H4 Semi-dwarf *M*

This is a member of the Pogonanthum Section of species characterised by their (unfortunately unscented) daphne-like flowers. Masses of bright-est pink flowers on a neat, tiny-leaved plant. Needs excellent drainage and a near-neutral soil. The equally fine *R. trichosto-mum* is later flowering and more tolerant of hot or dry conditions. This group of species and hybrids are sel-dom successful in areas with hot summers. 'Sarled' with cream flowers and the taller 'Maricee' with white flowers are perhaps slightly easier to please.

'Ptarmigan'
H4-5 Dwarf *E-EM*

The 'snow grouse', raised by the author's father, is a useful early-flowering hybrid which opens its pure white flowers over a long period, so avoiding frosts. A spreading plant which benefits from prun-ing when young.

racemosum
H3-5 Semi-dwarf/ Low/Medium E-M

This species is very variable in flower colour, hardiness and stature. Masses of small flowers from buds which form in the leaf axils vary from deep pink though pale pink to white. Some forms are straggly, needing pruning, while others are compact and dwarf. Tolerant of dry conditions and some forms may be heat-tolerant.

'Ramapo'
H7 Semi-dwarf EM

This has long been the most satisfactory low 'purple-blue' for very cold climates, and it is one of the few with a degree of sun and heat tolerance. Pale lavender-blue flowers on a fairly compact grower with fine grey-blue foliage. Its sister **'Purple Gem'** is less hardy but has darker flowers.

roxieanum
H5 Low EM-M

Usually sold as the form var. *oreonastes*, this is one of the finest slow-growing species. Narrow, pointed leaves with indumentum on the underside on a compact plant which is reminiscent of a porcupine. Rounded trusses of light pink to white flowers with red spotting. Often takes a while to start flowering but not as long as the closely related **R. proteoides** which has

smaller leaves and a very fine compact habit. **R. pronum** with a low, dense habit and fine bluish leaves, rarely flowers at all.

'Ruby Hart'
H3-4 Low M

A very fine hybrid for moderate climates with dark green leaves, a compact habit and very dark, black-red flowers.

sanguineum
H4 Semi-dwarf/ Low E-ML

A variable, low-growing species with flowers of red, pink, white, yellow or a combination of colours. It needs very good drainage and cool roots in summer and takes several years to flower freely. **R. dichroanthum** (ML-L) enjoys similar conditions and has orange flowers, or a combination of orange with yellow, pink or red.

Above: R. roxieanum var. oreonastes is one of the finest species for foliage effect. It has white flowers with red spotting

Above: 'Ruby Hart' has amongst the darkest red flowers of any rhododendron

Opposite: R. yakushimanum with its excellent foliage and compact habit and fine flowers has made it perhaps the most popular rhododendron species

'Schneekrone' (syn. Snow Crown')
H5-6 Low M-ML

One of the most popular 'yak' hybrids of this shade, pink buds open to white flowers with red spots. A vigorous, tough and free-flowering plant.

'Sneezy'
H5 Low M-ML

One of the seven dwarf 'yak' hybrids, this is larger-growing and the most vigorous. Full trusses of frilly, bright pink flowers, with red spotting, fade to pale pink. Not one of the best

of the 'yaks' for foliage. **'Bashful'** is very similar. **'Mardi Gras'** (H4-5) is more compact with pale pink flowers, fading to white. **'Hydon Dawn'** (H4) has pink flowers with a deeper centre and fine silvery young growth. **'Solidarity'** (H5-6) has large, deep pink flowers in a fine truss, which fade to pale pink and white. One of the most vigorous 'yak' hybrids. Highly rated in eastern parts of the U.S.A.

'Wee Bee'
H5 Dwarf EM

A terrible name for a fine plant with masses of rose-pink flowers, deeper on the outside, on a very compact grower with small, dark leaves. Everyone's favourite. Its sister **'Too Bee'** has darker flowers.

williamsianum
H4-5 Semi-dwarf/Low EM-M

The parent of many hybrids, this very attractive species is characterised by its pink, bell-shaped flowers and its small, oval leaves which are reddish-brown in young growth. Hardy, but the young growth is vulnerable to late frosts.

yakushimanum
H7 Semi-dwarf/Low ML

This is perhaps the best known species and certainly the most popular parent of all time, producing the 'yak' hybrids such as 'Dopey' and 'Schneekrone' listed above. Pink buds open to rounded trusses of white flowers. A very dense, compact grower having handsome leaves with thick indumentum on the underside and a silvery covering on the new growth. The clone **'Koichiro Wada'** F.C.C. is one of the best selections. **R. degronianum** (H5-6) with similar foliage is taller growing with pink flowers.

Larger Species

Although some of these are very tough and easy, the majority require a certain amount of shelter from wind and, in more southerly climates, a fair amount of shade. Many come into growth and flower in early spring, so are best with some frost protection. Species often take a few years to start flowering and, even then, some will not do so every year. Many of the species make up for this with their magnificent foliage, which is attractive all the year round. Those listed below are hardy enough for cultivation outdoors in the U.K. and Pacific North West of North America; some are suitable for colder climates. Less hardy species are covered in the 'tender rhododendrons' section. Seldom available from garden centres, larger species are best purchased from specialist nurseries. You are more likely to get them correctly named this way!

Left: The very variable *R. augustinii*, with masses of purple-blue flowers, is one of the finest species of this shade. Best in a woodland setting with some shelter

Right: The poor leaf retention and extremely free flowering probably indicates that this specimen of a fine red-flowered *R. arboreum* is dying

adenogynum
H5-6 Low-Medium E-M

This species is a member of subsection Taliensia whose members are prized by collectors for their foliage. All take a few years to flower and most need very good drainage and cool summer conditions. Pale pink to white flowers on a compact plant with fine foliage. *R. balfourianum* is similar with fine pink flowers.

arboreum
H2-4 Tall E-M

One of the most variable species, which is not surprising as its wild distribution extends from Sri Lanka through the Himalaya to Yunnan in China. This species is the dominant forest rhododendron (and the national flower) in Nepal, though much of the forest has been cut down. Capable of reaching 30m (100ft) in the wild, it can get very large in milder areas. Full, tall trusses of flowers vary from red though pink to white. Thick, stiff leaves have silvery or reddish-brown indumentum on the underside. The red forms tend to be the least hardy. *R. niveum* (H4) is a closely related, lower-growing species with distinctive purple flowers.

augustinii
H3-4 Medium EM-M

This species is one of the species in subsection Triflora. This subsection is characterised by fairly large-growing but small-leaved plants which are usually very free-flowering from a young age. *R. augustinii* is most commonly grown in its purple-blue flowered forms which can be very spectacular. Variable in hardiness and flower colour. The closely related *R. concinnum* is hardier and usually has purple or reddish-purple flowers in cultivated forms.

argyrophyllum
H5 Medium-Tall E-M

A very variable species from China with pink to white flowers. Usually grown as ssp. *nankingense* with fine pink flowers. *R. insigne* (L) is lower growing with pink flowers and a leaf underside covered with an metal-like indumentum.

auriculatum
H4-5 Tall *VL*

The latest of the larger species to flower, this magnificent plant has scented white flowers which open in late summer in the northern hemisphere. Under good conditions it grows into a huge, vase-shaped specimen. Its only drawback, apart from needing plenty of room, is that it grows very late in the season and is therefore vulnerable to early autumn frosts.

barbatum
H3-4 Medium-Tall
VE-EM

At its best this is one of the finest red-flowered species for moderate climates. Full, rounded trusses of brightest scarlet flowers on an upright plant with bristles on the leaf stalks and very fine, peeling, purplish bark. Needs some shelter. *R. argipeplum* differs only in the presence of indumentum on the leaf underside. *R. strigillosum*, also with early red flowers, has a more spreading habit and distinctive recurved leaves. The rare *R. exasperatum* has similar red flowers but is mainly grown for its wonderful purple tinged new growth and bristly leaves.

Left: For foliage, few species rival *R. bureavii* with thick reddish-brown indumentum on the stems and leaf underside, and whitish-fawn new growth

bureavii
H5 Low-Medium *EM-M*

One of the finest of all species for foliage: its dark green leaves are quilted beneath with thick reddish-brown indumentum which also covers the stems. Flowers are usually relatively small, white with reddish spots. The closely related *R. bureavioides* has larger flowers but the foliage is not quite so striking. *R. elegantulum* is lower-growing and more free-flowering with fine pink flowers and handsome narrow leaves.

calophytum
H5-6 Tall *E-EM*

The hardiest of the large-leaved species, this massive-growing, handsome plant has long, stiff leaves with large trusses of white flowers, strongly blotched red in the throat. The closely related *R. sutchuenense* (H5) has shorter leaves and pink flowers.

campanulatum
H4 Medium-Tall *EM-M*

This Himalayan species has variable lavender to white flowers. Foliage is usually handsome with indumentum on the leaf underside. **Ssp.** *aeruginosum* has fine, glaucous foliage. *R. wallichii* differs in its thinner or absent indumentum.

catawbiense
H7 Low-Medium *ML-L*

This north American native is one of the hardiest of all species and a parent of many of the hardiest hybrids. It is only worth growing in severest climates. Purplish-pink (occasionally white) flowers on a fairly tidy and compact plant which can take full exposure. *R. maximum* is equally hardy and is useful for its late white or pale pink flowers with a yellow blotch. Tolerant of quite deep shade.

cinnabarinum
H3-4 Medium-Tall *EM-L*

This very variable species is one of the most distinctive species with its clusters of pendant, tubular flowers in many different colours. All have fairly small leaves and a more or less upright habit and all are subject to powdery mildew disease, though some forms are more susceptible than others. Ssp. *cinnabarinum* usually has orange flowers, 'Roylei' Group has red flowers, ssp. *xanthocodon* has yellow flowers and 'Concatenans' Group has orange-yellow flowers and glaucous foliage.

dauricum
H6-7 Semi-dwarf-Medium *VE-E*

This very tough deciduous species is a parent of many of the hardiest hybrids such as 'P.J.M.' Purple, purplish-pink or white flowers, normally on the bare stems. The small leaves usually develop as the flowers are shed. The clone 'Midwinter' flowers in January in the U.K. *R. mucronulatum* (H5-6) is slightly less hardy, usually later flowering and is pink in most commonly cultivated forms. The forms grown as var. *chejuense* are low-growing with fine flowers and good autumn colour.

decorum
H3-4 Medium-Tall *M-ML*

This vigorous and easily grown species is useful for moderate climates for its scented pink to white flowers, and its tolerance of relatively dry conditions and near neutral soil. Variable in hardiness and flowering time. The variable *R. vernicosum* usually has pink or purplish pink flowers with little or no scent.

Above: One of the hardiest scented species, *R. fortunei* has been an important parent and is a popular plant in severe climates

Left: The pendulous bells of *R. cinnabarinum* never fail to attract attention. The form shown here is from the Roylei Group. Other forms have orange, yellow or bi-coloured flowers

fortunei
H5-6 Medium-Tall *ML-L*

This is the hardiest scented species and it has been much used in hybridising. Pale pink or pale lavender flowers fade to white. Smooth, glabrous leaves. Popular in eastern North America.

neriiflorum
H3-4 Low-Tall *EM-M*

A very variable species, usually grown in its red-flowered forms. Loose trusses of bright red flowers. Leaves usually glabrous.

orbiculare
H4 Low-Medium *EM-M*

A very distinctive species which has almost round leaves. Deep rose-pink or purplish-pink flowers.

oreodoxa
H5 Medium *E-EM*

This early-flowering species has white, lilac or pink flowers which are relatively frost-hardy. In most forms they will take a few degrees of frost. This species is most commonly grown as var. *fargesii* which usually has pink flowers.

pachysanthum
H5 Low *EM*

First introduced during the 1970s from its native Taiwan, this has become one of the most popular species, due to its outstanding foliage. The leaves are covered with a silvery or fawn indumentum on both upper and lower surfaces which, unlike most species, persists on the upper surface. A dense, compact grower with pale pink or white

flowers. *R. pseudochrysanthum* is closely related, with less indumentum but fine, pale pink to white flowers.

ponticum
H4 Medium *ML-L*

The infamous 'wild' rhododendron of the British Isles was introduced from E. Turkey over 200 years ago and has since become a serious invasive weed in areas of high rainfall. It now covers hundreds of acres of western Scotland, Wales and Cornwall and is very hard to eradicate. In drier parts of the U.K. it stays under control and may be a useful windbreak. Little grown outside the U.K.

rex
H4-5 Tall *M-ML*

This is the hardiest of the large-leaved species with indumentum, and is a very popular garden plant. Huge trusses of pale pink to white flowers with a deep red or purple spotting or blotch in the throat. Deep green, handsome leaves up to 45cm (18in) long. Worth attempting even in cold climates. **Ssp. *fictolacteum*** has slightly smaller leaves. Equally fine. *R. hodgsonii* (H4-5) is usually just as hardy. Fine, large leaves and attractive pinkish bark; flowers pink to magenta.

glischrum
H3-4 Medium-Tall *EM-ML*

A handsome species with bristly leaves and branches. Flowers pink or purplish-pink with a reddish-purple blotch in the throat, in fine rounded trusses. The related *R. adenosum* (H4) is a little-known species which should be more widely grown. Pink or white flowers on a tidy bush which is quite free-flowering.

hyperythrum
H5-6 Low-Medium *EM-M*

Usually pure white flowers in rounded trusses on a tidy plant with glabrous leaves which curve down at the edges. Cold and heat tolerant and should be used more as a parent.

lutescens
H3-4 Medium *E-EM*

This species has smallish, pointed leaves which are reddish or brown in the young growth. Bright yellow flowers in early spring. Rather early into growth, so needs shelter from frosts. The more compact *R. ambiguum* (H5) is hardier and flowers later.

Above: *R. glischrum* is an excellent plant for the woodland garden, with large leaves and showy pinkish-purple flowers with a deeper blotch in the throat

Right: The infamous *R. ponticum* has naturalised itself in wetter parts of the British Isles where it has become an invasive weed which is very hard to eradicate. Its purple flowers provide a spectacular sight in June

rubiginosum
H4 Tall _E-EM_

In moderate climates, this is one of the most vigorous species and it is useful as a windbreak or screen. Tolerant of near-neutral soil and fairly dry conditions. Small scaly, leaves and masses of lavender-pink to mauve flowers.

with a crimson blotch. Takes many years to flower. Requires plenty of shelter. _R. macabeanum_ has smaller, more oval leaves and fine yellow flowers.

sinogrande
H2-3 Tall _EM-M_

This species has the largest leaves in the genus, reaching a majestic 1m (3ft) in length in favourable conditions. Eventually growing enormous, with spectacular trusses of 20-50 cream-coloured flowers

smirnowii
H5-6 Low-Medium _ML-L_

A useful, tough species with rounded trusses of pink flowers on a fairly compact plant with indumentum on the leaf lower surface. Some heat and drought resistance.

Above: A white form of _R. souliei_ which has characteristic saucer-shaped flowers. It is often grown in pale and deep pink forms

Left:
R. yunnanense is a very common species in its native Yunnan where it covers huge areas. Very free-flowering in the garden and tolerant of dry conditions, but it is rather vulnerable to bark split as a young plant

souliei
H4-5 Low-Medium _M_

A beautiful species in its saucer-shaped pink or white flowers. Glabrous and glaucous leaves. Needs excellent drainage and dislikes hot summers, so seldom successful away from cooler northern areas.

thomsonii
H3-4 Medium-Tall _EM-M_

This fine species has rounded leaves and waxy, red flowers. It is also grown for its beautiful smooth, pinkish bark. Particularly prone to powdery mildew infection.

uvariifolium
H3-4 Medium-Tall _E-EM_

Pale pink flowers, usually with reddish spotting and/or a blotch in the throat. Pale indumentum on the leaf underside. Foliage is usually handsome. _R. fulvum_ is closely related, smaller in all parts, with pink flowers and leaves with a reddish-brown indumentum on the underside.

wardii
H3-5 Low-Medium _M-L_

Named after the plant collector Frank Kingdon Ward, this is one of the finest yellow-flowered species and it is the parent of most of the larger yellow hybrids. Pure yellow flowers, sometimes blotched or spotted red. Oval leaves. The Himalayan _R. campylocarpum_ is closely related and tends to have paler yellow flowers.

yunnanense
H3-4 Medium-Tall _M-ML_

One of the spectacular sights of Yunnan province of China are the hillsides covered in this very free-flowering, small-leaved species with pink or white flowers. Young plants are vulnerable to bark split. _R. davidsonianum_ is very similar, while _R. oreotrephes_ differs in its lower stature, glaucous leaves and usually purple-lavender flowers.

Larger Hybrids

These range from the ironclads, the toughest rhododendrons, bred for extremes of cold and often of heat also, to varieties suitable for woodland conditions in moderate climates. Most will start flowering at a relatively young age and flower reliably every year. In most cases the foliage is not as interesting or showy as that of the larger species listed above. Literally thousands of larger hybrids have been named and more are launched every year. Almost all the ones listed here are tried and tested and have been found reliable. One or two promising newcomers are also included. Listen to local advice as to which will grow best in your area, especially if your climate includes extremes of heat and/or cold. Most garden centres carry a range of hardy hybrids; these are not always well chosen for your area so take care!

'Anah Kruschke'
H5-6 Medium-Tall *ML-L*

Full trusses of reddish-purple flowers on a very vigorous plant with dark foliage. Heat and sun tolerant. Not a popular colour in the U.K. but a good doer in S.E. U.S.A.

'Blue Peter'
H5 Medium *M-ML*

Frilly pale lavender-blue flowers with a prominent reddish-purple flare in the throat. Rather untidy grower which is tough and easy to please. 'Blue Ensign' is similar. 'A Bedford' (H5) is an upright, leggy grower with fine, pale lavender-mauve flowers with a dark flare. Useful for its heat and sun tolerance.

'Britannia'
H4 Low-Medium *ML*

This old hybrid has long been popular, but I feel it has had its day. Rather pale red flowers with foliage that tends to look yellow, however well you treat it.

'Cadis'
H5-6 Medium *ML-L*

This hybrid, with ruffled, light pink, scented flowers, is popular in S.E. U.S.A. as it is heat tolerant and resistant to root rot. Narrow leaves give the plant a distinctive appearance. 'Caroline', one of Cadis' parents is equally heat tolerant and root-rot resistant. Lightly scented, pale pink flowers.

'Catawbiense Album'
H7 Medium-Tall *ML*

The toughest of the white, old ironclad hybrids, this is very widely grown in severest climates. Pure white flowers with a yellow-green flare. Sun, heat and wind-tolerant but takes a few years to flower freely. 'Boule de Neige' is equally hardy with pure white flowers with light green/ yellow spotting. Very popular in N.E. U.S.A. and E. Canada. 'County of York' (syn. 'Catalode') (H5-6) is a very vigorous hybrid with large trusses of white with a green throat. Sun and wind tolerant.

'Christmas Cheer'
H5 Low-Medium *E-EM*

One of the best early-flowering hybrids, though it only flowers at Christmas if it is forced inside. Full trusses of pink flowers gradually fade to cream. Trusses open over a long period of time, so even if some are frosted, there are usually more to come out. A dense and tidy grower and a first class plant.

'Crest'
H4 Tall *M-ML*

Amongst the yellow-flowered hybrids the flowers of 'Crest' have few equals, as they are large and pure yellow. The plant is upright and can look rather sparse. As with most yellows, it needs good drainage and it sometimes suffers from mildew.

'Cunningham's White'
H5-6 **Low-Medium** *M-ML*

This very old hybrid from Cunningham's nursery in Edinburgh is one of the most widely-grown throughout the world, due to its tolerance of poor or near-neutral soil, and its adaptability to full exposure. White flowers with a yellow throat. There are several clones in commerce. The most showy one has full trusses. The toughest and easiest clones have small, rather loose trusses. Used extensively as a rootstock for grafting. Good as a windbreak or screen.

'Cynthia'
H5-6 **Tall** *ML-L*

Another old favourite, this has large trusses of deep rose-pink with deeper crimson staining. Very tough: tolerant of sun and wind, and very free-flowering once it gets established.

'Erato'
H5-6 **Medium** *ML-L*

Very fine, pure red flowers in a full truss. A promising new hardy hybrid from Hachmann in Germany. 'Torero' is a very similar sister seedling.

Fabia Group
H3-4 **Medium** *ML-L*

There are several clones of this woodland hybrid with pendulous flowers in loose trusses of orange or salmon pink. Leaves have a light covering of indumentum on the lower surface. Tends to grow late, so best with some shelter. 'Medusa' has smaller, but more reddish-orange flowers.

Above: 'Hotei', named after a Japanese deity, is one of the deepest yellow hybrids. It takes a number of years to flower and needs perfect drainage

'Fastuosum Flore Pleno'
H5-6 **Tall** *L*

This is one of the few double-flowered hybrids. Pale bluish-mauve double-flowers (where the stamens have fused to form extra petals). A very tough and easy plant if fairly upright but tidy habit which is sun and wind tolerant.

'Golden Star'
H5 **Tall** *M-ML*

One of the best yellow hybrids for milder parts of the eastern seaboard of the N.E. U.S.A., this hybrid has large trusses of pale yellow flowers. Very vigorous and rather prone to

powdery mildew. Much used as a parent for hardy yellows.

'Goldflimmer'
H5-6 **Low-Medium** *L*

One of the few rhododendrons with variegated foliage, this has flecks of yellow in the leaves. Small trusses of purplish-pink flowers. *R. ponticum* 'Variegatum' has similar flowers while the narrow leaves have white variegation at the margins. 'President Roosevelt' (H4) has red and white flowers and bold variegation in the leaves, but it sprawls and the branches are brittle.

'Goldkrone'
H5 Low-Medium M

This hybrid has fine yellow flowers with reddish spotting on a fairly compact plant. It requires very good drainage and is better grafted in areas with hot summers. Very free-flowering.

'Gomer Waterer'
H5-6 Medium L

An outstanding, reliable and very tough hybrid which is sun, heat and wind-tolerant. White flowers, flushed lilac-pink at the edges, with a large yellowish flare. Free-flowering and useful for its late flowering time.

'Hotei'
H4 Medium M-ML

Named after a Japanese deity, this is one of the deepest yellow hybrids but it takes a few years to flower freely and it needs particularly good drainage.

'(The Hon.) Jean Marie de Montague'
H4 Medium M-ML

his has long been the standard red hybrid in the Pacific Northwest of North America. Fine crimson-scarlet flowers on a fairly upright plant. Free-flowering and useful for its sun and heat resistance.

'Right: 'Lady Chamberlain' is a favourite of all who see it, but it is particularly prone to powdery mildew

Below: '(The Hon.) Jean Marie de Montague' is one of the most popular of the old red hybrids and is a big favourite in western North America

'Lady Chamberlain'
H3-(4) Medium M

One of the most striking of all hybrids, this *R. cinnabarinum* hybrid has pendulous salmon-orange flowers on an upright plant with small leaves. Unfortunately this hybrid is extremely susceptible to powdery mildew as is its close relative **'Lady Rosebery'** which has pink flowers. Other *R. cinnabarinum* hybrids (all less susceptible to mildew) are **'Biskra'** (H4-5) with vermillion flowers, **'Alison Johnstone'** (H4) with peachy-apricot flowers and **'Conroy'** (H4) with bluish leaves and light orange and rose flowers.

'Lady Clementine Mitford'
H4 Medium-Tall ML-L

An old hybrid, still popular, with pink flowers fading towards the centre, with spotting, in a compact, rounded truss. New growth silvery. Heat and sun tolerant.

'Lem's Cameo'
H4 Medium *M-ML*

This extraordinary hybrid has revolutionised breeding and its many offspring are becoming increasingly popular in milder areas (see under 'Nancy Evans'). Frilly pink cream and apricot flowers with a red blotch in the base, in huge wide trusses. Rather sparsely clothed with leaves and reluctant to branch. Bronzy new growth. Free-flowering.

'Lem's Monarch'
H4 Tall *ML*

''The' hybrid for the 'large-is beautiful' brigade, this has trusses up to 30cm (12in) high, pale pink fading to white with a deeper rim round each flower. The extra thick foliage and stems allow the trusses to be held up well. A stunning hybrid which needs plenty of room. **'Point Defiance'** is very similar.

'Loderi'
H3-4 Tall *M*

The 'Loderi' grex or group is a range of sister seedlings renowned for their strongly sweet-scented flowers. Huge loose trusses of pale pink to white flowers. Long pale green leaves. For best results, wind shelter and filtered shade is advisable. The most popular clones are: **'King George'** with white flowers, **'Venus'** and **'Game Chick'** with pale pink ones.

Above: 'Lem's Monarch' has trick stems and leaves and large trusses of pale pink flowers, deeper on the rim of each flower.

Right: 'Mrs A.T. de La Mare' is a reliable old hybrid with fine scented white flowers

Opposite: Bred in the Pacific Northwest of the U.S.A., the cream, pink and red flowers have attracted many to 'Lem's Cameo'

'Lord Roberts'
H5-6 Medium *L*

A useful, very tough, late flowering hybrid with small trusses of dark crimson with a black flare.

'Madame Mason'
H5-6 Low-Medium *M*

Small, compact trusses of white flowers with a yellow blotch on a dense, spreading grower. Good in S.E. U.S.A.

'Markeeta's Prize'
H4 Medium-Tall *M*

Huge, densely textured trusses of bright red flowers on a vigorous but tidy plant with thick leaves. **'Halfdan Lem'** is similar but with a more untidy habit.

'Mrs A.T. de la Mare'
H5-6 Medium-Tall *M-ML*

This is one of the toughest scented hybrids. Lightly perfumed white flowers. Best in some shade to protect the flowers from the elements.

'Mrs. G.W. Leak'
H4 Medium-Tall *EM-M*

Rose-pink flowers, with a heavy brown and crimson flare in a full, conical truss. Upright in habit. The plant tends to suffer from leaf spot. There are many hybrids with similar pink flowers with a deeper blotch. Some of the most popular include **'Mrs Furnival'** (H5-6) sun and heat-tolerant, **'Furnivall's Daughter'** with a larger truss and round-ended, yellowish leaves, and **'Trail Blazer'** (H5), recently introduced with fine pink flowers and a compact habit.

'Mrs. T. H. Lowinsky'
H5-6 Medium *L*

Mauve buds open to off white flowers with a bold orange-brown flare. Vigorous and tough and useful for its late flowering. Heat-tolerant.

'Nancy Evans'
H3-4 Low-Medium *M*

The most popular of the many 'Lem's Cameo' hybrids now coming onto the market, this is an outstanding plant with very freely-produced rounded trusses of deep yellow flowers, marked orange as they first open. Fairly compact with bronzy new growth. Needs good drainage and a little shelter for best results. There are many new hybrids with multicoloured trusses coming onto the market. Time will tell which the best ones are. Some of these include the pale yellow **'Horizon Monarch'** and the yellow and pink **'Horizon Lakeside'**.

Naomi Group
H4-5 Medium-Tall *M-ML*

There are several named clones of this cross. The most popular is **'Naomi Exbury'** which has rounded trusses of white to yellow flowers, with a lilac-pink edging. Subject to powdery mildew.

The deep yellow 'Nancy Evans' is extremely free-flowering and is becoming popular as a garden plant in moderate areas

Nobleanum Group
H4 Medium *VE*

This group of hybrids are grown for their very early flowers, opening around or before Christmas in mild winters. Small trusses of scarlet-pink, pink or white flowers, depending on the clone. Pale green leaves have a thin layer of indumentum beneath. Habit is fairly compact but often rather irregular.

'Nova Zembla'
H6-7 Medium *M*

Long the standard ironclad red hybrid, this has slightly bluish-tinged red flowers on a well-behaved plant. Not worth growing in milder areas where better colours are available. Sun and fairly heat-tolerant as long as drainage is good. **'America'** is equally hardy, with a more spreading habit. Flowers are a rather harsh red.

'Odee Wright'
H4 **Low-Medium** *M*

Very fine trusses of pale yellow flowers with pink edging and on the reverse. Fairly compact and rather slow-growing.

'Pink Pearl'
H4 **Tall** *ML-L*

Long the standard, large pink hybrid for moderate climates, this upright grower with pale green leaves has tall pink trusses which fade out to off white. Two very similar hybrids are **'Betty Wormald'** with deeper pink flowers and **'Marinus Koster'** which is slightly more compact as is the popular **'Trude Webster'**.

Polar Bear Group
H3-4 **Tall** *VL*

One of the latest of the larger hybrids to flower, this large grower has fine trusses of scented white flowers which open in July or August. Best in light shade with shelter from wind and early autumn frosts which can damage the typically late growth.

'Purple Splendour'
H4-5 **Medium** *ML*

Deep purple, frilly flowers with an almost black blotch in full trusses. The plant itself is rather lacking in vigour and is prone to powdery mildew. It being gradually superseded by its hardier and more disease-resistant offspring such as **'Azurro'** and **'Jonathan Shaw'** which have almost as deep flowers.

'Naomi Exbury' is one of the best-known Rothschild hybrids from Exbury Gardens in England

'Roseum Elegans'
H7 **Tall** *ML*

One of the toughest and most reliable hybrids due to its hardiness and heat and sun tolerance. Rosy-lilac flowers in small trusses on a vigorous plant. Not worth growing in milder areas but an essential plant for severest climates of rhododendron-growing areas. **'English Roseum'** is similar with pinker flowers, while **'Catawbiense Boursault'** has purple flowers.

'Rubicon' Group
H3 **Low** *M*

One of the finest low reds ever raised, but only suitable for mild areas. Very fine trusses of bright red flowers. Handsome ribbed foliage on a compact plant. Heat-tolerant. Its parent **'Noyo Brave'** is taller growing with paler, pinkish-red flowers. Also good in warm climates.

'Sappho'
H5-6 Medium-Tall *ML-L*

This old hardy hybrid has very striking white flowers with a bold, reddish-purple flair but its deplorable straggly habit means that it should be sited at the back of a planting. Several newer hybrids such as 'Calsap' have similar flowers, but an improved habit.

'Scintillation'
H5-6 Medium *M-ML*

This hybrid consistently wins polls in Eastern North America as the most reliable hybrid in cold, but not the coldest, areas. Rounded trusses of pink flowers with a brown flare on a plant with a tidy habit and deep green leaves. Heat-tolerant but foliage can suffer sun burn in full-exposure. 'Janet Blair' (H5-6) has light pink flowers with a yellow-green flare. Free-flowering and heat-tolerant. 'Brown Eyes' (H6-7) has showy bright pink flowers with a large brown flare in the throat. Rather unattractive, twisted leaves.

'September Song'
H3-4 Medium *M-ML*

This is one of the finest orange-flowered hybrids we have seen. The flowers are a mixture of salmon and orange. Not all that bud-hardy, but free-flowering otherwise. There are several new orange hybrids coming onto the market. 'Mavis Davis' is one of the most promising.

'Sonata'
H4-5 Low-Medium *ML-L*

Small trusses of orange flowers with red centres. A compact, dense grower which is quite easy to please, as long as drainage is good. Quite free-flowering once established.

'Susan'
H4-5 Medium *M*

A popular hybrid with fine bluish-mauve flowers in rounded trusses. Dark foliage on a fairly compact bush. Somewhat hardier are 'Lavender Girl' (H5) lightly scented pale lavender flowers and 'Lavender Queen' (H5) with small rounded trusses of frilly, lavender flowers. 'Mrs Charles Pearson' (H4-5) has fine trusses of pale pinkish-mauve.

Opposite: 'Scintillation' consistently comes top of polls as the best larger hybrid for northeastern U.S.A. and eastern Canada. Well worth growing in other areas too

'Unique'
H4 Low-Medium *EM-M*

Consistently one of the most popular hybrids for its tight, dense habit, this old favourite has creamy-ivory flowers flushed pink and yellow. Seems to have some heat tolerance. Best in plenty of light for best habit. 'Bruce Brechtbill' is a sport of 'Unique', identical in foliage but with pale pink flowers. Very popular in areas of moderate climate.

'Vanessa Pastel'
H3-4 Low *ML*

One of the most attractive hybrids for mild areas, this has loose trusses which open salmon-pink and fade to cream, with a red blotch in the throat. Pale green leaves on plant of quite good habit which needs protection for its late growth. Somewhat prone to powdery mildew.

'Virginia Richards'
H4 Medium-Tall *EM*

Large trusses of bright pink flowers which fade to cream, with a red centre. Dark green leaves on a plant of good habit. Unfortunately this hybrid is very prone to powdery mildew which has decreased its popularity.

'Vulcan'
H5 Medium *L*

Brightest red flowers on a vigorous plant which should be in plenty of light for best habit. Shows good heat and sun tolerance but tends to produce rather yellowish late growth in the U.K. Very popular in North America.

Yellow Hammer Group
H4 Medium *EM-M*

This vigorous, upright hybrid has tiny leaves and masses of tubular yellow flowers from multiple buds up the stems. Needs a bit of pruning for best habit. It tends to flower quite well in Autumn, as well as spring.

Deciduous Azaleas

Hybridised throughout the last 200 years, these now come in a huge variety of colours. Some flower on the bare branches while others start to grow as the flowers open. Most are very hardy, and some such as the Northern Lights series are amongst the toughest plants in the genus. Often used for mass planting, in woodland or in borders, the hybrids have amongst the brightest flowers of all rhododendrons. Many varieties are scented and some have fine autumn colour. As most are relatively late-flowering, they seldom lose their flowers to spring frosts. Some of the white and yellow species and their offspring are subject to azalea powdery mildew (see page 66).

SPECIES

The species deciduous azaleas are becoming increasingly popular as garden plants; they are usually less flamboyant than their hybrid offspring, but with more character and often have features such as strong scent and fine autumn colour. They vary considerably in hardiness.

R. occidentale hybrid 'Exquisita' is grown for its pastel-coloured, sweetly scented flowers which open in early June

albrechtii
H5-6 Low-Medium EM-M

Brightest rose to deep rose-purple flowers on the bare stems. Although hardy, the rather early flowers and growth need some shelter.

arborescens
H5 Low-Medium ML-L

A fine, compact species with scented white to pale pink flowers with long red stamens and style. There are many Eastern American scented species of similar appearance: *atlanticum* (H5-6) has glaucous leaves and a low, spreading habit; *prinophyllum* (H7) has scented, pink flowers; *viscosum*

(H5-6) has very late small white flowers; *canescens* with pale to deep pink flowers is suitable for milder areas with hot summers only.

calendulaceum
H7 Medium-Tall L

This species is the source of much of the bright orange colour in the hybrids. Small, bright yellow or orange flowers. *cumberlandense* (H5-6) is very similar, with fine red forms; *prunifolium*(H5-6) with orange-red to vivid red flowers is late flowering and very heat tolerant; *austrinum* (H3-4) with yellow or orange yellow flowers is less hardy but very heat-tolerant. Good in its native S.E. U.S.A.

luteum
H5 Medium-Tall ML-L

This is the vigorous Pontic azalea, widely planted in the U.K. and elsewhere for its fine, sweetly scented, yellow flowers and its very good autumn colours.

molle ssp. japonicum (syn. Azalea mollis)
H7 Low-Medium M-ML

Red, orange, salmon, pink or yellow flowers. Very tough and easy. Widely grown under the name *Azalea mollis*.

occidentale
H4-5 Medium-Tall L-VL

The western American native azalea with large, sweetly-scented, white flowers, usually flushed pink, with a yellow flare, in quite large trusses. Not as hardy as most of the other species and subject to azalea powdery mildew and rust.

schlippenbachii
H7 Low-Medium EM

Very showy pink or white flowers on a compact plant with distinctive leaves. Although midwinter-hardy, its flowers and new growth are vulnerable to spring frost damage.

vaseyi
H5-6 Medium EM-M

A very distinctive azalea with attractive two-lipped, pink or white flowers on a bushy plant. Pointed leaves show good Autumn colour.

HYBRIDS

The following are the most commonly-grown named varieties in the various hybrid groups. Some, such as Mollis and Exbury, are often sold as seedlings to colour, rather than as named varieties.

Ghent
H6-7 **Medium-Tall**
M-ML

The oldest hybrid group, this contains tough, usually small-flowered cultivars, including the currently fashionable small, double-flowered varieties. The most commonly sold varieties are:
'Coccinea Speciosa' Orange-red with yellow, single
'Daviesii' White and yellow (two clones-one single and one double)
'Narcissiflora' Double pale yellow.

often sold as seedlings to colour. The most common named clones are:
'Adriaan Koster' pure yellow
'Christopher Wren' yellow, with orange flare
'Dr M. Oosthoek' vivid orange-red
'Koster's Brilliant Red' reddish-orange
'Lemonora' yellow, shaded pink

A white seedling Knaphill or Exbury axalea suitable for extreme climates. This group of azalea are available in a variety of colours from white, through yellow, salmon, pink, to orange and red

Mollis
H6-7 **Low-Medium**
M-ML

The earliest-flowering azalea group, these are mostly not hybrids but simply selections of the Japanese species *R. molle* ssp. *japonicum*. Colours range from red, though orange, salmon, pink to yellow. More compact and spreading than the other hybrid groups. Most

Exbury/Knaphill
H5-H7 **Medium-Tall**
ML-L

The most flamboyant of all the hybrid groups and containing the largest number of cultivars. Development of these hybrids began at Knaphill nursery and continued at Exbury (both in England). Subsequent work has followed in several parts of the world, including Ilam in New Zealand and Arensons and Girards in the U.S.A. Some varieties are scented. There are far too many named hybrids. Some of the most popular include:

'Balzac' Large trusses of orange-red flowers
'Berryrose' Pale pink with orange, fragrant. Bronzy new growth.
'Cannon's Double' Double pink with orange shading.
'Cecile' Salmon pink with a yellow blotch
'Chetco' Yellow with an orange blotch
'Fireball' Deep orange-red
'George Reynolds' Large, deep yellow flowers, orange spotting
'Gibraltar' The most popular orange-flowered selection

'Glowing Embers' Orange-red with an orange flare. Compact.
'Golden Sunset' Light yellow, tinged orange, orange flare
'Homebush' Double pink flowers in rounded, balled truss
'Hotspur' Reddish-orange flowers.
'Klondyke' One of the best yellows. New-growth coppery-red.
'Mount Saint Helens' Yellowish-pink with an orange flare, fragrant.
'Oxydol' Large white flowers with a yellow throat
'Persil' Pure white with a deep yellow flare'

Royal Lodge' Deep red with long, protruding stamens
'Satan' Not surprisingly this is deep reddish-orange
'Silver Slipper' White, edged pink, with yellow flare
'Strawberry Ice' Pink with a yellow blotch
'Syliphides' Light pink, with yellow shadings
'Whitethroat' Masses of smallish, scented white flower.

Northern Lights Azaleas
H7 or colder Medium-Tall *ML-L*

Bred for severest climates, the Northern Lights series are hardy to -34°C (-40°F) and are amongst the hardiest plants in the genus.

Above: 'Irene Koster' is one of the most popular of the *R. occidentale* hybrid deciduous azaleas, with its fine, scented pink and white flowers

Left: 'Golden Sunset' a fine yellow Exbury azalea which flowers in late May and early June

They have small flowers and are probably not worth growing in milder climates where less hardy varieties are suitable.
'Golden Lights' yellow, fragrant
'Lemon Lights' Bright yellow
'Mandarin Lights' Ruffled light orange flowers, light fragrance.
'Northern Hi-Lights' White with a yellow blotch, mildew resistant.
'Orchid Lights' Lilac flowers, low and bushy
'Rosy Lights' Pink with deeper shadings; fragrant
'Spicy Lights' Tangerine-orange, fragrant.
'White Lights' White, quite large flowers, fragrant.

occidentale
H4-5 Low-Medium *ML-L*

Bred from the species *R. occidentale*, these hybrids have pale-coloured flowers and most are scented. As the least hardy group, most are suitable for moderate climates only. Many are susceptible to azalea mildew.
'Delicatissima' White, flushed yellow and pink, blotched yellow, scented.
'Exquisita' White, flushed pink, orange blotch, scented.
'Irene Koster' Pale pink, fading to cream, deeper stripes, scented.
'Washington State Centennial' (syn. 'Centennial') White with huge yellow blotch.

Evergreen or Japanese Azaleas

Worldwide, these are the most popular members of the genus, making fine houseplants as well as garden plants, thriving in climates too hot or dry for other rhododendrons. The selection and breeding of azaleas goes back hundreds of years in Japan and hybridisation began here in the west as soon as many of the varieties were introduced, mostly in the early 1900s. Many evergreen azaleas are cold and heat-tolerant but are not successful in northern climates, where summers are not hot enough to ripen the wood. A number of the varieties which grow well elsewhere are not good performers in Scotland, Germany, Scandinavia and E Canada, for instance and breeders in these areas have produced hybrids to suit these of climates. Evergreen azaleas are subject to azalea gall and petal blight (see page 70).

The various breeding programmes divide the varieties into categories such as Satsuki, Kurume and Glenn Dale. Varieties with double flowers have fused stamens, giving a ruffled effect in the centre of the flower. Varieties described as 'hose-in-hose' have two rings of petals, one inside the other.

The various cultivar groups are listed in order of hardiness, with the tender ones listed first. Flowering times are hard to tie down, as in very mild climates, many will flower in winter and early spring, while in cold climates the same varieties may not flower till late spring.

A double flowered Indica azalea which can be grown outdoors in mild areas and which makes a popular houseplant in colder regions

Satsuki and Gumpo
H3 ML-L

The Japanese have been selecting and naming these spectacular azaleas for hundreds of years. Many of them have different colours of flowers on one plant with dots, spots, rings and other effects. This makes naming some of them a nightmare and a bit meaningless as you never know what colour you will get next. Most of the ones listed below are stable as far as flower colour is concerned. Best in partial shade to allow flowers to last. Very popular as pot plants and for bonzai. Very poor in areas without summer heat to ripen the wood.

'Flame Creeper' Single orange-red. Low, spreading habit.
'Gumpo' Large single white, low, dense
'Gumpo Pink' Single rose-pink flowers with deep flecks, low and dense.
'Higasa' Large single deep rose-pink flowers
'Shinnyo No Tsuki' Large white with pink flecks.

Kurume
H3-4 EM-M

These compact plants, first imported from Japan to the west by E. Wilson (as the Wilson 50), have masses of small flowers. Further hybrids were made of them in many parts of the world. Best in part-shade in warmer and more southern climates. Most are not reliably hardy in Scotland or similar northern climates; the hardier ones are noted.

'Addy Wery' Strong red, upright habit. Fairly hardy.
'Amoenum' Hose-in-hose, rosy-purple, low and spreading.
'Blauu's Pink' (M) Yellowish-pink, hose-in-hose, with a dark blotch.
'Coral Bells' Small, hose-in-hose, pink with darker centres. Small leaves.
'Hexe' Crimson hose-in-hose on a low spreader.
'Hino Crimson' Small, bright red flowers. Red winter foliage.
'Hinodegiri' (M) Small flowered, purplish-red. Quite hardy.
'Kirin' Hose-in-hose, two-tone pink. Good in S. England.
'Mother's Day' (L) Bright red, semi-double. Quite hardy.
'Mucronatum' Upright habit with large white flowers.

Gable, Kaempferi and Vuykiana
H4-(5/6)

This group contains many of the taller-growing and large-flowered hybrids raised from the species *R. kaempferi* and *R. poukhanense*. Many of the hybrids have inherited their parents' semi-deciduous nature and they can look rather sparse in winter. Many of them benefit from hardy pruning, especially when young. Many are suitable for colder climates such as Scotland and varieties such as 'Johanna' are amongst the most popular evergreen azaleas in Europe.

kaempferi (H3-5 M-L) This very variable Japanense species has reddish, orange-red, salmon pink, pink or, rarely, white flowers. Rather a rangy grower which tends to be semi-deciduous.

poukhanense. (syn. *yedoense* var. *poukhanense*) (H5-6 M) This Korean species is one of the toughest evergreen azalea species, and has been a very important parent of the some of the hardiest hybrids. Rose to pale lilac-purple flowers.

'Blue Danube' (M-ML) Fine deep purplish-red. Vigorous. Popular in U.K.

'Caroline Gable' (ML) Red, hose-in-hose, medium-tall.

'Fedora' (M) Deep-rose to salmon pink, single.

'Hardy Gardenia' ('Linwood') Double white, good foliage.

'Johanna' Carmine-red. Fine dark glossy foliage. Very popular.

'Palestrina' (H6) Large white flowers. Erect habit. One of the hardiest.

'Purple Splendour' (M-ML) Reddish-purple, frilled. Fairly compact.

'Rosebud' (ML) Double pink, like minature rosebuds. Compact.

'Rose Greeley' (M-ML) Hose-in-hose, white with greenish-yellow blotch.

'Orange Beauty' (M) Salmon-orange, tall, semi-deciduous.

The double-pink evergreen azalea 'Rosebud' is one of the most popular in many parts of the world. We find it a little tender in Scotland

'Stewartstonian' (H6 M) Large, single, bright red. Red winter foliage.

'White Rosebud' (KEHR) Double white, dense upright habit.

'Vuyk's Scarlet' (ML) Very popular in U.K. Large scarlet flowers.

Eastern American Hybrids, Glenn Dale Etc.
H4-5

The Glenn Dales, bred by Ben Morrison in Maryland, includes crosses made with many of the varieties previously mentioned. The hardiest ones are suitable for much of coastal N.E. U.S.A and they are very popular in the Pacific Northwest. A few are popular in Europe. Most not reliably hardy in Scotland.

'Buccaneer' (M) Large, brilliant orange-red. Upright. Needs shade.
'Chippewa' (VL) Late-flowering frilled bright pink. Compact. Hardy.
'Everest' (M-ML) One of the finest large-flowered, compact whites.
'Glacier' (M) single white, glossy leaves.
'Glamour' (M) Single bright rose-red. Bronze winter foliage.
'Martha Hitchcock' (ML) Very showy, white with reddish-purple margins.
'Megan' (L) Large purplish pink flowers. Needs pruning. Good in Scotland.

Eastern American Hardiest Hybrids
H5-6

This category includes the hardiest azaleas, suitable for extreme climates. Some of these have proven not to be hardy in milder, northern areas, due to lack of summer heat. This group includes varieties bred by Robin Hill, Shamarello.

'Cascade' (H6 M-ML) White
'Elsie Lee' (H6 M-ML) An upright grower with double lavender flowers. Good in U.K.

'Megan' is one of the most popular of the Glenn Dale azaleas from eastern U.S.A. Very showy, large purple flowers on a rather rangy bush which needs pruning when young

Girard's Hotshot'(syn. 'Hotshot') (H5-6 M) Single red, good foliage.
'Helen Curtis' (H6-7) Double-white flowers, spreading habit. Very hardy.
'Hino Red' (H6-7 M) Red, spreading but compact
'Nancy of Robin Hill' (H4-5) Hose-in-hose, semi-double pink. Low-growing.
'Red Red' (H6 M) Very fine red flowers. Not reliable in Scotland.

Kiusianum and Nakaharae & their Hybrids
H4-6

The dwarf species R. kiusianum and R. nakaharae have been crossed with larger-flowered but less hardy varieties to create selections satisfactory for Scotland, Scandinavia, Germany, E. Canada and other similar climates

where summer sun strength is not reliable. The most important hybridisers are Polly Hill (U.S.A.), Peter Cox (Scotland), and G. Ahrends, C. Fleischmann and H. Hachmann (Germany). Most are low-growing, tolerant of full exposure and fairly evergreen.

kiusianum (H5 M-L Dwarf). This deciduous, or semi-deciduous, species has tiny leaves and is usually slow-growing and compact. The masses of small flowers can be white, pink, purple, red or orange-red. Much used in hybridising.
nakaraharae (H5-(6) L-VL Dwarf). This Taiwanese species is useful for its low, creeping or spreading habit and its late flowers which range from salmon to orange-red and red. Very slow-growing and compact. 'Mt Seven Star' is perhaps the best clone.
'Alexander' (H5-6 L) Deep reddish-orange with deep blotch, creeping habit.
'Canzonetta' (H5-6) Hose-in-hose, brightest pink. Compact. Good In N. Europe.

'Squirrel' (H5 L) Masses of small scarlet flowers, good foliage. Good in Scotland.
'Susannah Hill' (H5 L) Strong red with deeper spotting, low and spreading.
'Wombat' (H5 ML-L) Bright pink flowers on a low, carpeting plant. Good in U.K.

'Diamant' (H5-6) A range of *R. kiusianum* hybrids in colours ranging from purple, red, pink to white. Compact and dense with small leaves and masses of small flowers. Very tough, and excellent in N. Europe.
'Geisha Orange' (H5 M) Salmon-orange, small flowered, compact and low.

'Kermesina' (H5-6 ML) A compact, small-leaved and small-flowered azalea popular in Europe. Bright pink flowers. 'Kermesina Rose' is a sport of the above with paink flowers, edged white. Very distinctive. 'Kermesia White' is white form of the above.
'Panda' (H5 ML) Compact with fine white flowers. Very popular in U.K.
'Pink Pancake' (H5 L) Low carpeter with single pink flowers. There are many similar selections from the same breeder.

Above:
R. kiusianum is a fine plant for the rock garden

Right:
The sport 'Kermesina Rose' is a very popular, low-growing evergreen azalea, ideal for northern. climates

Opposite:
'Canzonetta' is a tough, recently-named German evergreen azalea with double flowers of very bright pink and a low compact habit

Tender Rhododendrons

These fall into 2 categories: those which can take a limited amount of frost (temperate species) and those which must be kept more or less frost-free (Vireyas).

TEMPERATE SPECIES AND HYBRIDS

These species and their hybrids vary in hardiness from H3 to H1 and in mild climates such as the west seaboard of the U.K., and Ireland, parts of France and Italy, California and Vancouver Island, most of New Zealand and parts of S. Australia, they make superb garden plants, producing compact, free-flowering specimens with flowers ranging from lavender and pink though white to yellow. In colder climates, they make excellent indoor plants for the greenhouse or conservatory. Many of the plants listed below are scented. All appreciate good drainage and an open compost. (See page 35 for more details.) Unless you live in a mild climate, these varieties are likely only to be available from specialist nurseries.

burmanicum
H2-3 Low EM-M

The plant usually grown under the name *R. burmanicum* is actually a hybrid and is one of the best yellow hybrids for warm climates. Masses of yellow flowers on a fairly tidy plant with scaly leaves. There are many fine hybrids of this plant, such as **'Saffron Queen'** and **'Owen Pearce'**, which are similar in flower and habit.

edgeworthii
H2-3 Low-Medium EM-M

For both flowers and foliage, this is one of the finest choices. Usually sweetly scented, white or white-flushed-pink flowers in trusses of three. Deep green leaves have a distinctive rough upper surface

and the lower surface is covered with a layer of brown indumentum. Needs exceptionally good drainage, and good out outdoors in an old tree-stump or similar. Variable in hardiness; the hardiest forms are worth trying in a sheltered spot, even in climates such as eastern Scotland.

formosum
H2-3 Medium EM-L

A variable species in foliage, flowers and hardiness. Var. *formosum* tends to be hardier, with usually scented flowers, white, sometimes blotched yellow, flushed pink. The more tender var. *inaequale* has perhaps the strongest scent of the Maddenia species. Flowers white with a yellow blotch.

'Frangrantissimum'
H2 Medium ML-L

One of the most widely-grown hybrids of this type. White, pink-tinged flowers have a yellow throat and a fine nutmeg-like sweet scent. Very straggly, putting out long shoots which can be trained round stakes or trellis. Subject to rust and mildew. **'Lady Alice Fitzwilliam'** has a less powerful scent, but is much more compact, making a better indoor plant.

'Else Frye' from California has fine scented flowers, white, slightly flushed pink and yellow.

lindleyi
H2-3 Medium EM-M

Magnificent fragrant trumpets, up to 10cm (4in) long, in trusses of three to seven, are usually white with pink flushing. A rather ungainly, straggly grower which is best grown as an informal thicket, allowing the long shoots to scramble about. Rather too big and untidy for pot culture. Hardiest forms (often Ludlow and Sherriff collections) are worth trying outdoors in climates such as eastern Scotland in a favourable site. *R. dalhousiae* (H2) has creamy yellow flowers while *R. dalhousiae* var. *rhabdotum* (H1-2) has an extraordinary red stripe down the side of the corolla. *R. veitchianum* (H1-2) is variable in flower but usually has frilled white flowers, sometimes scented. Cubittii Group has fine white flowers, flushed pink, with a yellow-orange flare.

moulmainense
H1-2 Low-Tall _E-M_

This little-known species has huge potential as a garden plant in mild and hot areas such as California and New Zealand. Plentiful white, pink or violet flowers can produce a spectacular effect on a mature plant. Flowers are generally scented. It usually has a showy reddish-purple, smooth or peeling bark. This species is sometimes grown under names such as **R. ellipticum**. There are other equally fine, closely related species such as **R. stamineum** with tubular white flowers.

nuttallii
H1-2 Tall _E-M_

This species has amongst the largest individual flowers in the genus _Rhododendron_, up to 12.5cm (5in) long, in trusses of three to six. Flowers are white or cream, usually tinged pink and/or yellow and are strongly scented. Huge, wrinkled leaves, up to 24cm (10in) long, are bronzy or reddish in young growth. A vigorous, upright grower which needs a large space to grow indoors. Very popular in very mild rhododendron-growing areas. There are many named and unnamed hybrids of this species crossed with _R. lindleyi_ such as 'Mi Amor' and 'Tupare' which are equally finely scented and spectacular. The recently introduced species **R. excellens** also has large leaves but its flowers are not as large as those of _R. nuttallii_.

Clay pots are often used for growing Vireyas and other tender rhododendrons indoors. This is the scented vireya species R. suaveolens

VIREYAS

This group of rhododendrons are found on mountains in Indonesia, Papua New Guinea, Malaysia, The Philippines and other parts of S.E. Asia. There is one species in northern Australia. Unless you live in an area where frosts are almost unknown (Auckland and north of it in New Zealand, Los Angeles California, and other similar climates), you will have to grow these plants indoors, in a more or less frost-free greenhouse or conservatory. For sheer flamboyance with brightest yellows, oranges and reds, not to mention multicoloured flowers, the Vireyas have few equals, and anyone who sees them is captivated.

All are rated H0, though some varieties can take a degree or two of frost, for a short period. In the wild and outdoors, Vireyas can get to 5m (16ft) or more, but in cultivation, such large plants are seldom seen. Larger growers will reach 2m (6ft 7in), while some of the smaller ones scarcely reach 30cm (12in). As they come from near the equator, Vireyas tend not to respond to seasons and can therefore flower or grow at any time of year. There are several hundred species and many hybrids to choose from. Most are only available from specialist nurseries. The following is a small selection of some of the most commonly grown species and hybrids.

CELL SIZES

Cells vary greatly in size. As they are all microscopic, the scales of measurement normally used (metres, centimetres, millimetres) are too large to measure them. Therefore, a smaller measurement known as a micrometre is used to measure cells. There are 1000 micrometres (μm) to 1 millimetre (mm).

Fungal and bacterial cells are much smaller than typical plant and animal cells.

The table below shows the sizes of some cells.

Type of cell	Approximate size (μm)
E. coli – a bacterium	2
Yeast	3
Human red blood cell	9
Typical animal cell	10–30
Typical plant cell	10–100
Small amoeba	90
Human egg	100

DON'T FORGET

Micrometers are also known as microns.

ONLINE TEST

Test how well you've learned about the structure of plant and animal cells by taking the 'Cell structure' test online at www.brightredbooks.net/N5Biology

THINGS TO DO AND THINK ABOUT

1   Look at the following diagram of a cell and complete the table to identify the various organelles and their functions.

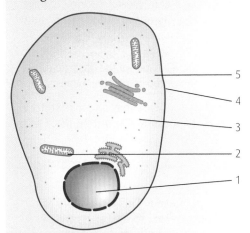

Part	Name	Function
1		
2		
3		
4		
5		

2   Compare this cell with the one shown on p7. Which of the cells is from a plant? Give evidence to support your answer.

3   You should be able to compare relative sizes of cells and convert sizes between micrometres (μm) and millimetres (mm):

- A measurement in mm can be converted to μm **by multiplying by 1000.**

- A measurement in μm can be converted to mm **by dividing by 1000.**

Complete the following table.

mm	μm
0·33	
	85
0·76	

TRANSPORT ACROSS CELL MEMBRANES

THE STRUCTURE OF THE CELL MEMBRANE

The cell membrane consists of **lipids** (fats) and proteins arranged as shown in the diagram.

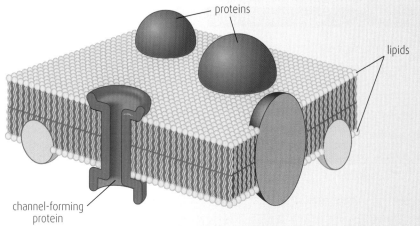

Structure of the cell membrane

The lipids form a double layer and are constantly moving, so the membrane is described as 'fluid'. The proteins vary in size and shape, and form a patchy mosaic within the lipid bilayer. For this reason, the membrane structure is referred to as the **fluid mosaic model**.

The proteins have a variety of functions:

● Some form channels, creating pores in the membrane. This allows the passage of molecules that are small enough to travel through the pores by passive means.

● Some proteins are partially embedded in the lipid layer or they may lie on its surface. Some of these act as receptors for chemicals such as **hormones** or **antibodies**. Others act as **enzymes** for chemical reactions.

● Other proteins act as carrier proteins for the process of **active transport** of materials across the membrane.

The cell membrane is described as being selectively permeable. This term refers to the property of allowing some molecules to pass from one side to the other, while other molecules are unable to pass through. Smaller molecules (such as water, oxygen and carbon dioxide) move freely through the cell membrane, slightly larger ones (for example **amino acids**, glucose and urea) move more slowly through it, but large ones (like proteins and **starch**) are unable to pass through.

PASSIVE METHODS OF TRANSPORT

Passive transport of materials does not involve energy expenditure by the organism for the process to take place. It relies on the fact that substances are found in different concentrations in different places. With passive transport, substances always move from a high to a lower concentration. This difference in concentration is known as a **concentration gradient**.

Diffusion

The definition of **diffusion** is the movement of molecules or ions from a region of high concentration to a region of lower concentration.

contd

Diffusion allows substances to move within a cell from one area to another, as well as allowing materials to enter and leave a cell. Diffusion continues until the concentration of the substance is even throughout.

Diffusion is important to organisms in many ways. For example, oxygen and glucose enter cells by diffusion for the process of aerobic respiration. The removal of waste products, such as carbon dioxide or urea, from cells also happens by diffusion.

Osmosis

The definition of **osmosis** is the movement of water molecules from a region of high water concentration to a region of lower water concentration through a selectively permeable membrane.

Osmosis is a special type of diffusion and only involves the movement of water molecules.

If there is a difference in water concentration between the fluids inside and outside of the cell, then water will either enter or leave the cell, moving from the higher to the lower water concentration. If the water concentration is equal on either side of the membrane, water molecules will still move from one side to the other, but in equal proportions. This is not osmosis, since osmosis (like diffusion) requires a concentration gradient to occur.

Osmosis is a very important cellular process as all cells require water to survive.

ACTIVE METHODS OF TRANSPORT

The definition of active transport is the movement of molecules and ions across a cell membrane against a concentration gradient.

Unlike diffusion and osmosis, molecules or ions do not move by themselves in active transport. Instead, they are moved by carrier proteins, which are a component of membranes. This process requires energy because molecules are being moved against the concentration gradient; that is from low to higher concentration. The energy is provided by **ATP** (adenosine triphosphate), which is produced during **respiration**. Therefore, anything that limits respiration will also limit the rate of active transport.

One example of the importance of active transport in animal cells is the reabsorption of glucose from the kidney tubules back into the bloodstream, ensuring that glucose is not passed out in the urine. An example of active transport in plants can be found in the fact that some seaweeds and corals can accumulate iodine from sea water in their cells to a concentration hundreds of times greater than that in the surrounding water.

VIDEO LINK

Have a look at the video on diffusion at www.brightredbooks.net/N5Biology

VIDEO LINK

Check out the simulation of osmosis at www.brightredbooks.net/N5Biology

DON'T FORGET

Diffusion and osmosis are two types of passive transport. Neither process requires energy expenditure by the organism

DON'T FORGET

Active transport goes against a concentration gradient and requires energy expenditure by the organism

ONLINE TEST

Test yourself on transport across cell membranes at www.brightredbooks.net/N5Biology

THINGS TO DO AND THINK ABOUT

The table shows the concentration of some substances in a cell and in the environment surrounding it. Identify the method of transport that would in each case move molecules of each substance into the cell.

Substance	Concentration in cell (%)	Concentration surrounding cell (%)
Glucose	5	10
Water	90	98
Oxygen	16	20
Carbon dioxide	3	2

EFFECTS OF OSMOSIS ON PLANT AND ANIMAL CELLS

Animal cells and plant cells react differently to the intake or loss of water. This is due to the differences in their structures.

OSMOSIS AND PLANT CELLS

As plant cells have a vacuole for water storage, any water gain or loss from a cell affects the size of the vacuole. This has an overall effect on the rest of the cell, as shown in the diagram below.

A plant cell in a solution which has an equal concentration to the solution in the vacuole will experience no net gain or loss of water. The cell will remain unchanged.

However, if the solution surrounding the plant cell has a water concentration greater than that in the cell, water passes into the cell from the surroundings, causing the vacuole to swell and press outwards against the cytoplasm. This, in turn, causes the cytoplasm to push against the cell membrane and cell wall. The cell wall is fairly rigid and strong enough the resist this pressure, preventing the cell from bursting. In this state the cell is described as **turgid**.

On the other hand, if the solution surrounding the cell has a water concentration lower than that in the cell, water passes out of the cell to its surroundings, causing the vacuole to shrink and pulling the cytoplasm inwards. This drags the cell membrane inwards too, but the cell wall remains in place. A gap develops between the membrane and the cell wall and, as the cell wall is fully permeable, the surrounding solution flows in to fill this gap. In this state, the cell is described as being **plasmolysed**.

Plant cells in various solutions

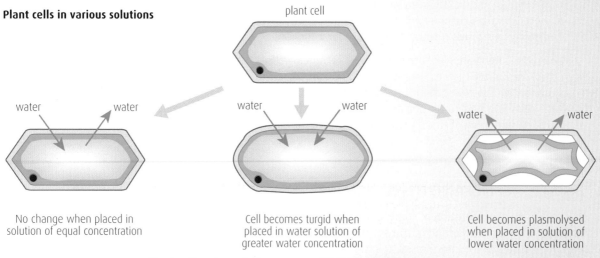

	plant cell	
water water	water water	water water
No change when placed in solution of equal concentration	Cell becomes turgid when placed in water solution of greater water concentration	Cell becomes plasmolysed when placed in solution of lower water concentration

Plant cells rely on being turgid to maintain their shape. Leaves can be seen to wilt if the cells are lacking the water content to keep them turgid. The cells become **flaccid** and no longer have enough pressure inside to maintain the upright position of the leaf. They can, however, recover if the plant is watered.

Wilted and recovered plants

OSMOSIS AND ANIMAL CELLS

Animal cells react differently to plant cells in terms of water gain or loss, due to the fact that they have neither a cell wall nor a vacuole.

An animal cell in a solution which has an equal concentration to the solution in the cell will experience no net gain or loss of water. The cell will remain unchanged.

However, if the solution surrounding the animal cell has a water concentration greater than that in the cell, water passes into the cell from the surroundings, causing the cell to swell up. As there is no cell wall to resist the continued stretching of the membrane, the cell eventually bursts.

On the other hand, if the solution surrounding the cell has a water concentration lower than that in the cell, water passes out of the cell to its surroundings, causing the cell to shrink and shrivel up.

As red blood cells are surrounded by a solution (blood plasma), it is important that the body has mechanisms in place to prevent the plasma becoming too concentrated or dilute as blood cells could burst or shrink.

DON'T FORGET

When referring to an increase in *water concentration*, this means that the concentration of the dissolved substance in the solution decreases. Therefore, water always moves by osmosis from a weak solution to a strong solution.

Red blood cells in various solutions

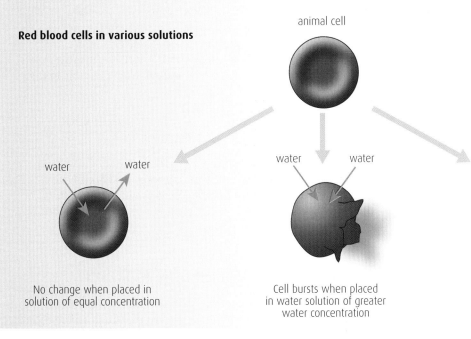

animal cell

water   water

No change when placed in solution of equal concentration

water   water

Cell bursts when placed in water solution of greater water concentration

water   water

Cell shrinks when placed in solution of lower water concentration

THINGS TO DO AND THINK ABOUT

Plants store the carbohydrate they produce during photosynthesis in the form of starch. Starch is a large molecule and is insoluble in water. Why is it important for the plant not to store carbohydrate as small soluble molecules of sugar?

ONLINE TEST

Test yourself on osmosis at www.brightredbooks.net/ N5Biology

PRODUCING NEW CELLS 1

MITOSIS

All new cells are produced from existing cells by the process of cell division. Cell division occurs in single-celled organisms in order for them to reproduce. Each new cell is a complete organism.

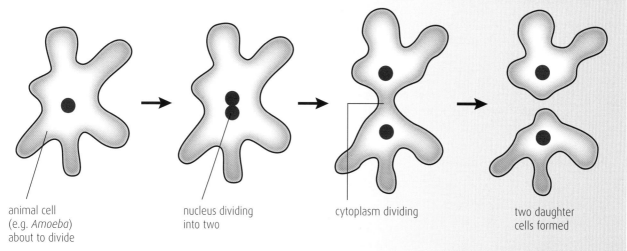

animal cell
(e.g. *Amoeba*)
about to divide

nucleus dividing
into two

cytoplasm dividing

two daughter
cells formed

In a multicellular organism, cell division is the process which increases the number of cells. This provides the means for growth and also for repair of damaged tissues.

An important part of cell division is the division of the cell nucleus. This is called **mitosis**. Mitosis ensures that each of the two daughter cells produced from the parent cell contains the same number of chromosomes as the parent cell and are genetically identical to it.

MAINTAINING THE DIPLOID NUMBER IN MITOSIS

The nucleus contains thread-like structures known as chromosomes. They carry information in the form of **genes** which determine the characteristics of an organism. Normally, the individual chromosomes in a cell cannot be seen, but as the cell begins to divide, the chromosomes untangle, becoming shorter and thicker. This makes them visible using a microscope and they become free to move around the cell.

In multicellular organisms all cells, apart from the sex cells, have two sets of matching chromosomes. Human cells have two sets each consisting of 23 chromosomes; that is they have 23 pairs. Each chromosome in a pair is an identical match to the other.

The number of chromosomes in this 'double' set is known as the **diploid number**. The diploid number in humans is 46. When a cell divides, it is essential that the diploid number is maintained so the new cells receive a full set of genetic information. This is because the genetic information controls cell development and all of the activities that cells carry out. It is therefore vital that none of the information is missing.

THE SEQUENCE OF EVENTS IN MITOSIS

The events that take place in the process of mitosis ensure each daughter cell has the diploid number of chromosomes.

The following diagrams show the sequence of events.

Sequence of events in mitosis

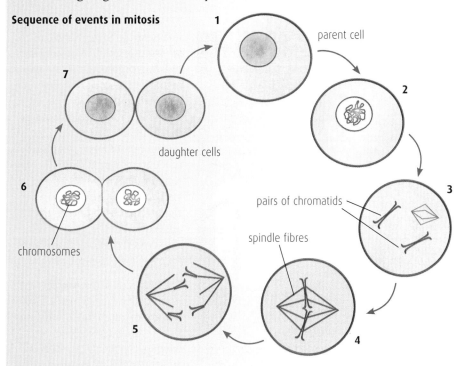

1   Each of the chromosomes, although not visible at this stage, makes a duplicate copy of itself (chromosomes are now pairs of **chromatids**).

2   The pairs of chromatids become shorter and thicker, and start to untangle.

3   The nuclear membrane disintegrates and the **spindle fibres** appear.

4   Each pair of chromatids attaches to one of the spindle fibres, at the **equator** of the cell.

5   The spindle fibres contract, separating the chromatids and pulling them to opposite ends of the cell.

6   A nuclear membrane begins to form around each group of chromosomes and the cytoplasm begins to divide.

7   Two new daughter cells form as the cell membrane divides the cells. Each new cell has an identical chromosome complement to the parent cell.

The sequence of events in mitosis is the same in both plant and animal cells. The main difference is found at the very end when the two newly formed cells separate from each other:

● In animal cells, the cell membrane pinches inwards from both sides until it meets in the middle, dividing the cytoplasm evenly.

● In plant cells, a new cell wall is formed as well, which divides the cell in two.

ONLINE TEST

Check how well you've learned about mitosis at www.brightredbooks.net/N5Biology

THINGS TO DO AND THINK ABOUT

Mitosis ensures that the diploid chromosome complement is maintained in the production of new cells. Explain why this is necessary.

PRODUCING NEW CELLS 2

CELL CULTURE

Large-scale industrial fermenters which could be used in the production of wine

It is possible to grow cells in laboratories, outside the bodies of living organisms, if suitable conditions for cell division and growth are provided. This is done for a variety of purposes including, for example, production of large quantities of identical plants, and in wine and beer production. **Cell culture** is also used in the production and testing of antibiotics, in the growth of new skin cells for skin grafting and for stem cell research.

The technique involves placing unspecialised cells into a culture medium and controlling factors, such as the level of oxygen, the pH of the medium and the temperature, to provide **optimum conditions**. The culture medium may be a nutrient broth or an agar jelly. If the conditions are satisfactory, the cells will divide.

Cell culture can be carried out in large **fermenters** with computers attached to monitor and control the conditions, automatically adjusting the conditions to maintain them at their optimum.

The diagram below shows the interior of a fermenter which is attached to a computer to monitor and control the conditions, maintaining them at their optimum. The paddle stirrers make sure that all of the contents are evenly distributed throughout the fermenter.

DON'T FORGET

In large industrial processes, the use of computers to monitor the conditions is essential. Factors such as oxygen concentration, temperature and pH are all checked constantly and the levels adjusted automatically, so that optimum conditions are maintained throughout the process. This would be difficult to do without the aid of computers.

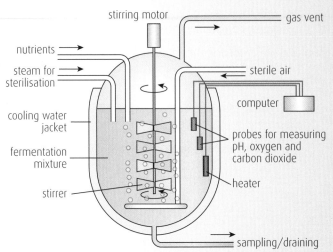

Internal view of an industrial fermenter

contd

In plants, small pieces of leaves or isolated cells are removed from a parent plant and placed in containers with the nutrients required for cell division. They eventually form a mass of unspecialised cells known as a **callus**. These can be transferred to appropriate growing media with all the nutrients needed to allow the cells to grow into whole plants.

In animals, the growing conditions for tissue culture are a little more difficult to achieve, but successful techniques have been developed using stem cells (see page 46). Rapid advances are being made in this area.

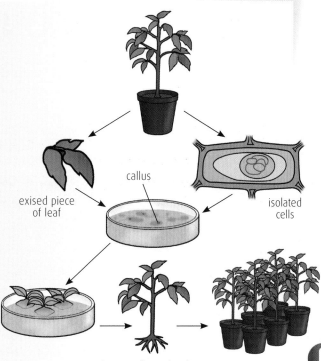

exised piece of leaf   callus   isolated cells

Tissue culture in plants

ASEPTIC TECHNIQUE

It is important that in any procedure using microorganisms or cell cultures, safety precautions are put in place to stop contamination and the spread of disease. The provision of a scrupulously clean environment is essential.

Any conditions that allow desirable cells to divide and grow will also be perfect for unwanted microbes. Therefore, scientists use **aseptic techniques** when carrying out work of this nature.

The main safety precautions involve:

- making sure that all equipment is sterile
- washing hands and benches thoroughly before any work is carried out
- using special techniques to transfer microorganisms or cells from one place to another
- sterilisation, by use of high temperature, to clean equipment prior to reuse or disposal.

The spores of bacteria and fungi are particularly resistant to normal hygiene procedures and industries that culture cells must take particular care to prevent contamination; appropriate chemicals and high temperatures are used. An autoclave is a device that is used to sterilise equipment with high pressure steam at 121°C for around 15–20 minutes. This kills bacteria and resistant spores which can survive treatment with boiling water.

THINGS TO DO AND THINK ABOUT

1 What factors need to be controlled in order to provide the optimum conditions for cell division and growth?

2 Why is it necessary to sterilise all equipment and work areas before using them for tissue culture?

3 If cells divide every 20 minutes, how many cells would be produced from one original cell after 3 hours?

VIDEO LINK

Check out the video 'Aseptic Technique' at www.brightredbooks.net/N5Biology

ONLINE

Have a look at the online guide to using aseptic technique in surgery at www.brightredbooks.net/N5Biology

DON'T FORGET

Any conditions that allow the successful growth of desirable cells are also ideal for the growth of unwanted bacteria and fungi. In some industrial processes, such as in the brewing industry, the growth of unwanted organisms would spoil the product and make it unusable. Contaminated beer would not be fit for consumption. It is essential, therefore, to use absolutely sterile equipment.

ONLINE TEST

For a test on cell cultures, visit www.brightredbooks.net/N5Biology

DNA AND THE PRODUCTION OF PROTEINS

Double helix of DNA

THE STRUCTURE OF DNA

Variation exists among the members of any given species. This is mainly due to differences in the information held in the genetic material and stored in the nucleus of their cells. The genetic information is in the form of chromosomes.

The nucleus of every cell contains thread-like structures known as chromosomes. They are made from a chemical called DNA (deoxyribonucleic acid). This is a double-stranded molecule twisted into a spiral known as a **double helix**. DNA carries the **genetic code** for making proteins. Each chromosome contains the instructions to make hundreds of different types of protein.

Each strand of the DNA molecule is made from a chain of subunits. Each subunit contains a type of base: Adenine (A), Thymine (T), Guanine (G) or Cytosine (C). The letters represent the names of the bases and each of the bases is a different shape. The shape of each base is complementary to one other base; thus, A and T have complementary shapes, and G and C are complementary to each other. The bases are linked by weak hydrogen bonds, holding together the two strands in the DNA molecule. The DNA double helix is like a ladder that has been twisted into a spiral and the bases make up the 'rungs' of the ladder.

In a DNA double helix, therefore, if A is on one side of the strand, T is always found opposite side. Similarly, if G is on one side, C will be held opposite by a weak hydrogen bond (A–T and G–C).

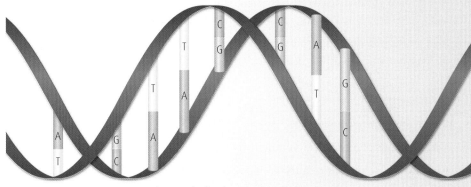

Thymine (Yellow) = T   Guanine (Green) = G
Adenine (Blue) = A   Cytosine (Red) = C

DNA double helix showing base pairing

ONLINE TEST

For a test on DNA and the production of proteins, visit www.brightredbooks.net/N5Biology

The sequence of the bases in a strand of DNA determines the sequence of amino acids which are joined together to make a protein. Different sequences of bases make different proteins. A chromosome is made up of hundreds of **genes**, each coding for a particular protein.

PROTEIN SYNTHESIS

All proteins are made of subunits called amino acids. These are chemicals which contain the elements carbon, hydrogen, oxygen and nitrogen. There are about 20 different amino acids. The sequence of these amino acids in a protein determines its structure and function.

A section of DNA which codes for a protein is called a gene. It can be hundreds of bases in length. The bases form groups of three, called triplets. Each triplet carries the code

for a particular amino acid. The amino acids must be arranged in the correct sequence to make a particular protein. The order of the triplets of bases determines this.

Using the DNA as a template, molecules called messenger **RNA** (mRNAs) are made in the nucleus. Base pairing ensures that these are complementary to the section of the DNA (a gene). The mRNA then leaves the nucleus and travels to a ribosome.

A protein can only be assembled within a ribosome. Ribosomes are found either individually or attached to a system of tubes in the cytoplasm. The ribosome 'reads' each triplet code on the mRNA in turn, ensuring that the correct amino acid is carried into place by a carrier molecule as it moves along the stand of mRNA.

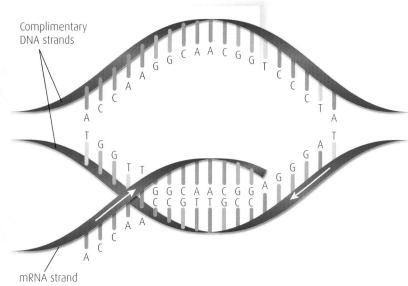

Complimentary DNA strands

mRNA strand

mRNA synthesis from a DNA molecule

As each amino acid is brought into line, it is joined to its neighbour by a chemical bond until a long chain (known as a polypeptide) is formed. These chains are then shaped into the form required for that particular protein.

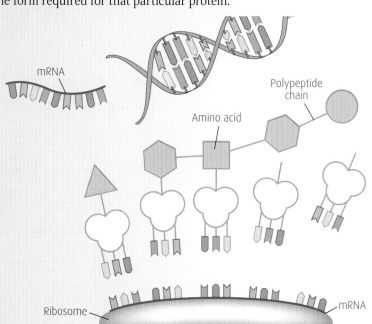

mRNA

Amino acid

Polypeptide chain

Ribosome

mRNA

Sequence of events in translation of the code into a protein

It can be seen that the sequence of the bases in the DNA in the nucleus determines the final structure of the protein made in the ribosome.

THINGS TO DO AND THINK ABOUT

1   What are the units that make up a protein?

2   How is the sequence of amino acids in a protein determined?

3   Why is the sequence of amino acids in a protein of importance?

VIDEO LINK

Watch the simulation of DNA replication at www.brightredbooks.net/N5Biology

VIDEO LINK

Watch the animation about protein synthesis at www.brightredbooks.net/N5Biology

DON'T FORGET

The order of the bases in the DNA determines the sequence of amino acids in a protein. It is the ability of nucleic acids to form base pairs that enables chromosome duplication during mitosis to take place. It also allows the transfer of the genetic code from the DNA to the mRNA and the carrier molecules during protein synthesis.

PROTEINS AND ENZYMES 1

DIFFERENT PROTEIN SHAPES AND FUNCTIONS

All proteins are made of amino acids. Each different protein is made of a different sequence of amino acids. Once the amino acids have been assembled into a long chain, they are folded in various ways to make a variety of shapes. Each particular protein has its own unique shape.

The shape of a protein is related to the function that it carries out. The shape is achieved by folding the strands of amino acids in certain ways after they leave the ribosome. Some are twisted into long strands, while others are wound into a roughly spherical shape, like a ball of wool.

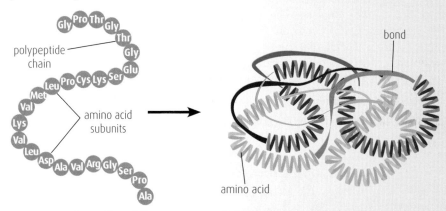

Formation of the enzyme amylase from several polypeptide chains

Some proteins have a **structural** function, like those found in body tissues such as muscles, ligaments and tendons.

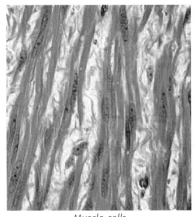

Muscle cells

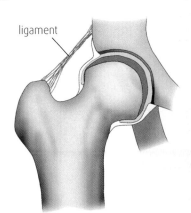

Ligaments

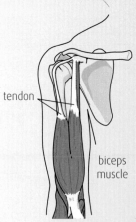

Tendons

Structural proteins

- Muscle cells contain long thin fibres of protein, allowing the cells to contract and relax.

- Ligaments are made of very strong, slightly elastic, fibrous proteins which hold bone to bone at a joint, preventing dislocation.

- Tendons have very tough fibres of protein which can withstand the pulling force of muscle on bone without stretching.

Other proteins, like antibodies, hormones and enzymes, are folded into a range of very specific shapes to suit their particular function.

contd

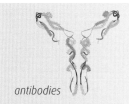

antibodies   hormones   enzymes

Protein shape is related to function

- Antibodies are proteins that are produced by the body's white blood cells in response to invasion by pathogens. Antibodies are Y-shaped and attach to the pathogen to prevent it attacking cells.

- Hormones are chemical messengers which target specific tissues to cause a particular response. There are a great many types.

- Enzymes are proteins folded in such a way that they have an **active site** which binds to another substance to bring about a reaction.

 DON'T FORGET

Proteins are three-dimensional structures and each type varies according to the sequence of its amino acids and the shape it is folded into.

ENZYMES

All enzymes are made of protein. They are made inside living cells by the process of protein synthesis. Each enzyme has a particular shape which determines its function.

Enzymes are biological **catalysts** and speed up chemical reactions. They:

- lower the activation energy required to start the chemical reaction

- speed up the rate of the chemical reaction

- remain unchanged after bringing the reaction about.

Enzymes are involved in all biochemical reactions. Living organisms exist at relatively low temperatures and are unable to tolerate the high temperatures required to bring about rapid chemical reactions. Enzymes allow essential reactions to take place at lower temperatures. Without the use of enzymes, the chemical reactions in cells would take place too slowly to sustain life. Since enzymes are not used up in a reaction, they can be used over and over again.

Enzymes can carry out two types of reactions:

1 **degradation** – breaking down a large molecule into two or more smaller ones

2 **synthesis** – building up two or more molecules to a larger one.

The substance with which the enzyme reacts is known as the **substrate** and the substance produced at the end of the reaction is called the **product**. Therefore, in an enzyme-controlled reaction:

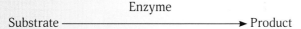

Enzyme

Substrate ─────────────────────────▶ Product

On the surface of an enzyme molecule is an area known as the active site. This is the area that the substrate molecule(s) binds to in order for the chemical reaction to take place. The shape of the active site is determined by the folding of the polypeptide chains which make up the enzyme protein. The active site and the substrate have complementary shapes, so that the substrate can fit into the active site of the enzyme.

 DON'T FORGET

Enzymes are folded into particular shapes, so that their active site only fits one substrate. Enzymes can be involved in degradation, as well as synthesis of molecules.

 **ONLINE TEST**

Test yourself on proteins and enzymes at www.brightredbooks.net/N5Biology

substrate

active site

enzyme

Enzyme with substrate that fits the active site

 THINGS TO DO AND THINK ABOUT

1 Try to find examples of different categories of proteins. Can you name two hormones and two enzymes?

2 What is haemoglobin? Where is it found?

PROTEINS AND ENZYMES 2

HOW ENZYMES WORK

Each enzyme is only able to act on one type of substance, due to the shape of its active site. It is said to be **specific** in its reaction. A substrate with a different shape will not fit into the active site, so will not be affected by the enzyme.

Enzymes and substrates are described as operating like a **lock and key**. A key only fits a specific lock and can change it from one state to another (locked to unlocked); the key remains unchanged and can, therefore, be used again. Similarly, an enzyme only fits a specific substrate and changes it into some sort of product, without being used up in the process.

An enzyme molecule binds with a substrate molecule to form an enzyme–substrate complex. This allows the chemical reaction to take place. At the end of the reaction, the product(s) detach from the active site and leave the enzyme. This means that the enzyme is now free to combine with another substrate molecule and catalyse the reaction again.

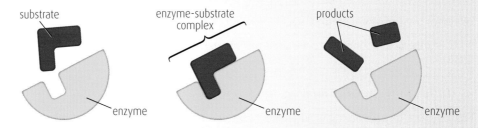

Lock and key hypothesis of enzyme action

ENZYME ACTION

Enzymes either break down or build up molecules.

Degradation (breaking down)

Some enzymes break down complex molecules to simpler ones. All of the enzymes involved in the process of digesting our food carry out degradation reactions, converting large insoluble molecules into smaller soluble ones which can be absorbed into the blood.

Examples of degradation enzymes are shown in the following table.

Substrate	Enzyme	Product
Protein	Pepsin	Peptides, then amino acids
Starch	Amylase	Maltose sugar
Fat	Lipase	Glycerol and fatty acids
Hydrogen peroxide	Catalase	Water and oxygen

Synthesis (building up)

Some enzymes build up simple molecules into more complex ones. A very important synthesis reaction is carried out by the enzyme phosphorylase. The substrate involved is a form of glucose found in plants, known as glucose-1-phosphate. Phosphorylase links glucose-1-phosphate molecules into long chains, which become molecules of starch. This is of benefit to the plant, enabling it to store food in its cells.

$$\text{Glucose-1-phosphate} \xrightarrow{\text{Phosphorylase}} \text{Starch}$$

FACTORS AFFECTING ENZYME ACTIVITY

The ideal conditions for an enzyme to work are called the optimum conditions. These include a suitable temperature, an appropriate pH and a plentiful supply of substrate. If any of these factors is inadequate, the enzyme will not be able to function at its best.

Effect of temperature on enzyme activity

As all enzymes are made of protein, any factor which affects protein will affect an enzyme. Temperature has a significant effect on proteins and, therefore, on enzymes. Most enzymes function best at about 40°C. This is their optimum temperature.

The graph shows how temperature affects the amount of starch digested by the enzyme amylase over a range of temperatures.

It can be seen that, as the temperature begins to increase towards 40°C, the activity of the enzyme increases. This is because the molecules of the substrate and enzyme move faster with the increased heat energy and collide more often. Therefore, enzyme molecules catalyse the conversion of substrate to product more frequently.

The temperature at which the maximum rate of reaction is reached is known as the optimum temperature.

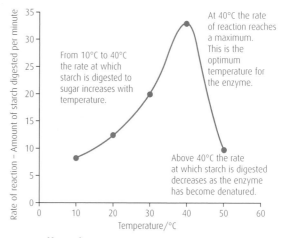

Effect of temperature on enzyme activity

From 10°C to 40°C the rate at which starch is digested to sugar increases with temperature.

At 40°C the rate of reaction reaches a maximum. This is the optimum temperature for the enzyme.

Above 40°C the rate at which starch is digested decreases as the enzyme has become denatured.

Further increase in temperature causes a decrease in enzyme activity. The increased heat energy begins to break the chemical bonds that hold the protein of the enzyme together, breaking the enzyme apart. The active site loses its shape and the substrate is no longer able to fit into it. In this damaged state, the enzyme is described as denatured.

Denaturation of an enzyme is an irreversible procedure and, as more enzyme molecules are damaged by the heat, enzyme activity will stop altogether.

Effect of pH on enzyme activity

Proteins (and, therefore, enzymes) are affected by the pH of their surroundings. The shape of an enzyme can be altered if the pH is too extreme and at certain pH levels enzymes become denatured.

Each enzyme works best at a specific pH, although most can operate within a range to either side of that optimum value. This is called the working range of the enzyme. The majority of enzymes work between pH 5 and pH 9 with an optimum of about pH 7, as shown by the enzyme amylase found in saliva.

However, there are exceptions. An example is pepsin, which is secreted by the lining of the stomach. Pepsin works best in the very acidic conditions found there, which are due to the presence of hydrochloric acid. The optimum pH for pepsin is 2·5.

Another exception is the enzyme arginase, which is found in the liver and is involved in the production of urea. It has an optimum pH of 10, which is highly alkaline.

Effect of substrate supply on enzyme activity

If the substrate is in plentiful supply and all other factors are at their optimum, the enzyme reaction will proceed at a rapid rate. However, as the substrate gets converted to product and is reduced in quantity, the reaction rate will slow. This is due to the fact that there are fewer collisions between the substrate and the enzyme's active site. Fewer enzyme–substrate complexes form, so fewer reactions take place.

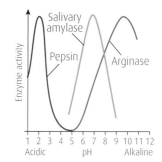

Effect of pH on the activity of different enzymes

 ## THINGS TO DO AND THINK ABOUT

The diagram on page 22 shows the process of degradation of a substance through the 'lock and key' action of an enzyme. Try to draw a set of diagrams to illustrate a synthesis reaction, such as the build up of starch by the enzyme phosphorylase.

GENETIC ENGINEERING

THE TRANSFER OF GENETIC INFORMATION

Genetic material can be transferred from one cell to another, either by natural means or artificially, through the process of genetic engineering.

NATURAL TRANSFER OF GENETIC MATERIAL

Scientists have studied the ways in which **viruses** transfer their nucleic acids into host cells. They found that viruses transferred their genetic material into the host so that it became attached to the host's DNA.

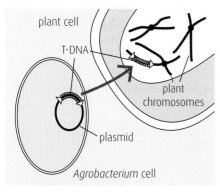

Research has shown that some bacteria living in the soil (species of *Agrobacterium*) are responsible for causing tumours to develop in plant tissue. Scientists have studied this process to see how it works. They found that the *Agrobacterium* actually transfers a piece of its own genetic material into the plant root, usually through a wound in the plant tissue. This genetic material is found in one of the bacterial plasmids and an area known as T-DNA is responsible for causing a tumour in the plant root.

Once in the plant cell, the bacterial DNA inserts itself randomly into the plant DNA, resulting in changes in the production of certain plant hormones. These can lead to the growth of tumours that weaken the plant, possibly killing it.

Transfer of DNA from *Agrobacterium* to plant root

Through research, scientists have developed ways to substitute the genes which cause tumours with other DNA and they are now able to introduce useful genes into *Agrobacterium*. The bacteria then pass these genes into the plant, allowing the plant to be **genetically modified** in certain ways.

When viruses and bacteria transfer their genetic material into cells, the behaviour of the cells changes; they are now able to make proteins which they previously could not. Scientists saw the potential of this and developed ways of using the technique to their advantage.

This technique has been used to create transgenic crops (plants with genes from another organism).

These crops have advantages over the natural varieties, such as increased yields or increased disease resistance, but controversy surrounds their use.

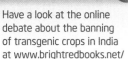

ONLINE

Have a look at the online debate about the banning of transgenic crops in India at www.brightredbooks.net/N5Biology

ARTIFICIAL TRANSFER OF GENETIC MATERIAL

The process of genetic engineering involves taking genetic material from one type of living organism and transferring it into another type of living organism. The organism with the altered genetic make-up is now 'reprogrammed', or transformed, to make different proteins which are useful to human beings.

Microorganisms, such as bacteria and yeast, are often reprogrammed to produce useful substances, including medicines and human proteins such as hormones. There are several advantages to using these single-celled organisms:

- They grow and multiply very quickly.
- Being individually small, they are easy to accommodate.
- They are relatively inexpensive to use.
- They are easier to reprogramme than more advanced organisms.

THE PROCESS OF REPROGRAMMING

The arrangement of the chromosomal material in a bacterium makes it an ideal organism for genetic engineering.

A bacterium has one large circular loop of chromosomal material, as well as several much smaller rings known as plasmids.

Plasmids are easily removed from bacteria. They are small enough to be removed, genetically altered and put back into a bacterium. When plasmids are used in this way, they are called **vectors**.

The stages involved in the reprogramming of bacteria to produce a human protein, such as insulin, are as follows:

1 The section of DNA in the human cell that has the required gene, is identified on its original chromosome.

2 The gene is cut out of the chromosome using an enzyme.

3 A plasmid is removed from a bacterium.

4 The plasmid is cut open using the same enzyme.

5 The required gene is inserted into the plasmid using another type of enzyme.

6 This is repeated many times.

7 The altered plasmids are then inserted into bacteria.

8 The reprogrammed bacteria are given the correct conditions to reproduce, making many identical copies.

The bacteria that have been genetically modified with the transferred gene make large quantities of the gene's protein, if given suitable conditions. These conditions are the same as those outlined for cell growth in the section on cell culture.

One of the important advantages of using bacteria in this way is the rapid rate at which they reproduce. This means that the mass production of the desired protein using this method is a relatively quick process.

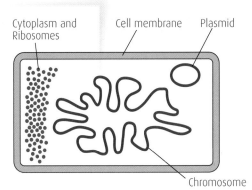

Cytoplasm and Ribosomes   Cell membrane   Plasmid

Chromosome

Genetic material in a bacterium, shown in red

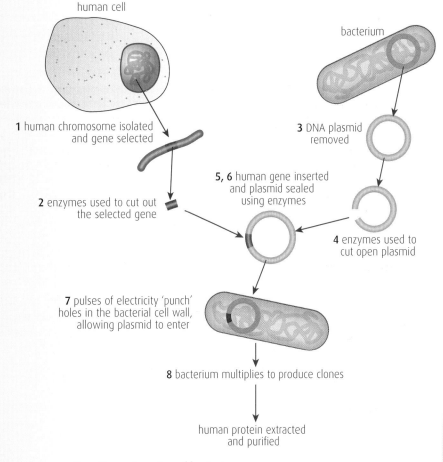

human cell

bacterium

1 human chromosome isolated and gene selected

3 DNA plasmid removed

2 enzymes used to cut out the selected gene

5, 6 human gene inserted and plasmid sealed using enzymes

4 enzymes used to cut open plasmid

7 pulses of electricity 'punch' holes in the bacterial cell wall, allowing plasmid to enter

8 bacterium multiplies to produce clones

human protein extracted and purified

Genetic engineering of bacteria

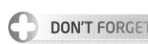

THINGS TO DO AND THINK ABOUT

Enzymes are used in several stages in the process of genetic engineering. Can you explain why the same enzyme can be used to cut the required gene from the human chromosome and to cut open the plasmid, but a different enzyme is required to put the gene into the plasmid?

DON'T FORGET

Genetic information can be transferred from one cell to another naturally or by genetic engineering.

ONLINE TEST

Test yourself on the transfer of genetic information online at www.brightredbooks.net/N5Biology

THE USES OF GENETIC ENGINEERING

Genetic engineering is growing in importance in our everyday lives. As new techniques are developed, more and more uses for genetic engineering are being discovered.

Genetic engineering has applications in medicine, as well as in commercial operations such as the food and drinks industry and in the manufacture of everyday materials like washing powders.

ONLINE

Read more about the history and development of insulin, from early versions made using animal proteins to the genetically engineered version we use today, at www.brightredbooks.net/N5Biology

MEDICAL APPLICATIONS

As people are living longer, more medical treatments are needed than ever before. Genetic engineering is used now to manufacture a variety of products. Genes are extracted from human DNA and inserted into bacteria or yeast, where they produce human forms of useful substances, as shown in the table below.

Product of genetic engineering	Medical application
Insulin	Used to treat people who cannot make sufficient insulin naturally due to type 1 diabetes
Antibiotics	Used to treat people with bacterial infections – antibiotics prevent the growth of these microorganisms
Human growth hormone	Used to treat children who cannot make enough growth hormone naturally – human growth hormone prevents reduced growth
Factor VIII	Used to treat people with haemophilia who cannot make Factor VIII (and whose blood is, therefore, unable to clot)

There are several advantages to using genetically engineered products, like those given above, for medicinal purposes. One of these is that it is possible to produce a pure form of the protein which is free from viral contamination. Also, as the products are made using human genes, many people are ethically more comfortable with them. Previously, they had objections to using products that were derived from animals. Another benefit is that fewer people have allergic reactions to the genetically engineered products than to other forms.

COMMERCIAL APPLICATIONS

Several industries now rely on genetic engineering to manufacture their products. Some examples are given here.

Crop production

- Tomatoes were one of the first food crops to be genetically engineered. Genes were inserted which gave the tomatoes enhanced flavour. Other genes were introduced which gave the tomatoes a much longer shelf-life without the quality of the fruit deteriorating.

- GM potatoes have been genetically modified to be resistant to the disease called potato blight. This disease can destroy whole fields of potatoes, spoiling the entire crop. It is, therefore, of great advantage to grow potatoes with resistance to this disease.

- Rapeseed is an increasingly important food crop, as the seeds are used to make rapeseed oil. In recent years, researchers started developing new rapeseed varieties with the advantage of rapid growth. Original varieties contained a bitter-tasting chemical, making the oil unusable in food production. A toxic chemical was also present which prevented the plant being used as animal feed. The new varieties produced by genetic engineering lack both of these undesirable qualities and have led to the rise in the growth of the crop.

- Genetic engineering has been used to create transgenic crops (plants with genes from another organism), including new strains of corn and soybeans. These crops contain

contd

genes which allow them to be resistant to certain herbicides. This means that farmers can spray their crops with herbicide to kill the weeds without damaging their crop plants. The crop field is kept free from weeds, increasing the crop yield. Resistance to herbicides has now been developed in a greater number of crop plants.

- β-carotene is a plant pigment which is important to humans because it is converted to vitamin A in our bodies. Rice plants produce β-carotene in their green tissues, but not in the edible part of the seed. Other valuable nutrients (for example, vitamin B and nutritious fats) are found in the outer coat of the rice grains, but are lost in the milling and polishing processes of white rice production. Unprocessed brown rice retains some of these nutrients, but is not suitable for long-term storage as it goes rancid. As rice is such an important part of the world population's diet, scientists wanted to improve its nutritional quality and turned to genetic engineering. Even though all the required genes to produce β-carotene are present in the grain, some of them are turned off during development. Scientists figured out how to turn on this complex pathway. Golden rice grains are easily recognisable by their yellow to orange colour. The stronger the colour, the more β-carotene is present.

White rice and golden rice

Other commercial applications

- UK scientists have created genetically modified chickens that do not spread bird flu. Bird flu is a disease caused by a virus and it spreads rapidly when poultry is produced in intensive conditions. An artificial gene has been inserted into chickens; this introduces a tiny part of the bird flu virus into the chickens' cells. They can still become infected but render the virus harmless to other poultry. Scientists believe that this genetic modification is harmless to the chickens and to people who might eat the birds. The researchers say that, in principle, the technique could be used to protect any farm animal from any disease. The eventual aim is to develop animals that are completely resistant to viral diseases.

- Making cheese involves curdling of milk. This was traditionally brought about by the use of an enzyme called rennin, which was extracted from the lining of calves' stomachs. Genetic engineers have now isolated the gene from the stomach lining and have transferred it to yeast cells. These yeast cells are grown in fermenters to produce large quantities of rennin, which is used by the cheese-making industry.

- Biological washing powders contain enzymes such as proteases to digest many of the stains that are found on clothing. These enzymes are produced by genetically reprogrammed bacteria. They are grown in large fermenters and the enzymes are extracted from them and added to the washing powders. These types of powders allow stains to be digested at lower temperatures, using less energy and saving money.

 DON'T FORGET

When a particular desirable characteristic is identified, it is only the gene(s) for that characteristic that is transferred between organisms and not whole chromosomes.

 ONLINE TEST

Test yourself on the uses of genetic information online at www.brightredbooks.net/N5Biology

 THINGS TO DO AND THINK ABOUT

There is much debate about the use of genetically modified crops. Many countries have banned them, while others are happy to grow them. Can you find out why?

LEAF STRUCTURE AND PHOTOSYNTHESIS

Photosynthesis is the process in which green plants make their own food using light as an energy source. The light for most plants is provided naturally by the Sun, but plants can also use artificial light for this process. The light required for the process to take place must be absorbed into the plant and this is done by a green pigment called chlorophyll, which is found in the chloroplasts of plant cells.

THE PROCESS OF PHOTOSYNTHESIS

Photosynthesis is a series of enzyme-controlled reactions and is divided into two stages. The first stage is dependent on light but stage two can occur in light or darkness.

As well as the presence of light, two raw materials are required for photosynthesis. These are the simple substances carbon dioxide and water – which are usually readily available to plants from the air and the soil. From these two ingredients, the plant can manufacture carbohydrates, which it uses as a food source to provide energy for the many processes that take place inside cells. A by-product of the process is oxygen.

The overall reaction of photosynthesis can be summarised by the following word equation:

$$\text{carbon dioxide} + \text{water} \xrightarrow{\text{light energy and chlorophyll}} \text{carbohydrate (sugar)} + \text{oxygen}$$

In this reaction:

- the carbon dioxide and the water are the raw materials
- the light energy and the chlorophyll are essential requirements
- the carbohydrate and the oxygen are the products.

Carbohydrates include such materials as sugars, starches and cellulose. They all consist of the chemical elements, carbon (C), hydrogen (H) and oxygen (O). To make carbohydrates, a supply of the elements involved must be available. The raw materials of photosynthesis provide these.

Carbon dioxide (CO_2) provides both carbon and oxygen. Water (H_2O) provides hydrogen. Using light energy trapped by the chlorophyll, these raw materials react to form carbohydrate. The oxygen from the water is a by-product of the reaction and is passed out of the cells.

HOW IS THE LEAF ADAPTED TO CARRY OUT THIS PROCESS?

Green leaf cells contain chloroplasts which have the ability to absorb light energy. They are shaped like a discus and contain a mixture of pigments including chlorophyll.

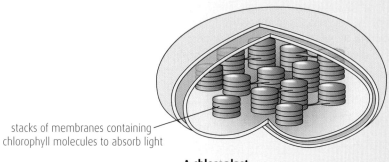

stacks of membranes containing chlorophyll molecules to absorb light

A chloroplast

contd

The light energy that is absorbed into the chloroplast is converted into chemical energy. This is initially in the form of a chemical called ATP (adenosine triphosphate) and then later in the form of carbohydrate (sugar).

Leaf structure

The leaf is well adapted to its role in photosynthesis, as the diagram shows.

As can be seen, the leaf consists of several layers of cells, each layer with an individual function (the specialisation of cells is described in more detail on page 44).

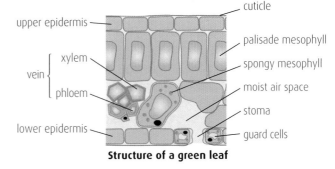

upper epidermis
cuticle
xylem
palisade mesophyll
vein
spongy mesophyll
phloem
moist air space
stoma
lower epidermis
guard cells

Structure of a green leaf

The cuticle found on the surface is made of a waxy substance and this acts as a waterproof layer, minimising water loss by evaporation from the upper surface of the leaf.

The cells of the upper epidermis are transparent, allowing the light energy to pass through them to the layers of cells below.

The cells of the **palisade mesophyll** are column shaped and packed tightly together, maximising the number present. These cells contain many chloroplasts and are mainly responsible for absorbing the light energy for photosynthesis. The raw materials of carbon dioxide and water arrive at these cells and photosynthesis takes place in their chloroplasts.

The cells of the **spongy mesophyll** are more irregular in shape and have fewer chloroplasts than the palisade cells. There are spaces between these cells which are filled with moist air. This allows carbon dioxide to dissolve before passing into the cells.

Veins in the spongy mesophyll layer transport water to the leaf for photosynthesis and to carry away the sugar which is produced, so that it can be distributed to other parts of the plant.

The lower epidermis contains a layer of cells similar to those in the upper epidermis, but also has sausage-shaped cells called guard cells. These surround an air gap known as a stoma (plural stomata) and are capable of opening and closing the stoma. The stoma allows carbon dioxide to enter the leaf and oxygen (the by-product of photosynthesis) to exit the leaf.

Generally, stomata are open during the day when light is available for photosynthesis and closed at night when photosynthesis stops and it is no longer essential to exchange gases with the surrounding air. When stomata are closed, water loss from the leaf is reduced. (See page 73 for more information on the opening and closing of stomata.)

The leaf is, therefore, well designed to meet the demands of photosynthesis – bringing the raw materials together, providing the energy for the reaction and removing the products. The reaction takes place in the chloroplasts of cells and requires many enzymes.

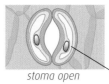

stoma open   guard cell

stoma closed

Stomata on the lower epidermis of a leaf

 DON'T FORGET

The veins in the leaf consist of two types of transport tissues. Xylem tissue is responsible for the transport of water and minerals, and phloem tissue transports sugar. More information about these tissues can be found on page 40.

ONLINE TEST

For a test on photosynthesis, visit www.brightredbooks.net/N5Biology

VIDEO LINK

For more on photosynthesis, watch the 'Biology of Plants' video at www.brightredbooks.net/N5Biology

 THINGS TO DO AND THINK ABOUT

Complete the following table about leaf structure by filling in the missing names and functions.

Name	Function
	Cells that form the upper surface of the leaf
Palisade mesophyll	
	Irregular shaped cells with moist air spaces between them
	Controls the size of the stoma
Vein	

THE CHEMISTRY OF PHOTOSYNTHESIS

Photosynthesis is a two-stage process. The first part of the reaction is dependent on the presence of light. The second part is not dependent on light, but it does require a continuous supply of the products from the light stage. The second stage is, however, temperature dependent.

STAGE ONE: THE LIGHT REACTION

The first stage of photosynthesis is often known as the **light reaction** or **photolysis**. The light energy is trapped by chlorophyll in the chloroplasts of cells and is converted into chemical energy, stored in molecules of ATP. This happens in a series of steps as shown in the diagram below.

Water (H_2O) consists of molecules of hydrogen and oxygen. The light trapped by the chloroplasts provides enough energy to split the hydrogen from the oxygen. The name of this process, photolysis, explains what happens: 'photo' means that light is involved, and 'lysis' means something is split.

The oxygen which results from this process is a by-product and is not required for the reaction to proceed. It is released from the cell, diffuses into the moist air spaces of the spongy mesophyll and then passes out of the leaf into the atmosphere.

The hydrogen, however, plays an essential role in the second stage of photosynthesis and must be transferred to that part of the reaction. The job of transferring the hydrogen is carried out by a hydrogen acceptor which picks up the free hydrogen. Once joined with the hydrogen, the acceptor is said to be reduced.

Not all of the energy trapped by the chlorophyll gets used up in the splitting of water. Some of the energy is used to join a molecule of Pi (inorganic phosphate) to a molecule of ADP (adenosine diphosphate) to form ATP (adenosine triphosphate). This 'stores' the energy until it is required in stage two of the photosynthesis reaction. This process is known as photophosphorylation ('photo' meaning light and 'phosphorylation' meaning that a phosphate has been added).

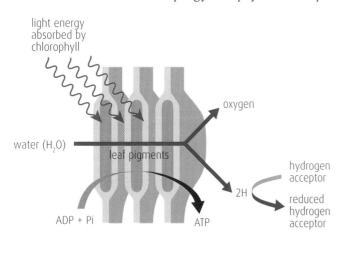

Light stage of photosynthesis

STAGE TWO: CARBON FIXATION

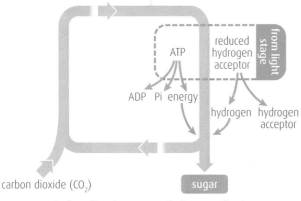

Carbon fixation stage of photosynthesis

This stage is known as **carbon fixation** and does not require light to proceed. The energy used to drive this reaction comes from the ATP molecules which were formed in the light reactions.

As with stage one (the light reaction) this second reaction also takes place in the chloroplasts of plant cells. Several different enzymes are involved and they control a series of reactions which take the form of a cycle. Although this stage of photosynthesis is not light dependent, it is temperature dependent; enzymes must be at their optimum temperature if they are to work efficiently.

contd

The raw material, carbon dioxide, goes through a series of reactions in which it eventually combines with the hydrogen from the light stage of the reaction. The hydrogen acceptor releases its hydrogen, which is then used to reduce the carbon dioxide to carbohydrate. The energy to do this comes from the ATP from the light stage. ATP is broken down to form ADP and Pi, releasing the energy 'stored' there.

The carbon from the carbon dioxide becomes 'fixed' into carbohydrate when it combines with the hydrogen. Carbon fixation results in the formation of sugar, often in the form of glucose.

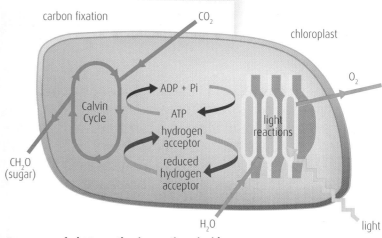

Summary of photosynthesis reactions inside a chloroplast

THE FATE OF CARBOHYDRATE PRODUCED IN PHOTOSYNTHESIS

The sugar formed may be used immediately as a food in the cell in which it is produced. In this case, it would be involved in the process of respiration which is explained on p 34. However, if not required for energy straightaway, it can be converted into other compounds.

Some of the sugar may be converted into cellulose for the construction of cell walls.

In many plants, excess sugar is converted into starch for storage. As starch is insoluble, it does not cause problems for the cell in terms of osmosis.

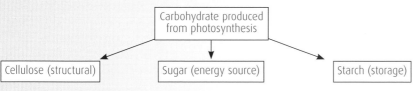

A leaf can be tested for the presence of starch as evidence that photosynthesis has taken place.

Iodine solution turns blue–black in contact with starch. However, leaves must be boiled in water to kill the cells and then be boiled in alcohol to dissolve the chlorophyll before the addition of the iodine solution.

VIDEO LINK

For a video explanation of this experiment, watch the clip at www.brightredbooks.net/N5Biology

DON'T FORGET

The first stage of photosynthesis requires light as an energy source and cannot take place in the dark. The second stage of photosynthesis uses the energy from the ATP which was formed in the first stage, so this stage can take place whether it is light or dark. However, in darkness, the supply of ATP and reduced hydrogen acceptor soon runs out and so even the light independent stage stops.

THINGS TO DO AND THINK ABOUT

ONLINE TEST

For a test on photosynthesis, visit www.brightredbooks.net/N5Biology

1   Chloroplasts consist of two main areas. One part is made up of stacks of photosynthetic pigments such as chlorophyll and the other part is a liquid which contains a great variety of enzymes. Can you identify in which of these parts of the chloroplast the light reaction must take place? Explain your answer.

2   What two substances from the light stage of photosynthesis are used in the carbon fixation stage?

3   What type of energy is light converted to during photosynthesis?

4   What are the chemical elements that are present in the final product of photosynthesis?

5   What is the by-product of photosynthesis and what happens to it when it is produced?

FACTORS AFFECTING PHOTOSYNTHESIS

There are several factors in the environment that have an influence on the rate at which photosynthesis takes place. These include the light intensity, the concentration of carbon dioxide and the temperature of the plant's surroundings. If any one of these factors is insufficient, it will limit the rate at which photosynthesis occurs in the plant. In turn, this affects the growth rate of the plant, as less sugar is produced for respiration to take place. These factors are important in crop production – growers need to provide the optimum conditions for maximum growth.

MEASURING THE RATE OF PHOTOSYNTHESIS

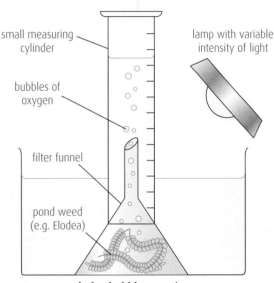

small measuring cylinder

lamp with variable intensity of light

bubbles of oxygen

filter funnel

pond weed (e.g. Elodea)

Elodea bubble experiment

There are various ways to measure the rate of photosynthesis in a plant. The mass of carbohydrate produced can be calculated, but the plant may be destroyed to get the measurement. Measuring the rate of uptake of carbon dioxide or the rate of production of oxygen are two methods which can be carried out without damage to the plant.

The diagram shows the apparatus which can be used to measure the rate of oxygen production.

By altering various environmental factors, this arrangement can be used to investigate how each affects the rate of photosynthesis.

The apparatus should be set up as shown and left to adjust to the environmental conditions for a period of time. Then, the number of bubbles of oxygen produced per minute from the cut ends of the *Elodea* pondweed is counted. This is repeated several times and an average calculated.

Measuring the effect of light intensity

To investigate the effect of light intensity on the rate of photosynthesis, the procedure is repeated at different light intensities. This can be done using a variable intensity lamp or by moving the lamp different distances away from the plant.

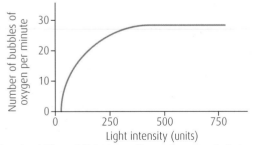

Graph showing effect of light intensity on the rate of photosynthesis

A graph of a set of results obtained from this investigation shows that, as the light intensity increases, the rate of photosynthesis (as shown by the increase in the production of oxygen bubbles) also increases – until it reaches a point at which it stops increasing. It then continues at a constant level. Further increase in light intensity has no effect because some other factor is now preventing the reaction from going faster. This factor, which is now in short supply, is called a **limiting factor**.

Measuring the effect of carbon dioxide concentration

To investigate the effect of carbon dioxide concentration on the rate of photosynthesis, the procedure is repeated at different CO_2 concentrations. This can be done by adding different quantities of sodium hydrogen carbonate to the water surrounding the pondweed. All other factors are kept at a constant level.

A graph of a set of results obtained from this investigation shows that, as the carbon dioxide concentration increases, the rate of photosynthesis also increases. At the start,

contd

it is the level of carbon dioxide which is the limiting factor. If given more CO_2, the rate of photosynthesis again increases, until it reaches a point where it stops increasing and continues at a constant level. Further increase in CO_2 concentration has no effect because again, some other factor is now preventing the reaction from going faster. The graph is a similar shape to the one for light intensity.

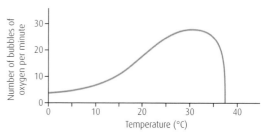
Graph showing effect of carbon dioxide concentration on the rate of photosynthesis

Measuring the effect of temperature

To investigate the effect of temperature on the rate of photosynthesis, again the same apparatus can be adapted. This time the light intensity and CO_2 concentrations are kept at a constant level and the whole apparatus is placed in a large temperature-controlled water bath.

A graph of a set of results obtained from this investigation shows a different pattern from the previous experiments. As the temperature increases, the rate of photosynthesis increases until it reaches its optimum. This is likely to be around 25–35°C, depending on the species of plant. Beyond the optimum temperature, the rate of photosynthesis falls sharply. This is due to the fact that photosynthesis is a series of enzyme-controlled reactions. As the temperature becomes higher, the enzymes are denatured and can no longer catalyse the reactions.

Graph showing effect of temperature on the rate of photosynthesis

FACTORS LIMITING PHOTOSYNTHESIS

All of the above graphs show results from investigations into how each of the three factors affect the rate of photosynthesis. However, at any one time, only one of the factors will be determining the rate. Any factor that is in short supply is known as a limiting factor.

The following graph shows the results of an *Elodea* bubbler experiment to investigate the effect of increasing light intensity, but carried out at two different temperatures. Most plants experience a range of temperatures and light intensities on a daily basis.

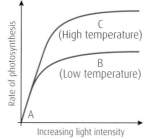

At point A on the graph, the limiting factor is light intensity, as increasing the light brings about an increase in the rate of photosynthesis. However, where the graph levels out, a further increase in the light intensity has no effect, showing that something else is limiting the rate of reaction.

Graph showing effect of increasing light intensity at two temperatures

By comparing the graph lines at points B and C, the limiting factor is shown to be temperature – the rate of photosynthesis increases when the temperature is raised.

THINGS TO DO AND THINK ABOUT

1   A variegated plant has green and white areas forming a pattern on its leaves. Compare the rate of photosynthesis in a variegated plant to a normal green plant. Give a reason for your answer.

2   Explain why the rate of the light reaction in photosynthesis is not affected by temperature, while carbon fixation is affected.

3   Why is an aquatic plant used to measure the rate of photosynthesis rather than a land plant?

VIDEO LINK

Have a look at the 'Exploring photosynthesis' clip for more at www.brightredbooks.net/N5Biology

 DON'T FORGET

When interpreting graphs of limiting factors, the part where the line is still rising in a slope indicates that the factor named in the label on the x-axis is the limiting factor. Where the graph levels out, it is a factor other than the one mentioned in the x-axis label that is acting as a limiting factor.

ONLINE TEST

For a test on photosynthesis, visit www.brightredbooks.net/N5Biology

THE PURPOSE AND IMPORTANCE OF RESPIRATION

ENERGY FROM FOOD

Energy that is locked up in food is released in all living cells to allow chemical processes to take place. Green plants are able to make their own food through the process of photosynthesis, but animals must consume food to obtain energy.

Human foods contain three main components: fats (and oils), proteins and carbohydrates. These contain large molecules that must be broken down into smaller basic units to be absorbed into the body. The breakdown of large food molecules is called digestion. The table gives the basic units of the three main food components and the chemical elements they contain.

Food component	Basic unit	Main elements present
Carbohydrate	Glucose molecules	Carbon Hydrogen Oxygen
Fat/oil	Fatty acids and glycerol	Carbon Hydrogen Oxygen
Protein	Amino acids	Carbon Hydrogen Oxygen Nitrogen

A simple experiment can be carried out to investigate the energy value of each of the food types.

A measured volume of water is placed in the test tube and the temperature noted. A 1 g portion of a food type is then set alight and the flame used to heat the water in the tube until the food is completely burned. The temperature of the water is recorded and the rise in temperature calculated.

By repeating this experiment with 1 g of each of the three food types, a comparison can be drawn.

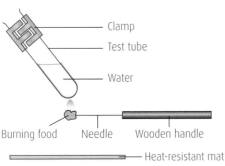

Clamp
Test tube
Water
Burning food Needle Wooden handle
Heat-resistant mat

Apparatus to measure the heat energy from a variety of food types

However, this method has several drawbacks:

- Not all of the heat energy from the burning food goes into the water. Some of it heats the test tube and the surrounding air.

- Not all of the food is burned. It is very difficult to make sure that the food stays alight until every last bit of energy is given out.

- It is very difficult to keep environmental factors from interfering with each experiment. For example, draughts in the room can blow the flame about.

For these reasons, a more sophisticated piece of apparatus called a calorimeter is used. This gives much more accurate energy values.

Using this method all of the heat energy released by the food is measured.

Results obtained from calorimeter experiments have shown that for equal quantities used, fat (or oil) contains about twice as much energy as protein or carbohydrate. This is why our bodies store energy as fat – more energy can be stored in a small quantity of material.

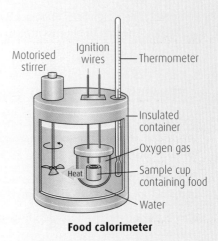

Motorised stirrer
Ignition wires
Thermometer
Insulated container
Oxygen gas
Heat
Sample cup containing food
Water

Food calorimeter

THE PROCESS OF RESPIRATION

To release the energy from food, living cells of both plants and animals must carry out a process known as **respiration**. The molecules which are broken down to release energy are known as respiratory substrates. The main respiratory substrate is glucose (a type of carbohydrate), but fats and proteins can be broken down if glucose is not available.

The carbohydrate, glucose, is a type of sugar. It consists of the chemical elements carbon (C), hydrogen (H) and oxygen (O); it can be broken down into these elements and reassembled into waste products, giving out energy in the process.

The overall reaction of respiration can be summarised by the following word equation:

glucose + oxygen → carbon dioxide + water + energy

In this reaction :

1   the glucose and the oxygen are the raw materials

2   the carbon dioxide and the water are the waste products

3   the purpose of the reaction is to release energy.

In the presence of oxygen, as shown by the equation above, glucose is broken down fully to release all of its energy and give the waste products, carbon dioxide and water. This is known as **aerobic respiration**.

Under certain circumstances, however, respiration can take place in the absence of oxygen and is then known as fermentation. Different waste products are formed in this type of respiration.

ONLINE TEST

Test yourself on this topic by taking the 'Purpose and Importance of Respiration' test online at www.brightredbooks.net/N5Biology

THE ROLE OF ATP

Adenosine triphosphate (ATP) is a chemical found in all living cells. It consists of a molecule of adenosine with three inorganic phosphate (Pi) groups attached in a chain-like fashion.

ATP acts as a type of energy management system in cells. Just as money is placed into a bank to keep and is withdrawn when it is required, energy can be 'banked' in molecules of ATP and released when needed. This takes place in the following way.

High-energy bond

Structure of ATP

The molecule of ATP is held together by bonds. The final bond, holding the end inorganic phosphate, can be easily broken and reformed. When energy is required by a cell, the bond attaching the end inorganic phosphate is broken, releasing energy. This leaves adenosine with only two inorganic phosphates attached and it is now known as adenosine diphosphate (ADP).

When glucose is broken down to release its energy, this energy is used to regenerate ATP by bonding an inorganic phosphate to ADP. This is, therefore, a reversible reaction.

Structure of ADP with unattached Pi

The series of reactions which are involved in respiration result in chemical energy being released and used to form ATP from ADP and Pi. The energy is stored in the bond. ATP is therefore an 'energy rich' compound. When the bond is broken again, the energy is released. This is a very rapid reaction, allowing energy to be available immediately on demand.

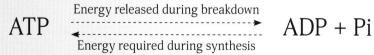

ATP   Energy released during breakdown → ADP + Pi

Energy required during synthesis

The energy released from the breakdown of ATP to ADP + Pi can be used in many cellular activities including muscle cell contraction, cell division, protein synthesis and transmission of nerve impulses.

THINGS TO DO AND THINK ABOUT

Explain why burning food in a calorimeter is a better method to use when investigating the energy value of food, compared to burning it on the end of a needle to heat water in a test tube.

THE CHEMISTRY OF RESPIRATION

The chemical energy stored in glucose is released by all cells through the series of enzyme-controlled reactions known as respiration.

Respiration takes place in several stages. The first stage always occurs in the cytoplasm, but further stages are dependent on whether or not oxygen is available.

AEROBIC RESPIRATION

Aerobic respiration is the term given to the type of respiration which involves the breakdown of glucose in the presence of oxygen. Carbon dioxide and water are the products of the process.

$$\text{glucose} + \text{oxygen} \longrightarrow \text{carbon dioxide} + \text{water} + \text{energy}$$

The process of aerobic respiration starts when a molecule of glucose is broken down into two molecules of **pyruvate** in the cytoplasm. This happens as a series of reactions, each of which is controlled by enzymes. This process is known as **glycolysis**. 'Glyco' refers to carbohydrate (glucose) and 'lysis' means splitting. Therefore, the name indicates that a carbohydrate (glucose) is being split.

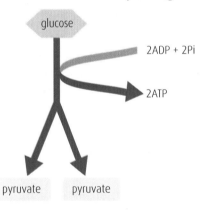

Splitting glucose (glycolysis)

During this series of reactions, enough energy is released to synthesise two molecules of ATP from ADP + Pi.

Like glucose, pyruvate also contains a lot of energy locked up in the molecule. Each molecule of pyruvate moves into a mitochondrion and, here, a further series of enzyme-controlled reactions gradually breaks down the pyruvate to release this energy. During these reactions, carbon dioxide and water are formed and a further 18 molecules of ATP are synthesised for every pyruvate that is broken down. The carbon dioxide and water are released as the waste products of respiration.

The complete set of respiration reactions is quite complex and a simplified version is shown below.

The reactions in the mitochondria allow the synthesis of 36 molecules of ATP (18 for each molecule of pyruvate). Add to this the two ATP molecules which were formed as glucose was split in the cytoplasm and it can be seen that *one molecule of glucose* yields a total of *38 molecules of ATP in aerobic respiration*.

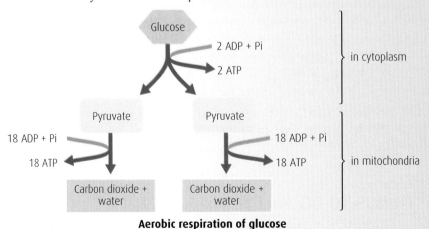

Aerobic respiration of glucose

RESPIRATION WITHOUT OXYGEN

A different type of respiration takes place if oxygen is not available.

The process begins in the cytoplasm in exactly the same way as in aerobic respiration: one molecule of glucose is broken down into two molecules of pyruvate and two molecules of ATP are synthesised. However, due to the lack of oxygen, the pyruvate molecules remain in the cytoplasm and the mitochondria do not become involved.

The pyruvate molecules are partially broken down by different chemical pathways depending on the type of organism carrying out the respiration.

Respiration without oxygen in multicellular animals

This type of respiration can occur in human muscle cells when a very heavy demand for more energy occurs and the oxygen supply is insufficient to meet the demand, for example when sprinting very fast.

In this case, pyruvate is only partly broken down, forming lactic acid, in a process called fermentation. No more ATP molecules are formed during this reaction. As the concentration of **lactic acid** builds up in the muscle cells, it causes muscle fatigue and pain. Since the muscles become inefficient, this process can only be maintained for a short period of time.

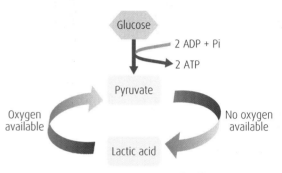

Fermentation in animal cells

In order to get rid of the lactic acid, oxygen is required. When oxygen becomes available, the lactic acid is converted back to pyruvate, which can then enter the mitochondria for aerobic respiration to take place.

Since the lactic acid can be converted back into pyruvate, fermentation in animal cells is described as a reversible process. It is not a very efficient process, however, as no ATP is produced during the breakdown of pyruvate. So, *one molecule of glucose* yields a total of *two molecules of ATP in fermentation in animal cells.*

Respiration without oxygen in plants and microbes

This type of respiration can occur in plant cells that are deprived of oxygen, for example in waterlogged root cells, and also in microbes, such as yeast cells, which are important in the brewing industry.

This involves the breakdown of pyruvate to ethanol (a type of alcohol) and the release of carbon dioxide gas. Again, no more ATP is formed in this reaction.

As carbon dioxide is released in the breakdown of pyruvate, fermentation in plants and microbes is an irreversible reaction. Again, it is not a very efficient process as no ATP is produced during the breakdown of pyruvate. So, *one molecule of glucose* yields a total of *two molecules of ATP in fermentation in plants and microbes.*

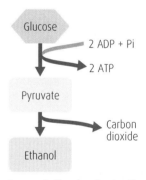

Fermentation in plant cells and microbes

COMPARISON OF RESPIRATION WITH AND WITHOUT OXYGEN

Respiration with oxygen	Respiration without oxygen
Glucose completely broken down	Glucose partly broken down
Carbon dioxide and water produced	Animals: lactic acid produced Plants and microbes: ethanol and carbon dioxide produced
38 molecules of ATP produced	2 molecules of ATP produced

 ONLINE TEST

Test yourself on this topic by taking the 'Chemistry of Respiration' test online at www.brightredbooks.net/N5Biology

THINGS TO DO AND THINK ABOUT

Explain why respiration with oxygen can be described as an efficient process, while fermentation is inefficient.

CELLS, TISSUES AND ORGANS: THE ORGANISATION OF CELLS AND MULTICELLULAR ORGANISMS 1

The basic unit of life is a cell. It is the smallest independent life form. Some cells exist as individual organisms and other cells are a part of more complex multicellular organisms.

UNICELLULAR ORGANISMS

Some organisms consist of only one cell, which must show all the characteristics of life and carry out all of the functions required for survival. These organisms are called unicellular organisms. Examples are bacteria, some algae, some fungi (including yeast) and a group of organisms called protozoa.

Unicellular organisms are unfamiliar to most of us as they are generally too small to be seen with the naked eye. Most protozoa are around 0·01–0·05 mm, although some can grow as large as 0·5 mm. They can, however, be easily seen using a microscope.

A few examples of unicellular organisms are shown here.

Unicellular organisms

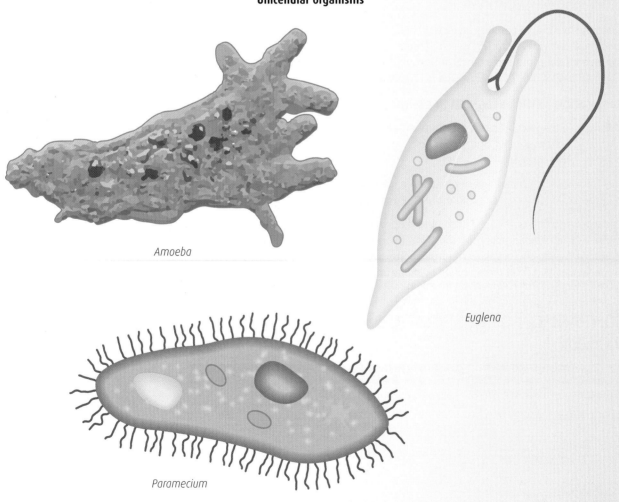

Amoeba

Euglena

Paramecium

contd

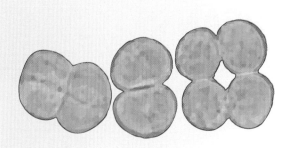

Pleurococcus

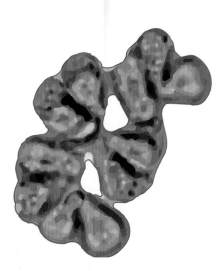

Single-celled algae

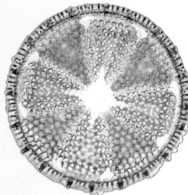

Diatom

As shown in earlier chapters, some unicellular organisms are extremely useful to humans, for example bacteria are used in genetic engineering and yeast cells are used in fermentation to produce alcohol. However, some are disease-causing cells and are known as pathogens.

MULTICELLULAR ORGANISMS

More familiar to us are organisms which are made of many cells. These are known as multicellular organisms. In multicellular organisms, it would be inefficient for every cell to carry out all the processes required for survival. Instead, a division of labour exists, where cells are specialised so that each type of cell carries out a particular function.

Each cell of a multicellular organism has a dual role to play. It must be independent and able to act at an individual level, as well as working together with neighbouring cells to perform a part in the operation of the whole organism.

At the individual level, cells must be able to absorb food, absorb oxygen, carry out respiration and manufacture proteins, for example. These are basic-level survival functions. In addition, however, the same cells must work together with groups of similar cells to perform a specialised function that benefits the entire organism, aiding its survival.

THINGS TO DO AND THINK ABOUT

1   Name one unicellular organism that is plant-like and one that is animal-like.

2   What type of organism is yeast?

3   Living organisms show seven different characteristics of life. Can you name them?

ONLINE

For more on this, check out the 'Unicellular v multicellular' link at www.brightredbooks.net/N5Biology

ONLINE TEST

Test yourself on this topic by taking the 'The organisation of cells and multicellular organisms 1' test online at www.brightredbooks.net/N5Biology

DON'T FORGET

In unicellular organisms, the cell must be able to carry out all of the functions of living things. In multicellular organisms, there is a division of labour, with each cell fulfilling a specific function.

CELLS, TISSUES AND ORGANS: THE ORGANISATION OF CELLS AND MULTICELLULAR ORGANISMS 2

CELL ORGANISATION

Groups of cells that are similar in structure and work together to carry out a similar function are known as **tissues**.

The diagram shows some of the tissues in the arm of the human body.

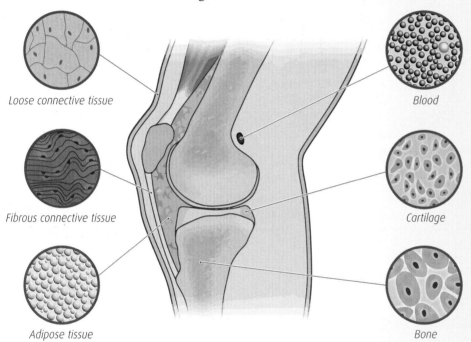

Loose connective tissue

Fibrous connective tissue

Adipose tissue

Blood

Cartilage

Bone

A structure such as the human arm contains a variety of different tissues

From the diagram, we can see that not all cells in a tissue have to be exactly the same, although this can be the case. For example, the cells which make up **cartilage** tissue can all be one type. In contrast to this are the cells which make up **blood**. Here different cell types (**red blood cells** and white blood cells) are present. These cells vary in shape, content, size and individual function, but still work together, having the overall function of transport in the body.

Plants also have a level of organisation in which cells operate together as tissues.

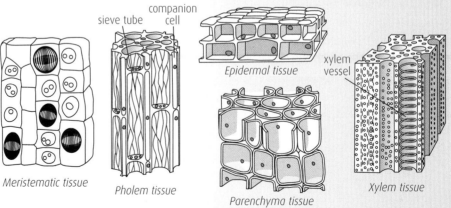

Meristematic tissue

sieve tube

companion cell

Pholem tissue

Epidermal tissue

Parenchyma tissue

xylem vessel

Xylem tissue

Plant tissues

As with animals, plant tissues can be made up of groups of cells that are all of a similar type, such as meristematic cells, or can consist of a variety of cell types working together. An example of this is **phloem** tissue, which consists of cells which form sieve tubes and cells called **companion cells**. These cell types differ in structure and content, but together deliver the overall function of transport of food materials in the plant.

contd

In order for efficient functioning of multicellular organisms, tissues are organised into organs, which are part of systems. Systems are coordinated together to perform as a whole functioning organism.

Thus, there is an organisational hierarchy of cells in a complex multicellular organism.

Hierarchy of organisation of cells

The stomach is an **organ** found in the human digestive system. It is made up of a variety of tissues which consist of many types of cells. The stomach is just one part of the digestive system.

An organ is a highly specialised structure in which a collection of tissues is joined in a structural unit to serve a common function. Some organs may have more than one function.

Examples of human organs are **heart**, **liver**, brain and lungs.

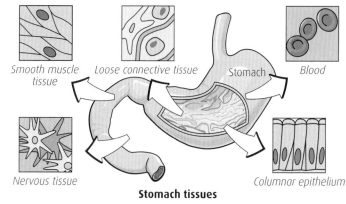

Smooth muscle tissue   Loose connective tissue   Stomach   Blood

Nervous tissue   Columnar epithelium

Stomach tissues

- The heart acts as a pump and consists of tissues such as muscle, nerve and blood.

- The liver breaks down poisonous chemicals and produces bile to aid digestion. It consists of connective tissue, blood and nerves.

- The brain processes information and examples of tissues found here include nervous tissue, blood and blood vessels.

- The lungs are involved in gas exchange and contain epithelial tissue, as well as blood.

DON'T FORGET

Multicellular organisms are much more complex than unicellular organisms and can, therefore, carry out more complicated functions.

Plants show similar organisation. Tissues work together to make organs which are part of systems.

Examples of plant organs are stem, leaves and roots.

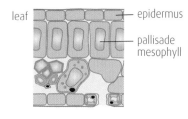

leaf — epidermus

pallisade mesophyll

- The stem supports the leaves of the plant. A variety of tissues such as **xylem** and phloem are found here.

- The leaves are the main photosynthetic organs of the plant and contain tissues such as **epidermis** and palisade **mesophyll**.

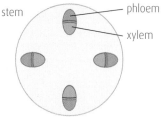

stem   phloem

xylem

- The roots anchor the plant, and absorb water and minerals through xylem tissue and receive food through phloem tissue.

THINGS TO DO AND THINK ABOUT

ONLINE TEST

Test yourself on this topic by taking the 'The organisation of cells and multicellular organisms 2' test online at www.brightredbooks.net/N5Biology

You should be able to name a tissue and the types of cells it contains, as well as being able to identify the organ it belongs to.

1   Name two types of cells found in the animal tissue blood.

2   Name two types of tissues found in a plant's transport system and for each tissue, state a cell type found there.

3   Why is it important that cells are specialised in a multicellular organism?

4   Starting with individual cells, describe the hierarchical organisation of cells in a living organism.

CELLS, TISSUES AND ORGANS: SPECIALISED CELLS AND THEIR FUNCTIONS 1

Multicellular organisms are made up of many different cell types, which are organised into tissues and organs. So, when cells are produced by cell division, they must undergo changes to become specialised for their particular function. Genes control the development of newly formed cells and bring about the many changes that produce the great variety of cells found in a complex multicellular organism.

The basic idea that a cell becomes modified to suit a particular function is important, although it is not necessary to know the individual details of how this happens. You don't need to memorise all of the examples which follow but you do need to have an awareness that cells differentiate to become specialised and you should able to give an example of this taking place.

SPECIALISATION OF ANIMAL CELLS

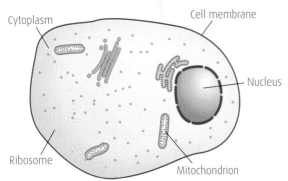

A newly divided animal cell

When an animal cell is produced, it has the same basic structure as all other animal cells. As it develops, its contents and shape are altered to make it specialised. Exactly what happens to each basic cell depends on where it is found in the organism, which organ it is associated with and the function it has to carry out.

A simplified version of a newly divided animal cell is shown in the diagram.

Let's look at some examples of how cells like this are modified to become specialised for a particular function.

Motor neuron

As can be seen from the diagram, many changes have taken place to make a motor **neuron** from an unspecialised cell. The function of this type of cell is to transmit electrical impulses from the **central nervous system** to the muscles or glands of the body, causing a response to some sort of **stimulus**. The cell might be very long in length as it may carry information from, for example, the spinal cord to the foot. Some of the specialised adaptations to form a motor neuron are:

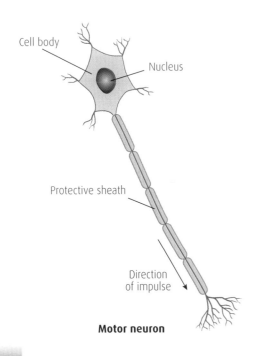

Motor neuron

- the main part of the cell has become elongated to form a conducting fibre

- extensions have been created at the ends so that connections can be made with other cells

- a protective sheath has formed to ensure that the electrical impulses travel from one end of the neuron to the other.

contd

Sperm cell

Again, many changes have taken place to create a sperm cell from the original unspecialised cell. The function of this type of cell is to carry half the genetic code to the egg and to fertilise it, creating a single cell called a **zygote**. This can go on to develop into an embryo. Some of the adaptations that take place to form a sperm cell are:

- the cell has become elongated and has three distinct areas

- the 'head' section has become small with the DNA tightly condensed in the nucleus

- many mitochondria have been produced and are found in the 'midpiece'

- the 'tail' section has developed to allow the sperm to swim

- organelles that are not required have disintegrated.

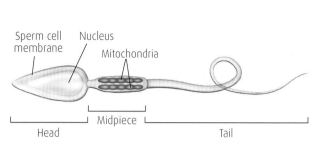

Human sperm cell

ONLINE

Check out the 'Cell specialisation' link at www.brightredbooks.net/N5Biology

Ciliated epithelial cell

The function of this type of cell is to sweep mucus containing trapped dust, bacteria and other foreign particles away. These cells are found in the **trachea** and bronchi of the respiratory system. Closely associated with the ciliated epithelial cells are goblet cells. They produce sticky **mucus** which traps the dust, bacteria and other particles, and then the **cilia** beat gently to push the mucus up towards the throat where it is swallowed. Modifications that are required to form a specialised ciliated epithelial cell include:

- the cell has become tall and thin (column shaped)

- small hairs, called cilia, have developed along the top of the cell.

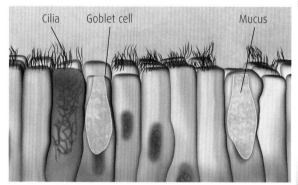

Ciliated epithelium

Red blood cell

The function of a red blood cell is to transport oxygen around the body. It is part of blood tissue, which forms part of the circulatory system. Red blood cells contain the pigment **haemoglobin**, which combines with oxygen to form **oxyhaemoglobin**. The specialisation required to form a red blood cell includes:

- the nucleus of the cell has disintegrated, leaving more space in the cell for the transport of oxygen

- haemoglobin has been produced

- the cell shape has been modified to become biconcave (curving inwards on both sides) to increase its surface area, allowing faster absorption of oxygen.

Red blood cells

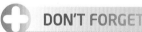

DON'T FORGET

Cells must become specialised so that they can take on a specific role in the efficient functioning of the whole multicellular organism.

ONLINE TEST

Test yourself on this topic by taking the 'Specialised cells and their functions 1' test online at www.brightredbooks.net/N5Biology

THINGS TO DO AND THINK ABOUT

1 You should be able to name a tissue and give an example of how the cells have become specialised to allow them to carry out their particular function.

2 Why does a red blood cell have no nucleus? Describe one other feature of this cell which allows it to carry out its role efficiently.

CELLS, TISSUES AND ORGANS: SPECIALISED CELLS AND THEIR FUNCTIONS 2

SPECIALISATION OF PLANT CELLS

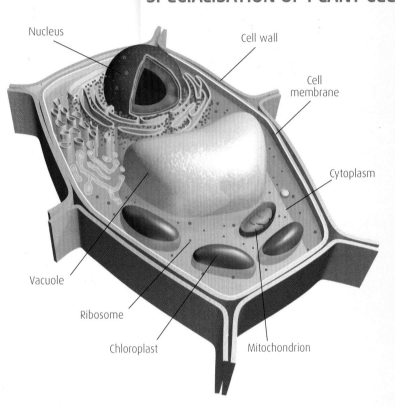

A newly divided plant cell

When a plant cell is produced, it has the same basic structure as all other plant cells until it undergoes the changes that make it specialised. As with animals, the exact detail of what happens to the basic cell depends on where it is found, which organ it is associated with and the function it has to carry out.

Plant cells are produced in certain areas of the plant known as **meristems**. A simplified version of a newly divided plant cell is shown in the diagram.

Although the diagram shows the presence of chloroplasts in the cell, not all plant cells possess these. This depends on whether the cell is positioned in an area of the plant which receives light and on whether it is involved in the process of photosynthesis.

Let's have a look at some examples of how plant cells become modified for a particular function.

A sieve tube cell

A sieve tube cell forms part of the phloem tissue. The function of the sieve tube cell is to transport sugar made in the leaves by photosynthesis. It allows sugar to be provided to areas that are unable to carry out photosynthesis, such as the roots. It also transports sugar to storage organs both above and below ground. Changes that happen to make a sieve tube cell specialised for this function include:

- cells have become elongated

- end walls have become perforated, forming sieve plates

- cell organelles which are not required have disintegrated.

Sieve tube cell

A palisade mesophyll cell

The function of this type of cell is primarily photosynthesis. These cells are found in columns near the uppermost surface of the leaf and are closely packed together, forming a continuous layer of cells that are specialised for the absorption of light for photosynthesis. Specialisation of these cells involves:

- cells have become column shaped

- a large quantity of chloroplasts have been made in the cell to provide more chlorophyll for maximum absorption of light.

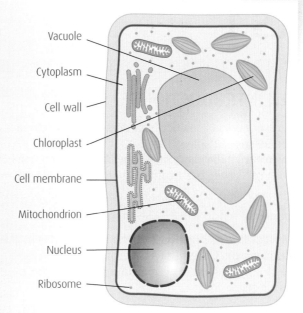

Vacuole
Cytoplasm
Cell wall
Chloroplast
Cell membrane
Mitochondrion
Nucleus
Ribosome

Palisade mesophyll cell

A ROOT HAIR CELL

This type of cell is, again, a modification of the basic unspecialised plant cell. Its function is to absorb water from the soil into the root of the plant. The plant cell has been specialised to make it more efficient at this task and the modifications include:

- no chloroplasts have been produced (this cell does not receive light, so cannot photosynthesise)

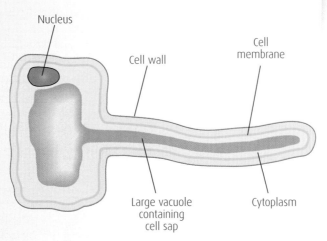

Nucleus
Cell wall
Cell membrane
Large vacuole containing cell sap
Cytoplasm

Root hair cell

- the cell has grown an 'extension', known as the **root hair**, to increase the surface area for water absorption

- the vacuole has extended into the root hair to maximise the osmotic difference between the cell and the surrounding cell water, to make the osmosis of water and the diffusion of dissolved minerals more efficient.

ONLINE

Check out the 'Root hair cells and osmosis' link at www.brightredbooks.net/N5Biology

DON'T FORGET

Although there are some organelles that are present in all living cells, the function of the cell determines the actual organelles that it needs.

ONLINE TEST

Test yourself on this topic by taking the 'Specialised cells and their functions 2' test online at www.brightredbooks.net/N5Biology

THINGS TO DO AND THINK ABOUT

1. You should be able to describe the way the cells in a tissue become specialised to allow them to carry out their particular function.

2. Describe the way in which a typical plant cell becomes specialised to carry out the function of absorbing water from the soil.

3. Why does a palisade mesophyll cell have more chloroplasts than other cells in a leaf?

STEM CELLS 1

AN INTRODUCTION TO STEM CELLS

As every cell in a multicellular organism arises from the original zygote formed at **fertilisation**, it follows that every cell has the full set of genetic information required to construct the entire organism. However, only some of the genes are 'switched on' in each cell, giving rise to differentiation or specialisation for a particular role.

It is this switching on and off of genes that allows the development of the great variety of specialised cells that exists in the tissues, organs and systems of an organism.

Most cells in an organism become specialised at a fairly early stage in their development. Once a cell has become altered to suit its function, it cannot revert back to its original form or develop into any other type of cell and is known as a permanent tissue cell.

Stem cells are different from permanent tissue cells. One of the main features of stem cells is that they have the ability to multiply, while still maintaining the potential to develop into other cell types. For example, stem cells can become cells of the heart, blood, brain, bones, muscle and skin. Stem cells can be sourced from different areas of the body, but all have this capacity to develop into multiple types of cells.

Stem cells are involved in the growth of an organism. They can produce any type of cell that is required. Even when growth has stopped, stem cells have an important role to play in replacing worn out and damaged cells and tissues.

Stem cells

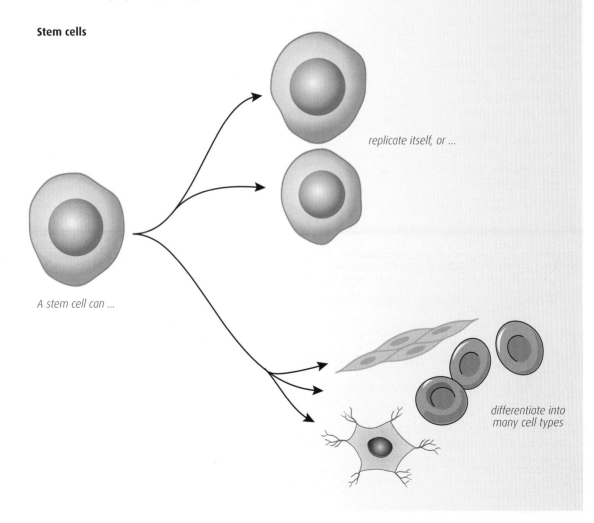

A stem cell can ...

replicate itself, or ...

differentiate into many cell types

TYPES OF STEM CELLS

- Embryonic stem cells are present in embryos. Embryonic stem cells form during the very early stages of development, when the zygote is dividing rapidly to form a ball of cells. These cells retain the capacity to divide for long periods of time and have the ability to make all of the various cell types required in the organism.

- Adult stem cells are obtained from some of the tissues in the body of an adult. Bone marrow, which is found in the long bones of a human, is a rich source of stem cells and it is used in the treatment of some types of cancer and blood diseases like leukaemia. Research by scientists has led to the development and isolation of stem cells from adult human skin cells and this work is still ongoing.

THE DISCOVERY OF STEM CELLS

The potential of stem cells to develop into any type of cell was recognised in the 1980s, but it was towards the very end of the 20th century that scientists found methods of isolating these cells from human embryos and growing them in the laboratory.

Most of the work was done using cells from embryos which had been created in the laboratory for the treatment of infertility. They were embryos which were 'left over' after the treatment and were no longer required for that purpose. This required consent from the individuals whose embryos were donated to this type of research.

A further development was the identification of conditions that allow some specialised adult human cells to be genetically reprogrammed to assume an embryonic stem cell-like state.

By using tissue culture techniques, stem cells can be induced to grow and divide in a controlled way, producing a collection of continually dividing undifferentiated cells. This collection is known as a stem cell line and has many potential uses. Once established, a cell line can be grown indefinitely in the laboratory and cells may be frozen for storage.

VIDEO LINK

For a video about stem cells, watch 'A stem cell story' at www.brightredbooks.net/ N5Biology

ONLINE TEST

Test yourself on this topic by taking the 'Stem cells 1' test online at www. brightredbooks.net/ N5Biology

DON'T FORGET

Adult stem cells can be found in several areas of the body such as in the blood, skin and brain. However, they are not as versatile as embryonic stem cells. Embryonic stem cells can develop into any type of cell, but in adults blood stem cells, for example, can only develop into the different types of blood cell.

THINGS TO DO AND THINK ABOUT

1 In what way are stem cells different from the cells which have become permanent tissue?

2 Why are stem cells involved in growth and repair of tissue?

STEM CELLS 2

THE USES OF STEM CELLS

Research and treatments

Stem cells are used in research to increase understanding of cell development. They are also important in the treatment of some conditions such as cancer and some birth defects.

Replacement of damaged tissues

Damaged or diseased organs are often replaced with transplants of healthy organs from a donor. However, the demand for such organs and tissues is far greater than the available supply. Research is taking place into the possibility of growing stem cells which are then directed to develop into specific types of cells, providing a source of new cells, tissues and even organs for transplant. This would be a renewable resource as stem cells can be grown continuously, given correct conditions. It is hoped that stem cells could be involved in the treatment of:

- Brain diseases – such as Parkinson's disease, in which damage to nervous tissues causes muscles to move continually, and Alzheimer's disease, in which damage to brain cells results in confusion and memory loss. Embryonic cells have been 'programmed' to develop into brain cells to replace damaged ones.

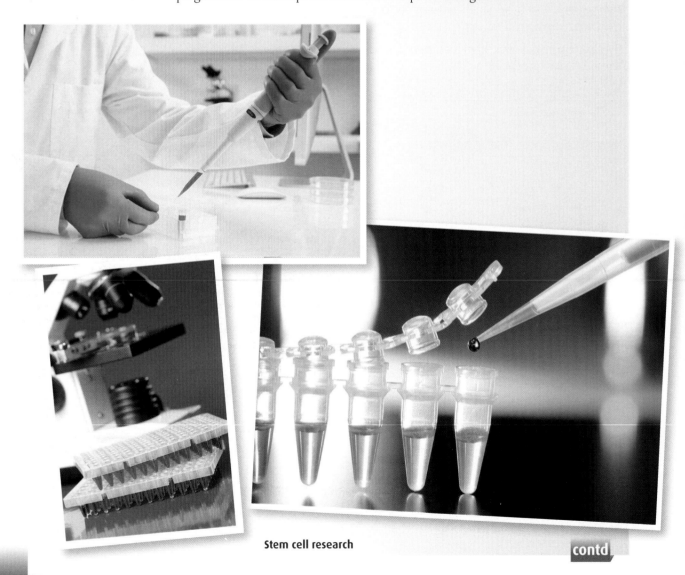

Stem cell research

contd

- Blood diseases – such as leukaemia, in which white blood cells grow and divide out of control, and sickle cell anaemia, in which red blood cells are misshapen and have reduced oxygen carrying capacity. As there are difficulties associated with bone marrow stem-cell extractions, treatment has been developed using the stem cells found in the umbilical cord and the placenta of newborn babies. This has led some scientists to suggest that an umbilical cord blood bank should be stored for future use.

- Heart disease – this is another area which is being explored for treatment by stem cells. For example, the possibility of growing heart muscle cells from stem cells in the laboratory is being investigated. These healthy muscle cells could be transplanted into patients who suffer from chronic heart disease.

- Type 1 **diabetes** – this results when the cells of the **pancreas** which normally produce **insulin** are destroyed by the person's own immune system. Investigations suggest that embryonic stem cells could be cultured to form insulin-producing cells which might then be transplanted into people with diabetes.

Testing of new drugs

Stem cells could be grown in the laboratory and used to test drugs and chemicals before they are trialled in people. This means that drugs could be tested on human cells, rather than on animals, resulting in safer drugs that are developed in a more ethical way.

Screening for toxins

Stem cells could be used to grow tissues for testing our response to certain chemicals. For example, stem cells could be used to investigate the effects of pesticides which are sprayed onto food crops. The pesticides could be applied to the stem cells to see if there were any adverse effects.

These are only some of the ways in which stem cells are being used or may be used in the future, and it is an area of continued significant research and development.

ETHICAL ISSUES

Stem cells have been used in medicine for many years, for example in bone marrow transplants.

Ethical issues about stem cells focus almost entirely on embryonic stem cells, and use of these cells does pose a dilemma. It forces a choice between two moral principles:

1 the sense of duty involved in preventing or relieving suffering

2 the sense of duty to respect the value of human life.

The basic problem is that, in using embryonic stem cells, the embryo is destroyed. This means the loss of potential human life. However, this has to be weighed up against the fact that stem cell research could lead to the discovery of new medicines and treatments that could alleviate suffering and prolong life.

Much debate has taken place at the highest court levels in many countries and this is still an area which is highly controversial.

THINGS TO DO AND THINK ABOUT

1 Where are stem cells found in humans?

2 Why are stem cells important?

3 Why might some people be against the use of stem cells for medical treatment while others are in favour of it?

DON'T FORGET

Stem cells differ from other body cells in that they retain the ability to divide and develop into any type of specialised cell.

ONLINE

Check out the US Department of Health and Information's guide 'Stem cell information' at www.brightredbooks.net/N5Biology

ONLINE TEST

Test yourself on this topic by taking the 'Stem cells 2' test online at www.brightredbooks.net/N5Biology

MERISTEMS

In animals, growth occurs all over the body during development. However, in plants, growth is restricted to specialised areas called meristems.

A meristem is a group of unspecialised plant cells which have the capability to divide repeatedly by **mitosis**. The undifferentiated cells which are produced in meristems have the potential to develop into any type of cell. There are two different categories of meristems:

- Apical meristems are found at the tips of the plant, that is at the shoot tips and root tips.
- Lateral meristems are mainly found between the phloem and the xylem and are important in plants which grow year after year (rather than completing their life cycle in one year). They are responsible for the increase in girth of the plant.

APICAL MERISTEMS

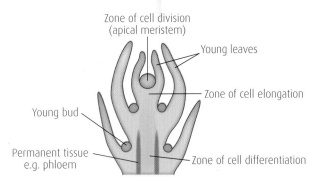

Zone of cell division (apical meristem)

Young leaves

Zone of cell elongation

Young bud

Permanent tissue e.g. phloem

Zone of cell differentiation

The apical meristem in a shoot

An apical meristem is found at the apex or tip of the shoots and roots of a plant. The structure is similar in both of these areas. The growth and increase in length of the shoots and roots depends on these cells dividing and elongating, before becoming specialised for their particular function.

Shoot growth

The growing point or shoot apex repeatedly undergoes mitosis, giving rise to a collection of unspecialised cells. These cells can be seen under the microscope in various stages of mitosis.

Once the cells have divided, they absorb water and each forms a vacuole, making the cells longer. This gives the name 'zone of elongation' to this part of the shoot. The cells in this area are still unspecialised and have the potential to develop into any type of plant cell.

It is only when the process of elongation is complete that the cells begin the next process of specialising, developing different structures in order to fulfil their function. Cells in this area are described as being in the 'zone of differentiation'.

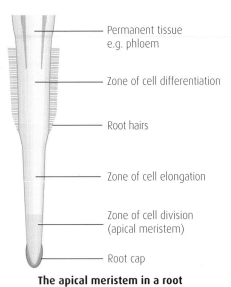

Permanent tissue e.g. phloem

Zone of cell differentiation

Root hairs

Zone of cell elongation

Zone of cell division (apical meristem)

Root cap

The apical meristem in a root

Root growth

The growing point at the tip or apex of the root shows the same meristematic pattern as the shoot. The cells at the tip of the root undergo the process of mitosis to make newly divided unspecialised cells. Water is then absorbed into the cells in the zone of elongation and the cells increase in length. Following this, in the zone of differentiation, the cells become specialised for their function and, at this point, they become permanent tissue. This means that they no longer have the potential to develop into other types of cells.

One difference between the apical meristem of the root and that of the shoot is that the root possesses a root cap in front of the cells that are dividing. This is simply a protective mechanism. As the root pushes its way through the particles of the soil, the delicate cells of the apical meristem are liable to become damaged and broken. The root cap prevents this from happening.

contd

A simple experiment can be carried out to show that growth of the root only takes place at the tip of the root and that, once the cells have become specialised, they do not have a role to play in growth.

As shown in the diagram, six spots of ink were spaced evenly at 1 mm intervals on the root of a recently germinated broad bean. It was left to grow for a few days and re-examined.

The results of the experiment are shown in the diagram. You can see that ink marks 1, 2 and 3 are spread out, but ink marks 4, 5 and 6 remain at 1 mm intervals. The area at the root tip has the root cap and the region where cells are dividing and elongating, causing growth of the root.

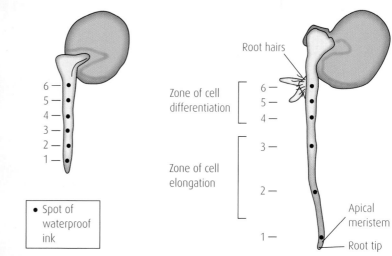

Ink marks on broad bean root

Growth of broad bean root

However, beyond mark 3, the cells are already fully elongated and are developing into specialised cells to fulfil their function (permanent tissue).

LATERAL MERISTEMS

Annual plants complete their life cycle in one year and then they die. They do not need particularly thick stems to support the plant. In contrast to this, many plants continue to grow year after year and must develop thicker stems in order to support the new growth each year.

The increase in girth of the plant is produced by the action of another type of meristem, known as a lateral meristem. This meristem ensures that plenty of xylem is produced from newly divided cells, so that the plant gets enough support and is able to transport lots of water and minerals from the soil to the living parts of the plant.

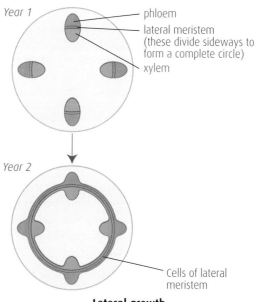

Lateral growth

THINGS TO DO AND THINK ABOUT

1 Compare the growth of animals to the growth of plants in terms of *where* growth takes place.

2 Why are meristematic cells important in a plant?

3 List three differences between cells found in the zone of cell division compared to cells from the zone of differentiation.

DON'T FORGET

Meristematic cells (of all types) can divide and have the potential to become other types of plant cells. They contribute to the growth of the plant.

ONLINE TEST

Test yourself on this topic by taking the 'Meristems' test online at www. brightredbooks.net/ N5Biology

ONLINE

For more on this, check out 'Plant meristems and growth' at www.brightredbooks.net/ N5Biology

CONTROL AND COMMUNICATION: NERVOUS CONTROL IN ANIMALS

THE NERVOUS SYSTEM

The cells, tissues and organs of the body do not work independently of one another; their activities are coordinated so that they work together. This means that they can perform their specific function as required by the body at any given time. This coordination is achieved by the nervous system.

The human nervous system is composed of three parts:

- the brain
- the spinal cord
- the nerves.

The brain and the spinal cord together make up the central nervous system (CNS). This is connected to all parts of the body through the nerves, which are made up of thousands of long thin nerve fibres.

In order to protect itself, the body must be able to detect changes which take place both internally and externally. These changes act as stimuli. Nerves lead to and from all of the organs and systems of the body, making sure that information is gathered and appropriate responses are made.

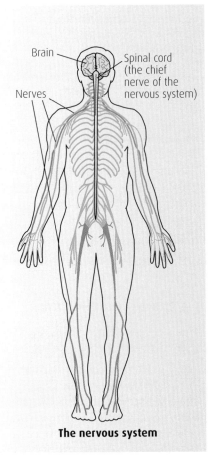

The nervous system

NEURONS

The nervous system is made up of nerve cells called neurons. These cells are specialised to carry electrical impulses. These impulses are only able to travel in one direction along the neuron. There are neurons that send impulses to the CNS, different neurons within the CNS to process impulses and other neurons which send impulses to organs which carry out responses.

There are, therefore, three basic types of neuron and each has a different function as summarised in the table.

Type of neuron	Function
Sensory neuron	To send information from the sensory receptors to the CNS
Relay neuron	To send information within the CNS
Motor neuron	To send information from the CNS to the muscles and glands

The flow of information follows a pathway as shown in the diagram.

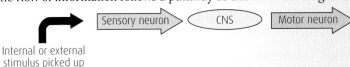

Internal or external
stimulus picked up
by **sensory receptor**

Response by muscle
or gland

Flow of information in the CNS

AREAS OF THE BRAIN

The brain is made up of millions of neurons which are coordinated to process information. There are three main areas of the brain: the **cerebrum**, the **cerebellum** and the **medulla**.

The cerebrum

This is the largest part of the brain and is divided into two halves or hemispheres. This part of the brain is responsible for receiving information from the sensory neurons, processing it and sending impulses to all parts of the body along the motor neurons in order to make some sort of response. It processes information from the senses such as sight and hearing. The cerebrum is also involved in mental and conscious thought processes such as reasoning, imagination, memory and thinking.

The cerebellum

This area of the brain is found towards the rear of the head. Its primary function is to control balance and coordinate muscle actions. Complex actions which require skill in both these areas, such as riding a bicycle, involve the cerebellum.

The medulla

The medulla is found at the top of the spinal cord. It controls involuntary body processes such as breathing, digestion, heart rate, swallowing and sneezing.

Communication within the brain is by short neurons which pass electrical impulses very quickly.

Coming from the main body of the cell are lots of tiny extensions which connect with other cells and receive information. This information (in the form of electrical impulses) is sent along a thin fibre which has a layer of insulation, preventing loss of the impulse as it travels to the other end of the neuron. Here, transmitters transfer the information to the next cell.

Neurons are highly specialised cells and, because they carry electrical impulses, they do not actually come into contact with one another. This means that there has to be a way of transferring the information across a gap between two neurons. This is carried out by chemical messengers called neurotransmitters in the following process:

1. An electrical impulse travels from the cell body of a neuron along the nerve fibre to the other end.

2. When it arrives, this triggers the nerve ending of that neuron to release chemical messengers called neurotransmitters.

3. The neurotransmitters diffuse across the gap between the first neuron and the next neuron. The gap is known as a **synapse**.

4. The neurotransmitters bind with receptor molecules on the membrane of the second neuron. The receptor molecules are specific to the chemicals released from the first neuron.

5. The second neuron now becomes stimulated to transmit the electrical impulse.

Synapses occur between all types of nerves and are necessary because the nerves do not touch each other directly.

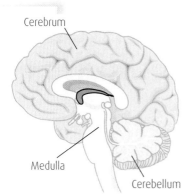

Parts of the human brain

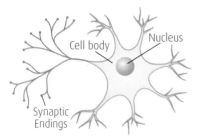

Neuron in the brain

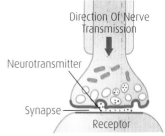

Direction Of Nerve Transmission

Neurotransmitter

Synapse

Receptor

A synapse

DON'T FORGET

The brain and the spinal cord make up the CNS (central nervous system). The brain is composed of many different areas and each area is responsible for a different function. The three main areas are the cerebrum, cerebellum and medulla.

THINGS TO DO AND THINK ABOUT

A synapse is found at the junction between two nerve cells. Describe what happens at a synapse.

CONTROL AND COMMUNICATION: NEURONS AND REFLEX ACTIONS

Nerves and the CNS provide communication within the body. Sensory neurons gather information about the internal and the external environment, pass the information in the form of electrical impulses to the CNS and then impulses travel along motor neurons to muscles and glands to make appropriate responses.

TYPES OF NEURON

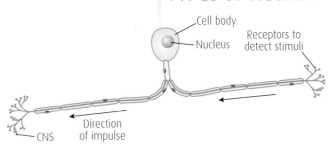

Sensory neuron

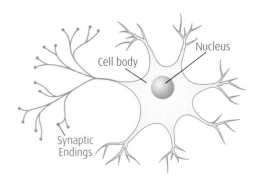

Relay neuron

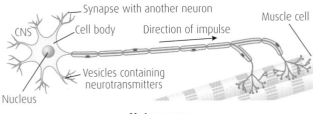

Motor neuron

Sensory neuron

The function of a sensory neuron is to send an electrical impulse to the CNS in response to a stimulus from a tissue or organ of the body. This could be an internal stimulus, such as the swallowing of food or an external one, such as the eye (as a sense organ) seeing a ball flying through the air.

A sensory neuron has extensions at the sensory end of the nerve fibre, where receptors detect sensory input or stimuli. This allows the gathering of information. The main body of the cell is part way along the length of the cell fibre and at the other end of the sensory neuron are more extensions, ready to send neurotransmitters across the synapse to the next cell.

Relay neuron

The function of a relay neuron is to send an electrical impulse within the CNS inside the spinal cord or within the brain. Relay neurons pass information from sensory neurons on to other nerves. They are generally shorter in size than the other neurons. Other terms which are used to describe relay neurons are 'intermediate neuron' and 'interneuron'.

Motor neuron

The function of the motor neuron is to send an electrical impulse from the CNS to the muscles or glands, which then make a response. This could be to produce an enzyme, such as pepsin in the stomach, or to cause muscles to contract in the arms and hands to catch a ball.

A motor neuron has extensions at the end of the nerve fibre and these are connected to the muscle or gland, allowing it to pass on an electrical impulse which will bring about a response. The main body of the cell is at one end of the fibre and has receptors to receive neurotransmitters which cross the synapses from neighbouring cells.

These three types of neurons work together, receiving stimuli, processing the information and making appropriate responses for the safe functioning of the organism.

VIDEO LINK

Check out the clip 'Structure functions and types of neurons' at www.brightredbooks.net/N5Biology

REFLEX ACTIONS

A **reflex action** is a type of response to a stimulus which does not need to be learned and which does not involve conscious thought. For example, if a person puts their hand down on something which is very hot, their response does not require thought or learning. The hand is automatically pulled away; it is an involuntary response. This action is known as a reflex action and it protects the body from harm.

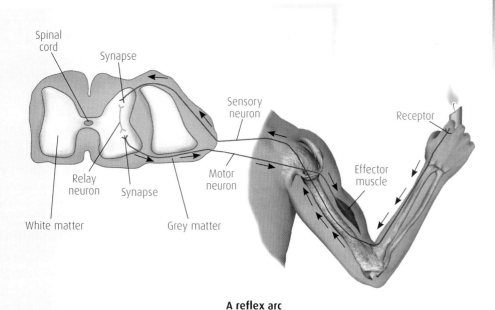

A reflex arc

The pathway that brings about a reflex action is called a **reflex arc** and is illustrated in the diagram.

The steps in the reflex arc are:

1 The stimulus is detected by the receptors in the skin (in the example above, pain receptors in the hand pick up the stimulus).

2 An electrical impulse is immediately sent along the sensory neuron towards the spinal cord.

3 The impulse crosses the first synapse and travels along the relay neuron.

4 The impulse crosses the second synapse and is picked up by the motor neuron.

5 The motor neuron conducts the impulse to the nerve endings in the muscle.

6 The muscle contracts, removing the hand from the stimulus causing the pain.

Reflex actions protect the body from damage. Other examples of reflex actions are:

- blinking when an object travels towards the eye

- the changing size of the eye's pupil in response to varying light levels

- swallowing when food reaches the back of the throat

- a jerking reaction when the knee is tapped.

Reflex actions often take place via the spinal cord and without involving the brain; this cuts down on the time that it takes to process the information, allowing a very fast response.

ONLINE TEST

Test yourself on this topic by taking the 'Control and communication 2' test online at www.brightredbooks.net/ N5Biology

DON'T FORGET

A reflex action is a rapid, involuntary response to a potentially harmful stimulus.

THINGS TO DO AND THINK ABOUT

1 Give a definition of a reflex action and explain why these actions are important.

2 Describe the pathway of information sent through a reflex arc from the moment a person stands on a sharp object, such as a tack, to the appropriate response being made.

3 Which of the following are examples of reflex actions?
   a) Sneezing when dust enters the nose.
   b) Kicking a ball in a game of football.
   c) Running to avoid an oncoming car.
   d) Blinking when a ball comes towards your head.
   e) The pupil of your eye constricting in bright light.

CONTROL AND COMMUNICATION: HORMONAL CONTROL

THE ENDOCRINE SYSTEM

In order to protect itself, the body needs to detect information about conditions – both internal and external – and then to make appropriate responses. The preceding chapters deal with how the nervous system plays a role in this function. Another system, the **endocrine system**, also has a role to play. Like the nervous system, this system is involved in communication around the body.

The endocrine system consists of several organs called glands. These glands release chemical substances, known as **hormones**, into the bloodstream. Hormones are chemical messengers. They carry information from one area of the body to another.

HORMONES VERSUS NERVE IMPULSES

Both hormones and nerve impulses work to coordinate the activities of the body, but they act in very different ways. When a nerve impulse is triggered by a stimulus, it travels along a particular route (the nerve fibre) to arrive at a specific muscle or gland. In contrast, when an **endocrine gland** is stimulated to release a hormone, the hormone enters the bloodstream and travels around the whole body. This means that the hormone is in the blood that arrives at every tissue, although they will not all react to it. So, to summarise, nerve impulses only travel along one particular route, while hormones travel around the entire body.

Consider this example. Imagine making a phone call to one of your friends. The information you tell that person goes straight to them and only them. That is similar to the way in which a nerve impulse travels – to one specified place. In contrast, however, if you were to go on television and deliver the same message, it would be broadcast to millions of people – but only those concerned about the message would respond. Similarly, hormones travel in the blood to all parts of the body, but only some parts respond.

Many hormones are proteins. They are secreted (released) following a specific stimulus. Although hormones are sent to all areas of the body, most of the tissues they arrive at 'ignore' their presence. It is only when a hormone arrives at a tissue which has the correct hormone receptor that the hormone has an effect.

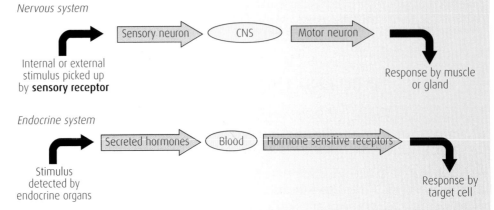

Nervous system

Internal or external stimulus picked up by **sensory receptor** — Sensory neuron — CNS — Motor neuron — Response by muscle or gland

Endocrine system

Stimulus detected by endocrine organs — Secreted hormones — Blood — Hormone sensitive receptors — Response by target cell

Comparing nervous and endocrine systems

HORMONE RECEPTORS

Hormone receptors are found embedded in the surface membrane of certain cells. When a hormone arrives at a cell with the correct receptor, having diffused out of the bloodstream, it attaches to the cell membrane. Each hormone only attaches to a matching receptor. In the diagram, the cell in tissue 1 has the necessary receptor sites for the hormone (and, therefore, is sensitive to it), but the cell in tissue 2 lacks the required receptor and does not react to the presence of the hormone.

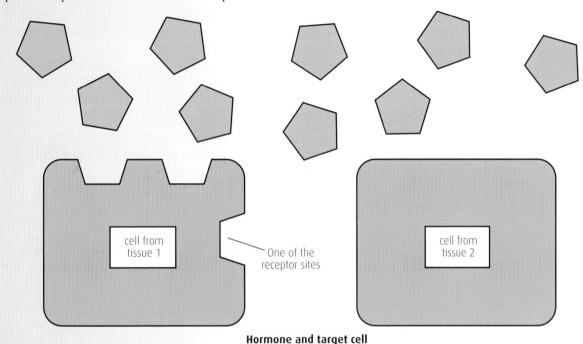

Hormone and target cell

Once a hormone has combined with the receptor on the cell membrane, a response occurs in the cytoplasm of that cell.

Although hormones are produced in tiny quantities, they have very important effects. The effects of some types of hormones can be long lasting. These are able to control the size to which the body grows, and can have an effect on mental development and personality. Other types of hormone have a more immediate effect and cause changes which last for a shorter period of time.

THINGS TO DO AND THINK ABOUT

1 Give two similarities and two differences between the control of body functions by the nervous system and the control by the endocrine system.

2 Place these statements in the correct order to show the sequence of events in hormonal control:

hormone binds to target cell receptors

stimulus is detected by endocrine organ

target cell makes a response

hormone is released

hormone travels in the bloodstream

3 Which of the control mechanisms, hormones or nerve impulses, is capable of having the longer lasting effect?

ONLINE TEST

Test yourself on this topic by taking the 'Control and communication 3' test online at www.brightredbooks.net/N5Biology

ONLINE

For more, check out the 'Endocrine system: facts, functions and diseases' at www.brightredbooks.net/N5Biology

DON'T FORGET

The nervous system relies on nerve impulses to carry information from one place to another in the body. The endocrine system operates by sending chemical messengers (hormones) in the bloodstream to travel to all parts of the body.

CONTROL AND COMMUNICATION: THE CONTROL OF BLOOD GLUCOSE LEVEL

It is essential that the conditions inside the body remain at the optimum for efficient function. There are systems in place that constantly monitor these conditions and that make sure that they are kept within tolerable boundaries. Some important conditions are body temperature, water content and blood sugar level.

A monitoring system in the brain detects the level of water in the blood and the core temperature of the body, and it makes adjustments if these are not within defined limits. The control of blood sugar is brought about by the action of the pancreas.

The body requires the release of energy in all cells. This is mainly achieved through the process of aerobic respiration. Glucose is continually being absorbed from the blood into cells for respiration.

MONITORING GLUCOSE LEVELS

To ensure that there is a constant supply of glucose for cell respiration, the body has regulating mechanisms. Glucose levels in the bloodstream are carefully controlled to make sure that there is sufficient sugar present in the blood for respiration to take place, but not so much that it stops the other systems of the body working properly.

When a meal is eaten, carbohydrates are digested. The final product of carbohydrate digestion, glucose, passes from the interior of the small intestine, through the villi walls and into the capillaries of the circulatory system. This causes a rise in the blood sugar level. The body has to be able to cope with the fact that we eat relatively large quantities of food at a time (raising the blood sugar level considerably) and then it can be quite some time before we eat again (causing the blood sugar level to drop substantially). The body monitors rising and falling glucose level and adjusts it accordingly.

THE PANCREAS

The pancreas is an organ situated just behind the stomach.

As well as producing digestive enzymes, the pancreas has a role to play in the regulation of blood sugar level. It is able to do this as it is an endocrine organ which produces two hormones, **insulin** and **glucagon**. These hormones are released directly into the bloodstream and have an immediate effect on blood sugar:

- insulin lowers the blood sugar level.
- glucagon raises the blood sugar level.

These two hormones work together to make sure that blood glucose is maintained at the correct level.

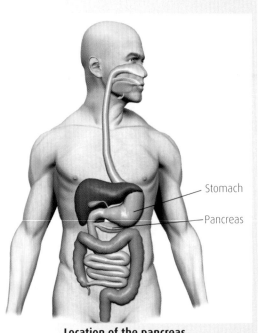

Stomach

Pancreas

Location of the pancreas

VIDEO LINK

For more on how the pancreas works, check out the clip 'Endocrine system, pancreas' at www.brightredbooks.net/N5Biology

THE LIVER

Another organ involved in the regulation of blood glucose is the liver. It is the largest internal organ in the body and is located just below the diaphragm, to the right of the stomach. It acts as a kind of storage facility for carbohydrate, removing glucose from the blood when the level is high and releasing glucose back into the blood when the level drops.

A rise in blood sugar to above the normal level is detected by receptor cells in the pancreas as blood flows through this organ. These receptor cells respond by producing the hormone insulin. The insulin is carried in the bloodstream to the liver. Here, insulin stimulates the liver cells to produce an enzyme that converts glucose to **glycogen** (a storage carbohydrate). About 100g of glycogen can be stored in the liver at any one time.

Glycogen is insoluble, making it a good storage compound. Because it is insoluble it has no osmotic effect. This is in contrast to glucose which, being soluble, can affect the balance of water in tissues.

If a long time has passed since a meal was eaten, the blood sugar level might drop below the normal level. This, again, is detected by a part of the pancreas as the blood flows through. A different response is triggered. The production of insulin slows down and a different hormone called glucagon is produced. This travels in the blood to the liver where it activates another enzyme that converts stored glycogen back to glucose. This is released into the blood from the liver, increasing the blood sugar level and returning it to the normal level.

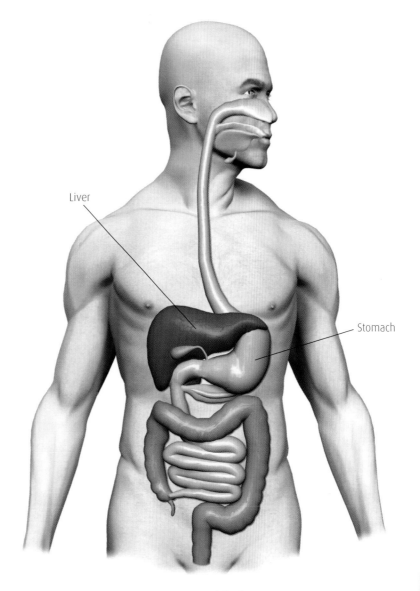

Location of the liver

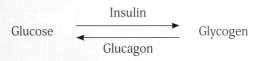
Glucose ⇄ Glycogen
Insulin
Glucagon

THINGS TO DO AND THINK ABOUT

Name the organ which is responsible for monitoring the blood sugar level and state its location in the body.

ONLINE TEST

Test yourself on this topic by taking the 'Control and communication 4' test online at www.brightredbooks.net/N5Biology

DON'T FORGET

Insulin lowers the blood sugar level by converting glucose to glycogen for storage. Glucagon raises the blood sugar level by converting glycogen back to glucose.

CONTROL AND COMMUNICATION: DIABETES

The disease diabetes is caused by the inability of some or all of the cells in the pancreas to make insulin. This lack of insulin causes the concentration of glucose in the blood to rise and remain above the normal level.

There are two main types of diabetes, known simply as type 1 and type 2.

ONLINE

Check out the NHS guide 'Diabetes, type 1' for more information at www.brightredbooks.net/N5Biology

TYPE 1 DIABETES

This type of diabetes is the form that is most common in children, but it can develop at any age. It is an autoimmune disease, meaning that the body's defence system mistakenly attacks certain cells in the pancreas, permanently destroying them. These cells can no longer produce insulin.

Without insulin, glucose cannot be moved out of the blood into the cells and the concentration of glucose in the blood increases. This can seriously damage the organs of the body. The body cells start to break down fat and muscle, leading to weight loss. Other symptoms include being very thirsty, needing to urinate often, feeling excessively tired and having skin infections.

The cause of type 1 diabetes is likely to be a combination of genetics and an environmental trigger. It is not yet fully understood why the body's immune system attacks the pancreas.

People with type 1 diabetes need to inject insulin regularly to manage their diabetes. It is a life-long condition and cannot be reversed. A carefully calculated diet, planned physical activity and regular blood glucose testing are required. Diabetes is a serious condition and it can lead to complications such as kidney disease, heart disease and stroke if left untreated.

TYPE 2 DIABETES

Type 2 diabetes occurs for one of two reasons: the cells of the pancreas fail to produce enough insulin to keep the blood sugar level normal or the cells of the body no longer react to the insulin that is produced, meaning that they cannot take up the glucose which is in the blood. This is known as insulin resistance.

Type 2 diabetes is a much more common disorder that type 1. It can potentially be avoided through correct exercise and diet. If a person develops extreme insulin resistance, they may need to take tablets or inject insulin to keep their blood sugar level stable.

This type of diabetes was once called adult-onset diabetes, but it is now becoming more common in children and teenagers. This increase has been linked to the increase in obesity. Other factors which can increase the risk of developing type 2 diabetes include having high blood pressure, having high cholesterol, being overweight and having a close family member with type 2 diabetes. The chances also increase with age.

Facts about type 2 diabetes:

- Type 2 diabetes is estimated to affect over 2·5 million people in the UK.
- If either parent has type 2 diabetes, the risk of inheriting it is 15%.
- If both parents have type 2 diabetes, the risk of inheriting it is 75%.
- Almost 1 in 3 people with type 2 diabetes develop the complication of kidney disease.

THINGS TO DO AND THINK ABOUT

1   Explain the roles of insulin and glucagon in maintaining a normal blood sugar level.

2   Describe what can go wrong in the body to cause diabetes.

DON'T FORGET

Diabetes is caused by a blockage in the hormone communication pathway due to a failure in the release of insulin or a failure to respond normally to insulin.

VIDEO LINK

Check out the NHS guide 'Diabetes, type 2' for more information at www. brightredbooks.net/ N5Biology

ONLINE TEST

Test yourself on this topic by taking the 'Control and communication 5' test online at www.brightredbooks.net/ N5Biology

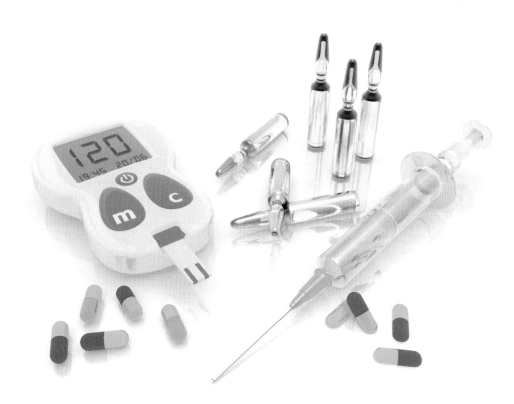

REPRODUCTION: THE STRUCTURES AND SITES OF GAMETE PRODUCTION

A **gamete** is a cell that fuses with another cell at fertilisation. Gamete is, therefore, another name for sex cell. Flowering plants produce gametes, as do animals that reproduce sexually.

GAMETE PRODUCTION IN PLANTS

Flowers are the organs of sexual reproduction in plants. Although the appearance of individual flowers can be quite different, the basic structures are the same. Most often, the flower contains both male and female parts. The diagram shows the main structures of a flower.

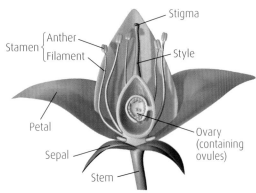

Structure of an insect-pollinated flower

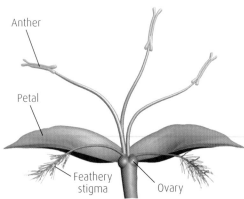

Structure of a wind-pollinated flower

Together, the filament and the anther make up the stamen. This is the male part of the flower and the anther produces pollen grains, which contain the male gametes.

The stigma, style and ovary make up the female part of the flower and the ovary produces ovules, which contain the female gametes.

The following table shows the function of each of the parts of the flower.

Part of flower	Function
Sepal	Protects the flower bud before opening
Petal	May be used to attract insects (often brightly coloured)
Stamen – anther	Produces pollen grains which each contain a male gamete
Stamen – filament	Holds the anther upright
Stigma	Traps pollen grains
Style	Leads from stigma to ovary
Ovary	Produces ovules
Ovule	Contains the female gamete

The type of flower shown in the top diagram has brightly coloured petals, may be pleasantly perfumed and has its sex organs (anthers and ovaries) inside the flower. These types of flowers are designed to attract insects for the process of pollination. Not all flowers have this structure. Some flowers are pollinated by the wind and, therefore, have no need for bright colours or strong scents. These flowers often have small greenish or brown petals and their sex organs hang out of the flower, exposed to the wind. The grass flower shown in the lower diagram is an example of a wind-pollinated flower.

POLLINATION

Once the flower has reached maturity and the pollen and ovules have been produced, the process of pollination takes place. Pollination is the transfer of pollen from the anther to the stigma. Usually, pollen from one flower lands on the stigma of another flower, but this can occur within the same flower. Insect-pollinated flowers have sticky stigmas, so that the pollen grains stay in place when they land there. Wind-pollinated flowers have stigmas that are feathery and hang out of the flower, acting like a net for trapping pollen grains.

Further development only takes place if the pollen lands on a stigma belonging to a flower of the same species.

FERTILISATION

After pollination has taken place, the pollen grain begins to grow a pollen tube. The tube grows through the tissues of the style and continues on towards the ovary. As it grows, the nucleus inside the pollen grain gradually makes its way down inside the tube. When the end of the pollen tube reaches an ovule in the ovary, it enters through a tiny hole. The tip of the pollen tube bursts, releasing the male gamete, which then fuses with the female gamete inside the ovule.

Fertilisation is the process by which the nucleus of the male gamete fuses with the nucleus of the female gamete to form a single cell. This is called a zygote. By repeated cell division, the zygote becomes a ball of cells which will eventually become an embryo plant. The ovule develops into a seed, acting as a food store for the embryo. The ovary, now containing the seeds, undergoes changes to become a fruit.

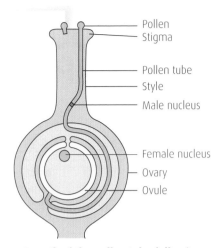

Growth of the pollen tube following pollination

GAMETE PRODUCTION IN ANIMALS

Like plants, animals produce gametes in specialised sex organs. In human males, sperm are produced in the testes and in females, eggs (or ova) are produced in the ovaries.

Sperm cells are the smallest human cells. They have a head containing a nucleus with a small amount of cytoplasm, some mitochondria and a long tail.

Millions of sperm cells are being produced in the testes at any one time. They are able to swim as long as they are in a fluid, by moving their tails backwards and forwards. They are released from the testes and travel along the sperm duct, leaving the male body through the penis.

Egg cells are the largest human cells. An egg has a nucleus and much more cytoplasm than the sperm cell. Egg cells are unable to move themselves and rely on other parts of the reproductive system to move them from one place to another.

Usually, only one egg cell is produced at a time. It is released from an ovary and cilia inside the oviduct help the egg to travel along towards the uterus. If the egg cell meets a sperm cell and fertilisation occurs in the oviduct, a zygote forms. This divides many times to form an embryo, which will then embed into the uterus wall to be nourished as it develops into a fetus.

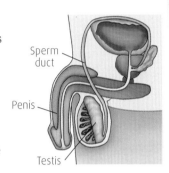

Male reproductive system

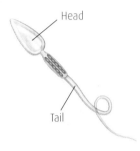

A sperm cell

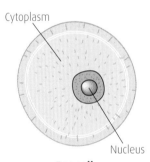

Egg cell

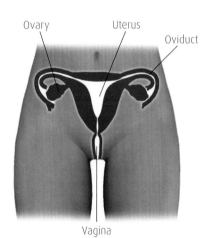

Female reproductive system

DON'T FORGET

'Gamete' is the name for any sex cell, whether it is produced by a plant or an animal.

THINGS TO DO AND THINK ABOUT

1   Name the sites of production of both the male and female gametes in a flowering plant.

2   What is pollination?

3   Name the male and female gametes in humans.

4   Give a definition of the term 'fertilisation'.

ONLINE TEST

Test yourself on this topic by taking the 'The structures and sites of gamete production' test online at www.brightredbooks.net/N5Biology

REPRODUCTION: DIPLOID BODY CELLS AND HAPLOID GAMETES

SEXUAL REPRODUCTION AND VARIATION

Variation can be categorised as **continuous** or **discrete** (this is explored in the next chapter). Sexual reproduction gives rise to the variation which exists among members of a species. This is because the single cell formed at fertilisation contains genes from each of the two parents and has, therefore, a new combination of genetic information.

The nucleus of every cell contains chromosomes. The number of chromosomes in cells varies from species to species, but is always the same in every body cell in a particular plant or animal. The number of chromosomes in each body cell is known as the **diploid** number. A diploid cell is one that contains two sets of chromosomes. One set of chromosomes comes from each parent.

The diploid number of a cell is known as 2n, where n represents the number of chromosomes in one set; so, 2n is a simple way of stating that the cell has two sets of chromosomes. In humans the 2n number is 46. This means that humans have two sets of 23 chromosomes.

A zygote forms when fertilisation takes place. The zygote is the result of two gametes joining together. Each gamete brings one whole set of chromosomes (the n number). When the gametes fuse, they create a zygote with two sets of chromosomes (the 2n number).

Organism	Diploid number (2n)	Haploid number (n)
Human	46	23
Chicken	78	39
Horse	64	32
Pineapple	50	25
Potato	48	24
Wheat	42	21
Lyon	38	19

While cells which contain two sets of chromosomes are described as diploid, cells such as gametes which have only one set of chromosomes are described as **haploid**. It is essential that gametes are haploid so that a zygote, produced by the joining of two gametes, can be diploid. As all body cells are produced from the repeated division of the zygote, all body cells have the diploid number of chromosomes.

Examples of diploid and haploid numbers of chromosomes of different organisms are shown in the table.

DON'T FORGET

The haploid number (n) is only found in the gametes; the diploid number (2n) is found in the nucleus of all other body cells.

HUMAN CELLS AS EXAMPLES OF ANIMAL CELLS

The male gamete, sperm, has one set of 23 chromosomes in its nucleus. The female gamete, the egg, also has one set of 23 chromosomes in its nucleus.

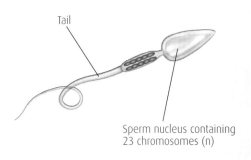

Tail

Sperm nucleus containing 23 chromosomes (n)

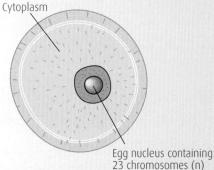

Cytoplasm

Egg nucleus containing 23 chromosomes (n)

Chromosome complement in human gametes

contd

When fertilisation takes place, both the male and female nuclei join together to form a zygote containing the chromosomes from each of the gametes. The zygote, therefore, has two sets of 23 chromosomes, making a total of 46 altogether:

- 23 is the haploid number of chromosomes in a human
- 46 is the diploid number.

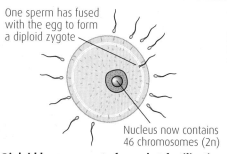
One sperm has fused with the egg to form a diploid zygote

Nucleus now contains 46 chromosomes (2n)

Diploid human zygote formed at fertilisation

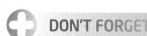
ROSE CELLS AS EXAMPLES OF PLANT CELLS

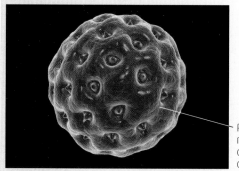

Pollen grain nucleus containing seven chromosomes (n)

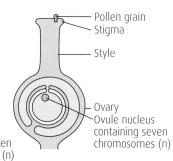

Pollen grain
Stigma
Style
Ovary
Ovule nucleus containing seven chromosomes (n)

Chromosome complement in rose gametes

When fertilisation takes place, both nuclei join together to form a zygote containing the chromosomes from each of the gametes. The zygote therefore has two sets of seven chromosomes, making a total of 14 altogether:

- 7 is the haploid number of chromosomes in a rose
- 14 is the diploid number.

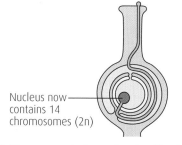

Nucleus now contains 14 chromosomes (2n)

Diploid rose zygote formed at fertilisation

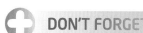

THINGS TO DO AND THINK ABOUT

1 The table shows various types of cells. Decide whether each of them contains the haploid or the diploid number of cells for that species and tick the correct box.

2 Explain why all gametes are haploid.

3 Complete the table to give the haploid or diploid number for each of the organisms shown.

Type of cell	Haploid number	Diploid number
Cell from a human liver		
Pollen grain from a daffodil		
Skin cell from a rabbit		
Cheek cell from a pig		
Sperm cell from a salmon		
Ovule from a daisy		

Type of organism	Haploid number	Diploid number
Red deer		68
Cotton plant		52
Earthworm	18	
Cabbage		18
Cow	30	
Cat	19	

VARIATION AND INHERITANCE 1

Shape of aspen leaves

Pattern of cone shells

Human faces

AN INTRODUCTION TO VARIATION

The members of a species are not identical, even though they all possess genetic information for the same range of characteristics. Individuals show variations which make them different from one another.

Some variations may be due to effects of the environment which influence the development of an individual. These variations are unimportant to the species as a whole because they are not passed on from parent to offspring.

Other variations are caused by differences in the genetic information of individuals and these can be inherited. Sexual reproduction involves combining genetic information from both parents. This allows mixing of genes in different ways and so contributes to variation. The photographs show some examples of variation between members of the same species.

Genes can exist in different forms, each capable of producing a variant of a particular characteristic. The different forms of a **gene** are called **alleles**.

DISCRETE VARIATION

Discrete variation of a characteristic shows only a limited number of distinct possibilities. This type of variation is found in characteristics that are coded by a single gene with a limited number of forms or alleles.

Discrete variation has been important in the study of inheritance. Characteristics which have easily recognised variants are observed in successive generations. The patterns of their inheritance have allowed researchers to work out the mechanism involved.

Examples of discrete variation in humans include:

● ear lobe shape

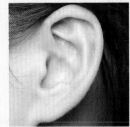

A) Free ear lobes

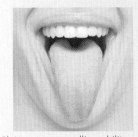

B) Attached ear lobes

● tongue-rolling ability.

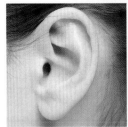

A) Tongue-rolling ability

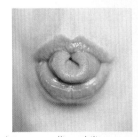

B) Non-tongue rolling ability

● blood groups

There are four possible blood groups. These are:

1 Group A   2 Group B   3 Group AB   4 Group O

CONTINUOUS VARIATION

Continuous variation of a characteristic shows a continuous range of possibilities between a minimum and a maximum value. There are no distinct groups and an individual's characteristic may have a value anywhere in the overall range of possibilities.

Continuous variation occurs because several different genes influence the same characteristic. Such a characteristic is said to be **polygenic**. When a number of genes contribute to a characteristic, it means that there are many different combinations of the various alleles involved. This produces many possible values for that characteristic, forming a continuous range of possibilities.

Examples of continuous variation include height, weight and hand span. Most visible characteristics are polygenic. It is probable that even some of those characteristics which show discrete variation and that are explained by single gene inheritance are influenced by more than one gene.

When the values for a polygenic characteristic are collected for a large number of individuals, it is found that they always show the same pattern of distribution. Relatively few individuals show values close to the extremes of the range. Most individuals show values close to the middle of the range, in other words a value close to the average.

This type of distribution is called a normal distribution. When it is plotted as a graph or chart, it shows a typical bell-shaped curve.

The photograph below shows a small group of people, all from the same university department, standing in order of their heights (in feet and inches).

The graph which follows it shows the distribution of their heights (in centimetres). The distribution is not a perfect normal distribution but the dotted line shows the overall pattern. If the sample size had been greater (more people included) then we would expect the pattern of height distribution to be closer to the typical normal distribution.

ONLINE TEST

Check how well you've learned about variation online at www.brightredbooks.net/N5Biology

DON'T FORGET

The production of haploid gametes from diploid body cells and the random combination of gametes at fertilisation both contribute to genetic variation.

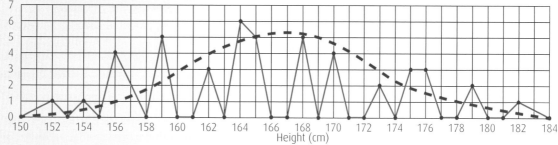

The distribution of heights in a group of people

THINGS TO DO AND THINK ABOUT

1   What is the most common height of the people in the group?

2   Can you calculate their average height to the nearest centimetre?

VARIATION AND INHERITANCE 2

INHERITANCE OF GENETIC INFORMATION

Inheritance is the passage of genetic information from parent to offspring. The characteristics that are coded in that information can be followed from one generation to the next. Organisms receive genetic information from both parents, giving them two complete sets of chromosomes (diploid). Therefore, they possess two pieces of genetic information (or two alleles) for every characteristic.

IMPORTANT DEFINITIONS FOR GENETICS AND INHERITANCE

Term	Definition
Phenotype	This is a description of a characteristic as it appears in an individual. For example, free ear lobes, green pea seeds and blood group A are all phenotypes.
Genotype	This is the inherited information of an organism. When studying inheritance, the genotype usually refers to the information for only one or two characteristics, rather than to all the genetic information of the organism. In other words, the genotype identifies the particular alleles of a gene that the organism possesses.
Dominant	When two *different* alleles of a gene are present in an organism, the dominant allele shows its effect and the effect of the other allele is masked. For example, if a person carries both the allele for tongue-rolling ability and the allele for non-tongue rolling, the person will be able to roll their tongue. This is because the allele for tongue-rolling is dominant over the allele for non-tongue rolling.
Recessive	This is the opposite of dominant. It refers to the allele which does not show its effect when two different alleles of a characteristic are present. For example, the allele for non-tongue rolling is recessive to the allele for tongue rolling.
Homozygous	If the two alleles that an organism possesses for a characteristic are the same, the organism is said to be homozygous for that characteristic. For example, if a person has two alleles for tongue-rolling ability, they are homozygous for tongue rolling. If they have two alleles for non-tongue rolling, they are homozygous for non-tongue rolling.
Heterozygous	If the two alleles that an organism possesses for a characteristic are different, the organism is said to be heterozygous for that characteristic. For example, if a person possesses one allele for tongue-rolling ability and one allele for non-tongue rolling, they are heterozygous for tongue rolling. They will be able to roll their tongue because this is the dominant trait.

DON'T FORGET

Your understanding of all the definitions given in the table is crucial for you to be able to understand and answer questions on genetics.

VIDEO LINK

For more information about Gregor Mendel and his work, watch the video at www.brightredbooks.net/N5Biology

GREGOR MENDEL

Gregor Mendel was an Austrian monk and a scientist. He carried out experiments on inheritance using garden pea plants. For his experiments, Mendel established groups of pea plants with a particular characteristic which was always inherited by their offspring when they were crossed together. He referred to these plants as 'true-breeding'. We would now refer to them as being homozygous.

The characteristics showed discrete variation, each having only two possible phenotypes.

The characteristics Mendel studied in his experiments were seed shape, seed colour, flower colour, pod shape, pod colour, flower position and stem length.

One of Mendel's experiments was to cross homozygous purple-flowered plants with homozygous white-flowered plants. Mendel called these the parental generation (P generation).

All the offspring had purple flowers. Mendel called this the first filial generation (F_1 generation).

F_1 plants were crossed together to produce a second filial generation (F_2 generation).

contd

The F$_2$ generation contained both purple-flowered plants and white-flowered plants in a 3:1 ratio.

Mendel carried out this investigation many times and did the same using homozygous plants with the other pairs of characteristics. His results were always the same. The F$_1$ generation always showed one phenotype (the dominant one) and the F$_2$ generation always showed a 3:1 ratio of the dominant:recessive phenotypes.

From these results, Mendel produced his first law of inheritance in 1866. It states that, during the formation of reproductive cells (gametes), pairs of hereditary factors (genes) for a specific trait separate so that offspring receive one factor from each parent. In other words, his pea plants contained two alleles for flower colour and each had an equal chance of being passed on to the offspring.

Characteristic	Seed shape	Seed colour	Flower colour	Pod colour
Possible phenotypes	Round seeds	Yellow seeds	Purple flowers	Green pods
	Wrinkled seeds	Green seeds	White flower	Yellow pods

Mendel's peas: four of the seven characteristics studied by Mendel

THE MECHANISM OF INHERITANCE

Symbols are used to represent the alleles involved in a genetic cross. An upper-case letter is used for a dominant allele and the same lower-case letter is used for the recessive allele.

- Y represents the allele for yellow seed colour.
- y represents the allele for green seed colour.

P generation phenotypes yellow-seeded plants × green-seeded plants
P generation genotypes **YY** × **yy**
P generation gamete genotypes all **Y** all **y**
F$_1$ generation genotype all **Yy**
F$_1$ generation phenotype all yellow-seeded plants
F$_1$ generation genotypes **Yy** × **Yy**
F$_1$ gamete genotypes 50% **Y** and 50% **y** 50% **Y** and 50% **y**

F$_2$ generation genotypes can be the result of a number of different possible gamete combinations at fertilisation. These can be represented using a Punnett square.

F$_2$ genotypes **YY Yy Yy** **yy** (1:2:1 genotype ratio)
F$_2$ phenotypes yellow-seeded plants green-seeded plants (3:1 phenotype ratio)

Punnett squares can be used to predict the results of any cross where the genotypes of the parents are known.

		Gametes from first parent	
		Y	y
Gametes from second parent	Y	YY	Yy
	y	Yy	yy

Possible F$_2$ genotypes

 THINGS TO DO AND THINK ABOUT

Use a Punnett square to predict the phenotype ratios of the offspring from the following crosses:

1 a heterozygous purple-flowered plant with a white-flowered plant

2 a heterozygous purple-flowered plant with a homozygous purple-flowered plant.

THE NEED FOR TRANSPORT IN PLANTS 1

PLANT TRANSPORT SYSTEMS

Plants have two types of transporting tissue:

1 **xylem** tissue, which is responsible for the movement of water and minerals from the roots to the leaves of the plant

2 **phloem** tissue, which is responsible for transporting sugar throughout the plant.

THE MOVEMENT OF WATER AND MINERALS

There is a continuous movement of water from the roots of a plant to the leaves. The movement is always in that one direction and it is responsible for supplying plant cells with water and minerals. This movement of water involves a number of structures and processes.

The entry of water into plants

Plants obtain water and minerals from the soil through structures called root hairs. Root hairs can be seen on germinating seedlings such as radish. Each root hair is part of a specialised cell.

The root hairs come into close contact with the layer of water which surrounds soil particles. They provide a large surface area for the efficient uptake of water and minerals. Water enters root hair cells by osmosis. Minerals enter these cells by active transport.

The movement of water from cell to cell in plants

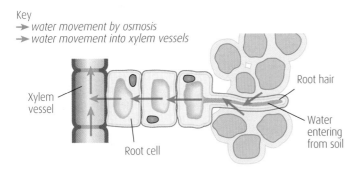

Key
→ water movement by osmosis
→ water movement into xylem vessels

Xylem vessel
Root cell
Root hair
Water entering from soil

Water movement across roots

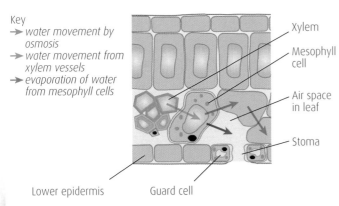

Key
→ water movement by osmosis
→ water movement from xylem vessels
→ evaporation of water from mesophyll cells

Xylem
Mesophyll cell
Air space in leaf
Stoma
Lower epidermis
Guard cell

Water movement in leaf

Once water has entered a plant, it moves through the cells of the root by osmosis. The root hair cells have a higher water concentration than cells further inside the root because of the water they have absorbed from the soil, so there is a continual movement of water by osmosis across the root from the outermost cells to the inner cells adjacent to the xylem vessels in the centre of the root. Water movement in the xylem is always in the same direction, from the roots to the leaves. Minerals are carried in solution in the xylem. It is from the xylem that cells throughout the plant receive both the water and minerals they require.

There is a similar continual movement of water by osmosis in the leaves of a plant. Water evaporates from mesophyll cells of the leaf into the leaf air spaces. The cells which lose water have a lower water concentration than other cells. Osmosis takes place from cells which obtain water from xylem vessels to the cells which have lost water.

The water which evaporates from the mesophyll cells diffuses to the outside air through pores called **stomata** (singular – stoma) which are found in the lower epidermis of plant leaves. This loss of water from plant leaves is called **transpiration** and it is the main cause of the movement of water up the xylem vessels in the plant.

contd

Water movement in xylem vessels

Xylem vessels are formed from elongated cells which have died, losing their contents and their end cell walls. The remaining cell walls become strengthened with deposits of **lignin** in characteristic patterns. The lignin is deposited on the inside of the cell walls in rings or spirals. Gradually, the deposits of lignin become more widespread until most of the inner walls of the xylem vessel are covered. The dead cells of the xylem form continuous hollow tubes which run from the roots of a plant, up the stem and into the leaves.

The upwards movement of water in plants can be demonstrated by placing a stalk of celery in coloured water. The colour eventually appears in the leaves of the celery, showing that it has been transported upwards from the base of the stalk. If the celery is cut, the location of the xylem vessels can be clearly seen.

The overall movement of water through a plant is known as the transpiration stream. It is represented in the following diagram by the blue arrows.

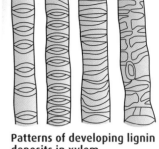

Patterns of developing lignin deposits in xylem

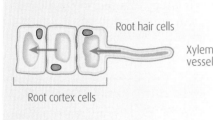
Root hair cells
Root cortex cells

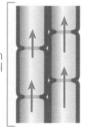
Xylem vessel

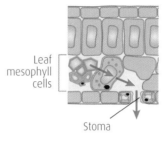
Leaf mesophyll cells
Stoma

The transpiration stream

THE TRANSPORT OF SUGAR

Sugar is produced in the leaves of plants by photosynthesis. Plants use sugar for a number of different functions.

sugar
- used in respiration to release energy for use by cells
- converted to cellulose for the formation of cell walls
- converted to starch for storage
- used in the manufacture of other substances such as proteins and fats

This means that sugar is transported in a plant according to its requirements at any given time. Transport of sugar can be in any direction.

The transport of sugar takes place in phloem tissue. Like xylem, phloem tissue is formed from elongated cells which become arranged into vessels. However, the cells which form phloem vessels are still living, although they are highly adapted to enable them to transport material efficiently.

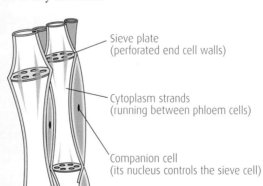
Sieve plate (perforated end cell walls)
Cytoplasm strands (running between phloem cells)
Companion cell (its nucleus controls the sieve cell)

Phloem vessels

THINGS TO DO AND THINK ABOUT

1 Apart from the transport of water and dissolved minerals, suggest one other benefit a plant gains from having vessels strengthened with lignin running up its length from roots to leaves.

2 In a potato plant, suggest two reasons why sugar sometimes moves downwards from the leaves to underground parts of the plant and one reason why it moves upwards from underground parts.

THE NEED FOR TRANSPORT IN PLANTS 2

TRANSPIRATION

As stated earlier, transpiration involves evaporation of water from the mesophyll cells in the leaves of plants. This means transpiration is affected by the same abiotic factors that influence evaporation. The rate of evaporation from plants and the effect of these factors can be measured using a piece of apparatus called a potometer. Diagrams of two types of potometer are shown below.

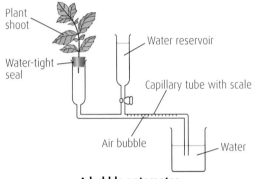

A bubble potometer

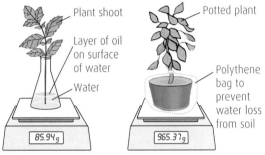

Weight potometers

Bubble potometer

Bubble potometers measure the rate at which water is absorbed by the plant shoot. When water is lost by transpiration from the leaves, more water moves from the leaf xylem into the leaf mesophyll cells. This causes upwards movement of water in the xylem vessels, causing water to be drawn into the bottom ends of the xylem vessels.

The rate of this uptake of water can be measured by the rate of movement of the air bubble along the capillary tube. The water reservoir on the potometer allows the air bubble to be reset so that repeated measurements can be taken.

Weight potometer

Weight potometers measure the rate at which water is lost from the leaves of the plant or plant shoot. This is done by recording the weight of the plant or the shoot over a period of time. It is important that only water lost from the leaves is measured. To make sure of this, if a plant shoot is being used, a layer of oil is put on the surface of the water in the container to prevent evaporation.

If a whole plant is used, a polythene bag is secured around the stem of the plant and its pot for the same purpose.

FACTORS AFFECTING TRANSPIRATION

The effects of abiotic factors on transpiration

Once the rate of transpiration from a plant has been measured several times and an average value calculated, the effects of various abiotic factors can be investigated by changing the conditions and taking more measurements. Details are shown in the table.

Abiotic factor	How the factor is altered	Effect of an increase in the factor on the rate of transpiration
Temperature	Move the apparatus to a warmer or cooler situation	Increase
Humidity	Enclose the whole apparatus in a transparent container	Decrease
Air movement	Place a fan close to the apparatus	Increase
Light	Place additional lamps close to the apparatus (Use a heat shield to avoid causing an increase in temperature when doing this.)	Increase

The effects of changes in temperature, humidity and air movement on the rate of transpiration are to be expected, since these factors affect evaporation in the same way. However, changes in light intensity do not affect evaporation but do affect transpiration. This is because of the response of the **guard cells** surrounding the stomata to changes in light intensity. Stomata are open when it is light and closed when it is dark.

STOMATA

Stomata are the tiny pores found in the epidermis of plant leaves, mainly on the lower leaf surface. They are important in allowing carbon dioxide to enter the air spaces, so that it can be absorbed and used in photosynthesis. The number and shape of stomata vary from one plant species to another. Typically there are between 100 and 1000 stomata per square millimetre of leaf surface area.

Each **stoma** is surrounded by two specialised guard cells. The shape and structure of the guard cells cause them to bend when they are turgid. This opens a gap between them. The gap is the open stoma. When the guard cells are flaccid, they become closer together and so the stoma is closed.

Stomata from two different plants

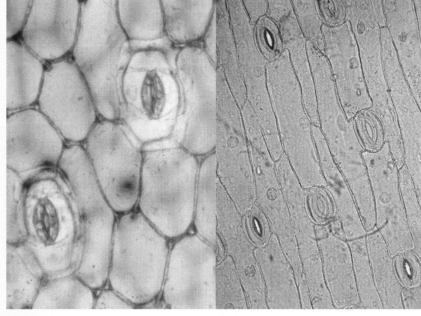

Cranberry   *Rockcress*

Water vapour passes out of the stomata during transpiration. The ability of the guard cells to open and close the stomata is important because it allows the stomata to close at night when photosynthesis does not take place. This reduces water loss from the plant at a time when it has no requirement for carbon dioxide uptake.

The appearance and relative number of stomata differ from species to species.

Opening and closing of stomata

The mechanism of stomata opening and closing is complex. Guard cells are the only cells of the leaf epidermis to contain chloroplasts. The part of the cell wall of a guard cell which borders the stoma pore is much thicker than the cell wall elsewhere in the cell. Both these facts are involved in the mechanism.

A model stoma can be made using dialysis tubing to demonstrate the opening and closing.

Two dialysis tubing bags are partially filled with strong sugar solution

The bags are held together at each end with elastic bands

The bags are then immersed in water.

Water enters the bags by osmosis making them turgid.

As this happens the bags swell and bend apart.

VIDEO LINK

For more on stomata, watch the video at www.brightredbooks.net/N5Biology

ONLINE TEST

Test yourself on transpiration at www.brightredbooks.net/N5Biology

THINGS TO DO AND THINK ABOUT

1 Why are the stomata found mostly on the lower surface of leaves?

2 What type of plant leaves have stomata only on the upper surface?

THE BLOOD CIRCULATORY SYSTEM IN MAMMALS 1

THE ROLE OF THE BLOOD IN TRANSPORT

Blood consists of two parts:

- liquid plasma which contains dissolved materials
- blood cells.

Both the plasma and the red blood cells are important for the transport of materials around the body.

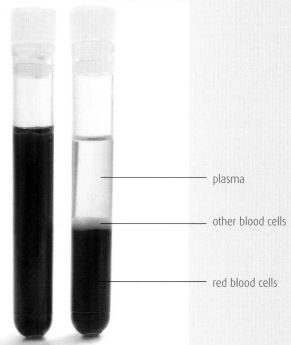

plasma

other blood cells

red blood cells

Unseparated and separated blood

The role of the blood circulatory system in the transport of hormones that are involved in the control and regulation of body processes has been mentioned earlier. In addition to the transport of hormones, blood is used to transport nutrients, oxygen, carbon dioxide and urea. Some details of these transport functions of blood are shown in the table.

Substance	Where it enters the blood	Where it leaves the blood	How it is transported	Use in the body
Glucose	Small intestine	Body cells	In solution in the plasma	Used as an energy source in respiration. Excess is stored in the liver as glycogen or converted to fat.
Amino acids	Small intestine	Body cells	In solution in the plasma	Used to make proteins. Excess is broken down in the liver to produce waste urea.
Oxygen	Lungs	Body cells	In the red blood cells	Used in respiration to release energy from glucose.
Carbon dioxide	Body cells	Lungs	Most in the plasma and a little in the red blood cells	Waste material produced during respiration.
Urea	Liver	Kidneys	In solution in the plasma	Waste material produced from excess amino acids.

RED BLOOD CELLS

Red blood cells are the most numerous type of cell in our blood. Approximately one quarter of all our body cells are red blood cells. Our blood contains about 6 million red blood cells per cubic millimetre (mm^3). A red blood cell lasts for about 120 days before it is broken down and replaced. Our bodies produce about 2·4 million new red blood cells every second.

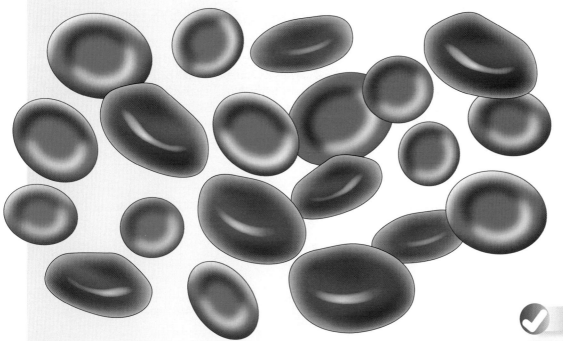

Red blood cells

Red blood cells are very small but, even so, they can only pass through the smallest blood vessels, the capillaries, in *single file*. They are described as being biconcave in shape. This means they are flattened discs that are thinner in the middle than at the edge.

The function of red blood cells is to carry oxygen from the lungs to the body cells. They are able to do this because they contain a chemical called haemoglobin, which reacts with oxygen to form a temporary complex molecule called oxyhaemoglobin. At the lungs, oxygen from the air reacts with the haemoglobin and is carried by the red blood cells. At the body tissues, the oxyhaemoglobin releases the oxygen which is then available to the cells of the body.

This can be represented as a chemical equation.

in the blood capillaries of the lungs

oxygen + haemoglobin $\xrightleftharpoons{}$ oxyhaemoglobin

in the blood capillaries of the body tissues

Red blood cells do not have a nucleus. This is the reason why they have a short life span and need to be replaced.

THINGS TO DO AND THINK ABOUT

Suggest how the lack of a nucleus and the distinctive shape of a red blood cell both contribute to its efficiency in transporting oxygen from the lungs to the cells of the body.

ONLINE TEST

Test yourself on transport functions of blood at www.brightredbooks.net/N5Biology

VIDEO LINK

Watch the clip on how oxygen is transported in blood at www.brightredbooks.net/N5Biology

DON'T FORGET

1 Red blood cells transport oxygen and a little carbon dioxide. All other materials are transported in solution by the plasma.
2 In addition to the transport of materials, the blood is also important in distributing heat around the body.

THE BLOOD CIRCULATORY SYSTEM IN MAMMALS 2

THE STRUCTURE OF THE CIRCULATORY SYSTEM

Blood is pumped round the body by the muscular heart. The blood passes through the heart twice in one complete circuit. This is important because it means that the blood pressure remains high as the blood carries its contents to the body cells. One loop of the circuit takes the blood from the heart to the lungs and back to the heart. In the lungs the blood gains oxygen and loses waste carbon dioxide. The second loop of the system takes the freshly oxygenated blood from the heart round the rest of the body and back to the heart. As the blood travels round this loop, the body cells gain oxygen and nutrients, and get rid of carbon dioxide.

Heart structure

The following diagram shows the structure of a dissected heart and it's major blood vessels.

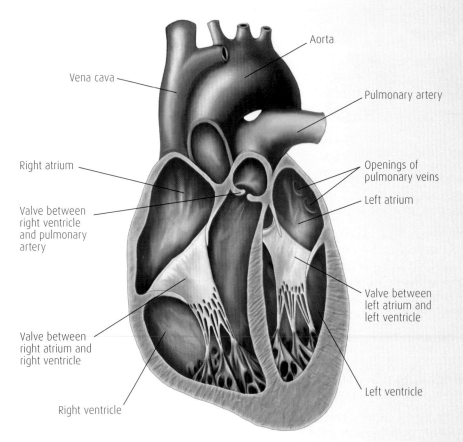

Dissected heart

Notice the much thicker muscular wall of the left **ventricle** compared to the right ventricle. This is because the left ventricle has to pump blood round the whole of the body, whereas the right ventricle pumps blood only to the lungs.

The heart contains four **valves** which prevent the blood from flowing backwards during the heart contractions. There is a valve between the **atrium** and the ventricle on each side of the heart and a valve between the ventricle and the main **artery** which leaves the ventricle. In the photograph, the valve between the left atrium and left ventricle can be seen, as can the valve between the left ventricle and the **aorta**.

contd

The pathway of blood round the body

The following diagram shows the route taken by the blood around the body.

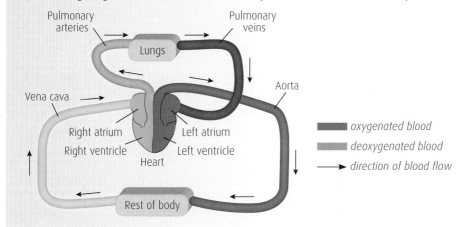

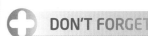

DON'T FORGET

1 Arteries always carry blood away from the heart. Veins always carry blood towards the heart.
2 The atria (singular atrium) are the receiving chambers of the heart. The ventricles are the pumping chambers.
3 The left ventricle has a thicker muscular wall than the right ventricle because it needs to pump the blood further than the right ventricle.
4 Diagrams showing body structures are always presented as though the organism is facing you. This means that the right-hand side of the diagram represents the left-hand side of the organism.

BLOOD VESSELS

Blood is carried round the body in three different types of blood vessel. The different blood vessels have different structures to match their different functions.

Arteries

Arteries carry blood away from the heart. This blood is under high pressure and so arteries have a relatively narrow channel and thick muscular walls to help maintain the pressure of the blood as it travels round the body.

The pulmonary arteries carry deoxygenated blood from the right ventricle to the lungs where it gains oxygen.

The largest artery is the aorta which carries oxygenated blood from the left ventricle. Smaller arteries branch from the aorta to carry the blood to particular areas and organs.

The first branch from the aorta is the **coronary artery**. This is located within the wall of the heart and supplies the heart muscle with nutrients and oxygen.

Veins

Veins carry blood towards the heart. The blood is returning from tissues and organs of the body. The **pulmonary veins** from the lungs carry oxygenated blood to the left atrium of the heart, so that it can be pumped to the rest of the body. Veins from these other parts of the body feed into the largest vein, called the **vena cava**, which takes the deoxygenated blood to the right atrium.

The blood in the veins is at low pressure and so veins have a thinner muscle layer in their walls and a wider channel than the arteries. This means that the veins do not create much resistance to the flow of blood. Veins also have valves at intervals along their length so that the slow-moving blood does not begin to flow backwards.

Capillaries

Capillaries are the blood vessels which link the arteries and veins. They form a network of vessels in the tissues of the body. Capillaries are microscopic in size and have very thin walls, only one cell thick at their finest. A network of capillaries produces a large surface area for the efficient exchange of materials between the blood and the body cells.

VIDEO LINK

Watch the clip for a video on capillaries at www.brightredbooks.net/N5Biology

Cross-sections of blood vessels

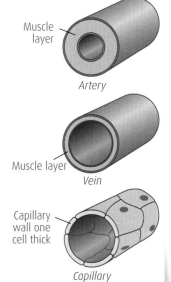

Muscle layer

Artery

Muscle layer

Vein

Capillary wall one cell thick

Capillary

ONLINE TEST

Test yourself on the structure of the circulatory system at www.brightredbooks.net/N5Biology

THINGS TO DO AND THINK ABOUT

Using the names of the major blood vessels and the chambers of the heart, describe the path of a red blood cell from the time it leaves the lungs until it returns back to the lungs.

GAS EXCHANGE IN THE LUNGS OF MAMMALS

The blood circulatory system is responsible for transporting both oxygen and carbon dioxide. The exchange of these gases between the blood and the air takes place in alveoli, or air sacs, in the lungs.

THE MOVEMENT OF AIR INTO AND OUT OF THE LUNGS

Before gas exchange can take place, air must enter the lungs from the atmosphere. This is achieved by the actions of the ribs and the diaphragm. The ribs are connected to the bones of the spine at the back and to the breast bone at the front. Together these form a protective cage-like structure which surrounds the lungs. The diaphragm is a muscular sheet underneath the lungs. Movement of the ribs and the diaphragm increase and decrease the volume of the lungs. This forces air in and out.

The breathing system

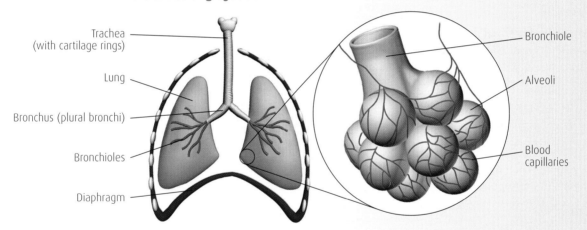

The mechanism of breathing

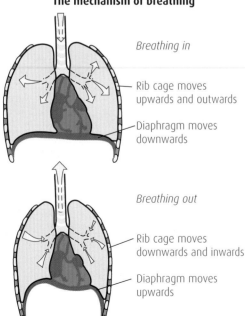

Air passages in the nose and mouth are connected to the trachea. This divides into two bronchi, one going into each lung. Each **bronchus** divides repeatedly into smaller and smaller air tubes called **bronchioles**. The trachea is strengthened by rings of cartilage which prevents it from kinking when moving the neck. Cartilage rings are also present in the bronchi and the larger bronchioles to prevent these air passages from collapsing during inhalation.

Finally the bronchioles end in microscopic bubble-like air sacs called alveoli.

The breathing mechanism

Contraction of muscles between the ribs causes the ribs to move upwards and outwards. Contraction of the muscles of the diaphragm causes it to be pulled downwards. These movements increase the volume of the lung cavity and reduce the pressure in the lungs. Air is forced into the lungs from the outside. The lungs expand as air flows through the trachea, bronchi, bronchioles and into the alveoli.

When the muscles of the ribcage and diaphragm relax, the reverse happens and air is forced out of the lungs.

These actions are shown in the diagram.

GAS EXCHANGE IN THE ALVEOLI

The alveoli of the lungs are microscopic. They are bubble-like structures with walls that are only one cell thick. Together they provide a very large surface area for gas exchange. Capillary blood vessels form a network over the outside of the alveoli. Gas exchange takes place between the blood in the capillaries and the air in the alveoli.

There is a higher concentration of oxygen in the alveolar air than in the blood, so oxygen diffuses from the air into the blood. It has only to pass through the wall of the **alveolus** and the wall of the blood capillary, both just one cell thick. At the same time, carbon dioxide diffuses in the opposite direction because the blood has a higher concentration of carbon dioxide than air.

The difference in the concentration of each of the two gases in the air compared to the blood is always maintained. This is because the air in the alveoli is always being replaced with fresh air from the outside and the blood is always being replaced as it continues to move through the capillaries.

The large number of alveoli and the extensive network of blood capillaries which surround them create a large surface area for the diffusion of gases between the blood and the air in the alveoli.

Gas exchange in an alveolus

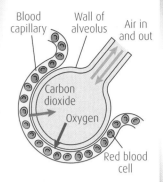

KEEPING THE LUNGS CLEAN

The trachea, bronchi and bronchioles of the breathing system are lined with a layer that contains two specialised types of cell:

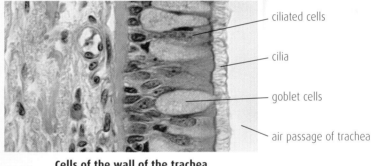

Cells of the wall of the trachea

- Ciliated cells have hair-like projections called **cilia** which can move with a whip-like action.

- Goblet cells produce sticky mucus which is secreted from the cells onto the walls of the air passages.

The mucus is important because it traps particles of dirt and any microorganisms which are breathed in. The constant movements of the cilia sweep the mucus and any trapped material away from the lungs and towards the back of the throat. We are not normally aware of this and we swallow the mucus. Any harmful materials are destroyed by the acids and enzymes of the stomach.

DON'T FORGET

It is the movements of the rib cage and the diaphragm which cause the expansion and contraction of the lungs. Which of these actions is predominant during periods of shallow breathing?

 THINGS TO DO AND THINK ABOUT

The breathing movements involve the creation of low pressure in the air passages. This could cause the walls of the air passages to collapse inwards, cutting off the flow of air. Bending the neck could cause a kink in the trachea with the same result.

Look at the diagram of the breathing system above. Notice the stripy pattern on the trachea and other air passages. This is due to C-shaped bands of tough cartilage on the outside of the air passages.

1   Suggest a function for the bands of cartilage.

2   What similar example have you come across from the structure of plants?

 VIDEO LINK

Watch the video on lung structure and the cleaning system at www.brightredbooks.net/N5Biology

 ONLINE TEST

For a test on gas exchange in the lungs of mammals visit www.brightredbooks.net/N5Biology

THE DIGESTIVE SYSTEM

DIGESTION

The digestive system is responsible for the breakdown of large insoluble molecules in our food to smaller soluble molecules, which can then be absorbed into the blood. The overall reactions of digestion can be summarised as:

1 complex carbohydrates → glucose

2 proteins → amino acids

3 fats → fatty acids and glycerol

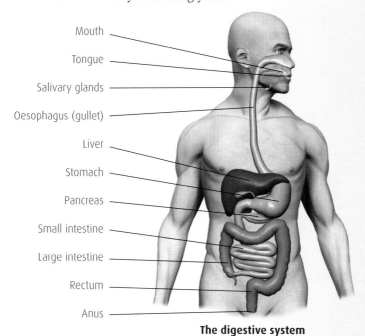

Mouth
Tongue
Salivary glands
Oesophagus (gullet)
Liver
Stomach
Pancreas
Small intestine
Large intestine
Rectum
Anus

The digestive system

The reactions of digestion take place in the mouth, the stomach and the first half of the small intestine. Enzymes break down food particles into their products. The products are then absorbed into the blood. This takes place from the second half of the small intestine.

The various parts of the digestive system and some associated organs are shown in the diagram.

PERISTALSIS

Food is moved through the digestive system by a process called **peristalsis**. This involves the contraction of circular muscles in the walls of the digestive system immediately behind food material. The contractions take place with a wave-like action and the food is pushed along in front of the wave. The muscles in front of the food relax to allow it to pass.

The process is shown in the diagram.

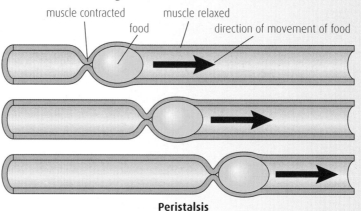

muscle contracted   muscle relaxed
food   direction of movement of food

Peristalsis

ABSORPTION OF FOOD

Digestion of food is complete by the time it reaches the second half of the small intestine. This part of the digestive system is adapted to absorb the digestion products into the blood. The inner lining of the small intestine is covered in small projections called **villi** (singular **villus**) that are about 1 mm in length. This gives the inner lining of the small intestine a greatly increased surface area, enabling the absorption of the digestion products to take place efficiently and quickly.

Structure of a villus

Villi have a number of features that help to absorb the products of digestion. These can be seen in the diagram.

Internal structure of a villus

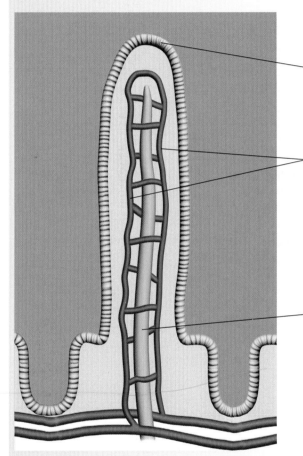

Thin wall (one cell thick) – enables digestion products to diffuse quickly from the small intestine to the transport vessels

Blood capillaries – absorb glucose and amino acids

Lacteal (lymph capillary) – absorbs the products of fat digestion (fatty acids and glycerol), which are less soluble than other digestion products

 THINGS TO DO AND THINK ABOUT

Copy and complete the following table to summarise the actions of three digestive enzymes.

Enzyme	Substrate	Products	Where it is produced	Where it acts
Amylase			1.	1.
			2.	2.
Pepsin				
Lipase				

EFFECTS OF LIFESTYLE CHOICES ON HEALTH: SMOKING

It is known that cigarette smoke contains about 4000 different chemicals, many of which are harmful. These include: tar, arsenic, benzene, cadmium, formaldehyde, nicotine and carbon monoxide.

Smoking has several health risks.

EFFECTS OF SMOKING ON THE CIRCULATORY SYSTEM

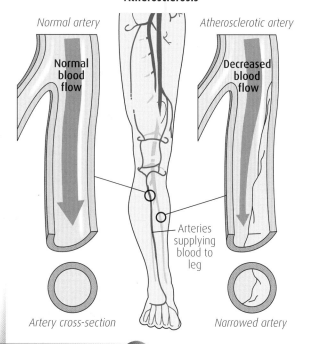

Atherosclerosis

Normal artery

Normal blood flow

Atherosclerotic artery

Decreased blood flow

Arteries supplying blood to leg

Artery cross-section

Narrowed artery

- Heart disease – smoking is a major cause of coronary artery disease in which the heart's blood supply becomes narrowed or blocked. This starves the heart muscle of nutrients and oxygen, eventually resulting in a heart attack. Smokers in their 30s and 40s are five times more likely to have a heart attack than non-smokers.

- Stroke – smoking can lead to damage or blockage of the arteries of the brain. Parts of the brain can be deprived of nutrients and oxygen, becoming permanently damaged.

- Raised blood pressure and heart rate.

- Constriction (tightening) of blood vessels in the skin, resulting in a drop in skin temperature.

- Less oxygen carried by the blood.

- Stickier blood, which is more prone to clotting.

- Damage to the lining of the arteries, which is thought to be a contributing factor to atherosclerosis (the build-up of fatty deposits on the artery walls).

- Reduced blood flow to extremities, such as fingers and toes.

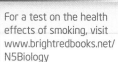

ONLINE TEST

For a test on the health effects of smoking, visit www.brightredbooks.net/N5Biology

EFFECTS OF SMOKING ON THE BREATHING SYSTEM

- Irritation of the air passages, which causes coughing.

- Reduced lung function and breathlessness due to narrowing of the air passages and the accumulation of mucus.

- Damaged cilia mean that harmful materials are not removed from the lungs, making the smoker more at risk from infections.

- Damaged alveoli mean that gas exchange becomes less efficient.

Effect of smoking on lungs

Lung from a non-smoker

Lung from a smoker

VIDEO LINK

Have a look at the clip about how smoking affects your lungs at www.brightredbooks.net/N5Biology

These effects can lead to lung diseases such as chronic bronchitis, asthma and emphysema which make it increasingly difficult for the sufferer to breathe.

OTHER HEALTH EFFECTS OF SMOKING

Cancers

The most obvious cancer caused by smoking is lung cancer. This is difficult to treat and long-term survival rates are low. Several other types of cancer are associated with smoking. These include cancer of the mouth, stomach and kidney.

Infant problems

Smoking in pregnancy increases the risk of miscarriage. Babies tend to have lower birth weights and their physical and mental development may be impaired. Smoking by parents can increase the risk of infant respiratory illnesses, such as bronchitis, colds and pneumonia.

If you smoke for a lifetime, there is a 50% chance that your eventual death will be smoking-related. Half of all these deaths will be in middle age.

HEALTH EFFECTS OF STOPPING SMOKING

Many of the health risks associated with smoking are reversible. The table shows some of the effects of stopping smoking

Time since stopping smoking	Beneficial effects
20 minutes	Pulse returns to normal.
8 hours	Nicotine levels in the body reduce by 90%. Carbon monoxide levels in the body reduce by 75%.
24 hours	Nicotine levels in the body almost zero. Carbon monoxide levels in the body almost zero. Cilia in the lungs begin to recover.
48 hours	All nicotine removed from body. Sense of taste and smell improves.
72 hours	Air passages in the lungs begin to dilate. Breathing becomes easier.
2 to 12 weeks	Blood circulation improves.
1 month	Skin colour improves, becoming less grey. Wrinkles lessen.
3 to 9 months	Coughing and wheezing lessen.
1 year	Increased risk of a heart attack reduced by 50%.
10 years	Risk of lung cancer falls to 50% of that of a continuing smoker.
15 years	Risk of a heart attack falls to that of someone who has never smoked.

DON'T FORGET

Passive smoking can cause the same health problems as active smoking. There are 600 000 deaths every year across the world caused by second-hand smoke.

THINGS TO DO AND THINK ABOUT

The table shows the total number of deaths in England from a number of diseases during 2010, together with the number of those deaths that were caused by smoking.

Disease	Number of deaths	Number of deaths caused by smoking
All cancers	65 820	37 500
Respiratory diseases	45 911	22 300
Circulatory diseases	138 436	20 600
Digestive system ulcers	2 340	1 200
Total	255 801	81 600

1 Calculate the percentage of all deaths caused by smoking, to the nearest whole number.

2 Of the cancer deaths, 28 044 were cases of lung cancer and 23 100 of those were caused by smoking. Use this information to calculate the percentage of lung cancer deaths caused by smoking and suggest a reason for the difference between it and the percentage for all cancers.

EFFECTS OF LIFESTYLE CHOICES ON HEALTH: ALCOHOL

TYPES OF ALCOHOL

The range of alcoholic drinks is vast and the alcoholic content varies enormously. This means that it is difficult for an individual to know how much they have consumed.

Alcohol is produced by fermentation of starchy or sugary foods using yeast. The drinks which come from this basic fermentation include beer, lager and wine. The alcoholic content of these varies from 3·5% to 7% for lagers and beers, and from 10% to 15% for wines.

Fortified wines such as sherry and port have an alcohol content of about 19%. They consist of wine that has been strengthened by the addition of alcoholic spirits such as brandy.

Spirits such as whisky, vodka and gin are made by distilling products of fermentation to produce drinks with an alcohol content of 38% to 56%.

In an attempt to simplify comparison of alcoholic drinks and to help people keep track of their alcohol intake, alcoholic consumption is normally measured in 'units' of alcohol.

Recommended maximum limits on alcohol consumption

Men should drink no more than 21 units of alcohol per week, no more than 4 units in any one day and have at least two alcohol-free days a week.

Women should drink no more than 14 units of alcohol per week, no more than 3 units in any one day and have at least three alcohol-free days a week.

These guidelines are for adults. Anyone under 18 and pregnant women are recommended not to drink alcohol at all.

Alcohol content of drinks

Drink	Beer	Alcopops	Wine	Spirit	Spirit	Cider	Cheap wine
Volume	1 pint	275 ml	175 ml	35 ml	25 ml	1 pint	1 litre
Alcohol content (%)	4·4%	5%	12%	40%	40%	5·2%	5%
Units of alcohol	2·5	1·4	2	1·4	1	3	5

ONLINE TEST

For a test on the health effects of drinking alcohol, visit www.brightredbooks. net/N5Biology

EFFECTS OF ALCOHOL ON THE CIRCULATORY SYSTEM

Alcohol has almost instant effects on the body, making a drinker feel more relaxed and sociable. Studies in adults have shown that a glass of alcohol (beer, wine or distilled spirits) each day can help heart function. Drinking alcohol in moderation can help keep the balance of fat in the blood in the right proportions. This can lower the chances of developing blocked arteries or blood clots.

However, drinking more than the recommended maximum each day may cause harm. Large amounts of alcohol can affect how the heart works. If the heart isn't pumping blood throughout the body effectively, other organs may suffer from lack of oxygen or nutrients.

EFFECTS OF ALCOHOL ON THE BREATHING SYSTEM

Excessive drinking of alcohol can lead to serious illnesses such as pneumonia and acute respiratory distress syndrome. Alcohol disrupts proteins that keep fluids out of the lungs and interferes with the body's immune defences. Alcohol also reduces the effectiveness of antioxidants in preventing damage to cells. Alcoholism may double the risk of respiratory distress.

OTHER HEALTH EFFECTS OF ALCOHOL

Drinking too much alcohol on a regular basis can have extremely damaging effects on the body. These may be permanent and can cause severe health problems. The liver is particularly at risk from excess alcohol because it is responsible for breaking down the alcohol into safe products. Liver damage can result if it is asked to perform this function on too great a scale. Some liver damage is reversible if alcohol consumption stops, but the liver tissues can become permanently damaged. This is called cirrhosis and can lead to death.

ONLINE

Have a look at the NHS page 'Liver Disease' for more information on how alcohol affects the liver at www.brightredbooks.net/N5Biology.

Stages in liver damage

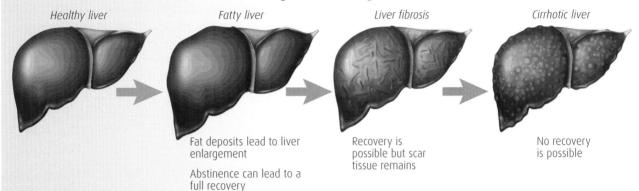

| Healthy liver | Fatty liver | Liver fibrosis | Cirrhotic liver |

Fat deposits lead to liver enlargement

Abstinence can lead to a full recovery

Recovery is possible but scar tissue remains

No recovery is possible

There are no recognised *safe* limits for alcohol consumption because the effects of alcohol vary from one person to another, and other contributing factors are involved. However, there are recommended guidelines and broad categories of risk associated with different levels of alcohol consumption. These are shown in the table below. Alcohol is addictive and so the health risks increase for someone who does become dependent.

There are several other health implications not covered in the table because of the individual nature of these effects. These include:

- infertility
- heart disease
- stomach ulcers
- osteoporosis (thinning of the bones)

- pancreatitis
- stroke
- dementia
- brain damage

- damage to a fetus
- mental health problems such as depression and anxiety

DON'T FORGET

One simple fact about alcohol is that it has a high energy value and regular drinking makes a significant addition to the energy intake of an individual. A measure of gin contains about 70 calories (290 joules) and a pint of lager contains about 220 calories (920 joules). A 'beer belly' is a fact of life for many drinkers.

Risk level	Alcohol consumption (maximum)	Health effects
Low risk	Men: 3–4 units per day Women: 2–3 units per day plus at least 3 alcohol-free days per week.	Very few or none
Increased risk	Exceeding the recommended limits on a regular basis and drinking every day or most days of the week.	Risk of cancer of the throat, neck or mouth increases by up to 2·5 times. Risk of high blood pressure increases by 1·5 times. Risk of breast cancer increases slightly for women. Risk of cirrhosis of the liver doubles for men.
High risk	Men: more than 8 units per day Women: more than 6 units a day and drinking every day or most days of the week.	Risk of cancer of the throat, neck or mouth increases by up to 5 times. Risk of cirrhosis of the liver increases by up to 10 times. Risk of irregular heartbeat doubles. Risk of high blood pressure increases by 4 times for men and doubles for women. Risk of breast cancer increases by 1·5 times for women.

There were over 8700 alcohol-related deaths in the UK in 2010.

THINGS TO DO AND THINK ABOUT

A man goes to the pub on Friday night and drinks four pints of lager. On Saturday he has a pint of lager before going to the football and a pint afterwards. He shares a bottle of wine with his wife over dinner and has two large whiskies later in the evening. On Sunday he shares another bottle of wine over dinner (350 ml each). On Wednesday he has one pint after work.

Comment on his drinking behaviour in terms of health risks.

DON'T FORGET

Binge drinking is defined as consuming more than twice the recommended maximum daily allowance in one session. Binge drinking is a significant contributor to accidents and violent behaviour.

EFFECTS OF LIFESTYLE CHOICES ON HEALTH: DIET

FAT

Fat is an essential component of our food. It is needed for the transport of some vitamins around the body. It is a source of essential fatty acids. Some of these help to lower cholesterol levels in the blood. It is important as a component of cell membranes. It helps protect body organs by acting as a cushion and an insulator. It is easily stored and acts as an energy reserve.

Lard

It is widely accepted that high levels of blood lipid (fat) increase the risk of coronary artery disease and heart attacks. The levels of blood lipids are determined by your diet.

A diet that is high in saturated fats (found in animal products such as cheese and fatty meat) and trans fats (oils that have been processed to turn them into semi-hard fats for use in cakes and biscuits) leads to increased levels of cholesterol. High levels of cholesterol in the blood can lead to atherosclerosis. This is a thickening of the inner walls of arteries due to fatty deposits, restricting the blood flow and causing high blood pressure. Blockages of the arteries can result in heart attacks and strokes.

Unsaturated, polyunsaturated and monounsaturated fats are beneficial for heart health. They are present in fish, nuts, seeds and vegetables.

However, *total* fat intake is also important. Even if all the fat you eat is unsaturated, it should never account for over 35% of the total energy value of your food. If it does, then the risk of cardiovascular disease increases. Saturated fats should never account for over 10% of the total energy value of your food.

SALT

Salt (sodium chloride)

Salt consists of the chemical sodium chloride. Sodium is needed as part of the mechanism for controlling the water content of the body and for keeping the pH of the blood at normal levels. It is needed for the transmission of nerve impulses and the contraction of muscles. An adult needs an intake of about 6g of salt per day.

Salt can act as a preservative for foods and it is often used as flavouring. It is easy to develop a taste for salt and this often leads us to add excessive amounts to our food. Most natural foods contain some salt, but many processed foods contain large quantities – the average quantity eaten by most people exceeds the daily requirement.

High salt intake is a cause of high blood pressure. This can increase the risk of strokes and heart attacks.

SUGAR

Sugar is an important chemical. Glucose sugar is the end point of carbohydrate digestion and it is the fuel our body cells use to gain energy. So why is it dangerous? The answer is that most people eat too much of it. Sugar is added to many processed foods to make them more appealing. It is added to sweets, chocolate, cakes, some fizzy drinks and fruit juices. Sugar is added to foods in many disguises. It may be called glucose, sucrose, maltose, corn syrup, honey, hydrolysed starch, invert sugar or fructose.

Sugar – how much is good for you?

The main risk associated with sugar is that it has a high energy value. One teaspoon (4 g) of sugar contains 16 calories (676 joules) and so it is a major contributor to obesity. Being overweight increases the risks of health problems such as heart disease and type 2 diabetes.

It is difficult to estimate our sugar intake because it is found in so many processed foods and given so many different names. A basic strategy to avoid eating too much sugar is not to add sugar to any food or drink, and to avoid processed foods when the nutritional label indicates the 'Carbohydrates (of which sugars)' has a value of more than 10 g of total sugar per 100 g of food.

Sugar can cause tooth decay because it encourages the growth of bacteria in the mouth and these produce acidic waste products which can damage tooth enamel. That's why it's always a good idea to clean your teeth after taking sugary foods, even healthy ones such as natural fruit juices.

ONLINE

For more on healthy eating, check out the link at www.brightredbooks.net/N5Biology

ONLINE TEST

For a test on the health effects of diet, visit www.brightredbooks.net/N5Biology

THINGS TO DO AND THINK ABOUT

Information from the nutrition labels of six processed foods is shown in the table.

Food (100 g)	Dry cured ham	Walnut whip	Salmon and broccoli quiche	Cheese twist	Blackberry and apple snack	White bread	Guideline daily amount (GDA) for an adult
Energy (kJ)	990	2080	885	2155	1515	1005	
Energy (kcal)	235	500	210	515	359	240	2000
Protein (g)	29·9	6·2	7·3	12·5	3·5	8·4	45
Carbohydrate (g)	0·5	56·0	14·5	51·0	69·0	48·3	230
of which sugars (g)	0·5	51·5	2·0	3·5	33·0	3·5	90
Fat (g)	12·8	27·1	13·9	29·0	8·0	1·1	70
of which saturates (g)	5·0	15·0	6·0	17·5	3·0	0·3	20
Sodium equivalent as salt (g)	4·52	0·18	0·80	1·90	1·00	1·00	6

1   Which food contains almost 25% of the daily adult GDA of energy per 100g?

2   Meat does not contain sugar. Explain the 0·5g of sugar per 100g of cured ham.

3   Identify two reasons why Walnut whips may be best avoided by some people.

EFFECTS OF LIFESTYLE CHOICES ON HEALTH: EXERCISE

Many people in the UK are physically inactive. This means that they take less than 30 minutes of exercise, intense enough to make them feel warm and out of breath, in one week. It is estimated that 7 out of 10 women in the UK and 6 out of 10 men are not active enough to gain any health benefits.

ONLINE

Have a read through the article stressing the importance of physical activity for good health at www.brightredbooks.net/N5Biology

EFFECTS OF LACK OF EXERCISE ON HEALTH

The most important effects of exercise concern the heart. The heart is a muscle and needs exercise in order to be able to work efficiently. In the UK, 19% of deaths from heart disease are caused by smoking but 37% are related to lack of physical activity.

Exercise helps to prevent heart disease in a number of ways including:

- lowering blood pressure and so reducing the risk of a heart attack
- reducing the cholesterol levels of the blood
- reducing body weight
- reducing the risk of developing type 2 diabetes
- reducing the risk of blood clots.

Exercise has other beneficial effects, such as relieving stress, reducing feelings of anxiety, improving sleep patterns, reducing the risk of osteoporosis and making you feel more energetic.

Lack of exercise is bad for you

WHAT SORT OF EXERCISE IMPROVES HEALTH?

The heart gains most benefit from aerobic exercise. That means exercise in which the muscles of the arms or legs are moving for a prolonged period. The level of activity should make you feel warm and slightly out of breath. This increases the demand for oxygen – the heart and lungs need to work harder to satisfy this demand. The breathing system and the circulatory system become more efficient as a result and stamina improves. Activities such as jogging, brisk walking, cycling, dancing and swimming are all forms of aerobic exercise.

Useful exercise does not have to be formalised. Activities such as climbing stairs instead of using a lift, getting on or off a bus a couple of stops early, housework and washing a car all contribute to physical activity.

Ideally, 30 minutes of this sort of exercise should be carried out five times per week. The periods of exercise can be broken up into a number of shorter blocks, but they should still be long enough to get you breathing hard. Someone who has been physically inactive should build up to this level of activity.

The bottom line is that any increase in the amount of exercise is going to be beneficial and, within reason, the more the better.

Aerobic exercise has health benefits

THINGS TO DO AND THINK ABOUT

1 Recovery time is the time taken for the body to return to normal after a period of exercise. Vigorous exercise results in the production of lactic acid by the muscles.

The graph shows the concentration of lactic acid in the blood of an athlete before, during and after a period of exercise.

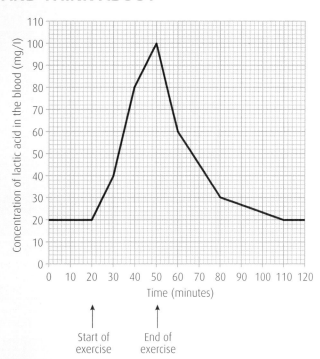

(i) Calculate the maximum percentage increase in the concentration of lactic acid in the blood as the result of the exercise.

(ii) What was the recovery time of the athlete following the period of exercise?

(iii) Following a period of training, the athlete found that the same level of exercise caused a smaller increase in blood lactic acid and that his recovery time decreased.

Explain these improvements in his fitness.

(iv) Suggest an easier method for measuring recovery time.

2 The table shows the changes in the number of capillaries supplying blood to the heart muscle of a person during a period of regular training by running.

Total distance run (km)	0	50	100	150	200	250
Number of capillaries per mm² of heart muscle	2000	2100	2250	2500	3000	3200

(i) Complete the graph using the results from the table.

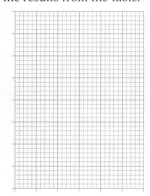

Total distance run (km)

(ii) Calculate the total distance run by the person in order to produce a 25% increase in the number of capillaries in the heart muscle.

(iii) Explain the benefit obtained by increasing the number of capillaries in the heart muscle.

BIODIVERSITY AND THE DISTRIBUTION OF LIFE 1

FACTORS AFFECTING BIODIVERSITY

Biodiversity refers to the range of different **species** present in an **ecosystem**. It also includes the different variations that exist within each species. Therefore, biodiversity covers the whole range of genetic information present in any environment.

Biodiversity can refer to an individual ecosystem, but it is sometimes used with reference to a larger system such as a **biome** or even the whole planet. The greater the biodiversity, the healthier and more stable the ecosystem.

Various factors can affect biodiversity and we will consider these in the next few pages.

ONLINE TEST

Take the 'Biodiversity and the distribution of life 1' test at www.brightredbooks.net/N5Biology

THE EFFECT OF BIOTIC FACTORS ON BIODIVERSITY

Biotic factors involve living organisms. There are many ways in which organisms can affect other species in an ecosystem. If the effect is extreme, it may have an impact on the biodiversity of the ecosystem.

Grazing

Grazing animals can reduce or increase biodiversity:

- Overgrazing – in severe cases, overgrazing can result in soil erosion, causing a loss of plant species from the land.

- A less drastic effect of overgrazing may be the loss of some of the less abundant plant species. As the grazing animals compete for diminishing food sources, such plant species may be eaten out of existence.

- Undergrazing – this can also reduce plant biodiversity. Vigorous plant species are able to grow unchecked and are able to dominate their surroundings at the expense of less vigorous species.

- Moderate grazing – this can maintain or increase plant biodiversity in grasslands. This is because vigorous plant species will be eaten by the grazing animals and they will not become too dominant. Less vigorous species will be able to survive and spread in the area.

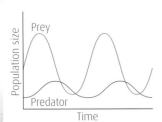

Soil erosion due to overgrazing

Predation

Predation is the feeding of one organism (the predator) on another organism (the prey). There are many different types of feeding relationships which may be described as predation, but in true predation the predator kills and eats the prey.

Predators reduce the numbers of their prey and in extreme situations this can lead to the loss of a prey species. However, in a stable ecosystem predation results in fluctuations in the numbers of both the predator and the prey species in such a way that both species survive. The predators are obviously dependent on the prey for their survival, but the prey species also needs the predators. Without the predators, the prey **population** would increase to a point where its food supply would be completely used up. This could cause widespread starvation.

This can be seen in graphs which plot the populations of a predator species and its prey.

When the prey population is high, the predator population increases because the food supply is plentiful. As predator numbers increase, there will be increased predation and a resulting fall in prey numbers. The decrease in the prey population means less food for the predators and so their numbers will fall. The prey population will then start to increase, and so on.

VIDEO LINK

To watch a video about predation visit www.brightredbooks.net/N5Biology

A typical predator–prey relationship

THE EFFECT OF ABIOTIC FACTORS ON BIODIVERSITY

Abiotic factors do not involve living organisms. They are the chemical and physical components of an ecosystem that can determine which species are able to survive there.

- Chemical components include oxygen concentration, soil mineral concentration and water availability.

- Physical components include light intensity, pH and temperature.

pH

pH is a measure of the acidity or alkalinity of liquids. Most natural aquatic environments have a pH value in the range 6–8, which is around neutral. Most fish are adapted to live in this pH range.

Many rivers, lakes and oceans are showing signs of acidification due to **pollution**. The changes are small because there are natural substances which buffer acidic pollutants, reducing their impact. However, long-term changes in pH will affect the distribution of fish in affected waters.

Some fish are adapted to live in very extreme pH conditions:

- The black piranha lives in the Rio Negra, which is a tributary of the Amazon River in Brazil. The waters there are acidic with a pH of 3·5 to 4·5.

- The Magadi tilapia lives in Lake Magadi in Kenya. The lake is alkaline with a pH of 10.

Temperature

Oceans are undergoing rising temperatures as a result of climate change. This is having an effect on the distribution of some fish species.

In the North Sea some species such as sardines and anchovies, which are adapted to cold waters, are reported to be moving further north as water temperatures increase. At the same time, species which are adapted to warmer waters, such as red mullet and sea bass, are moving northwards into the North Sea.

Extreme survivor: black piranha

THINGS TO DO AND THINK ABOUT

The pictures show the pellets of an owl, which is a predator. Predation is a biotic factor affecting biodiversity.

Owls regurgitate pellets which contain the undigested parts of the animals they have eaten. If the pellets are separated, the bones they contain can be used to identify the prey of the owl.

Can you think of any other examples of biotic and abiotic factors which affect biodiversity?

3 cm

An owl pellet   **Contents of a pellet**

DON'T FORGET

The term 'biotic' refers to living organisms and so biotic factors include food sources, predation and diseases caused by other living things such as bacteria and fungi. Abiotic refers to non-living factors.

BIODIVERSITY AND THE DISTRIBUTION OF LIFE 2

HUMAN INFLUENCES ON BIODIVERSITY

Changes to **habitats** occur naturally as a result of changing environmental conditions. Natural changes normally take place slowly and organisms may adapt or evolve with the changes. Humans have been responsible for altering their environment for thousands of years and these changes have always had an impact on biodiversity:

- Agricultural development has involved clearing forests and woodlands to make room for the cultivation of crops. Keeping herds of grazing animals has involved the removal of other grazers which would compete with domesticated cattle and sheep. It has also led to the elimination of natural predators such as wolves.

- The development of large towns and cities has reduced biodiversity in the areas concerned.

- The rapidly increasing human population means that these pressures on the environment are increasing.

DON'T FORGET

Carbon dioxide and methane are known as greenhouse gases. This is because of their effect in preventing the escape of heat from the earth's atmosphere. By doing this, both gases are contributing to global warming.

AIR POLLUTION

Some of the main pollutants of the atmosphere are:

- sulphur dioxide and oxides of nitrogen – these gases come from the burning of fossil fuels, such as coal and oil, and they combine with moisture in the air to form acids

- carbon dioxide and methane – the burning of many fuels produces carbon dioxide gas; methane is released from a number of sources including sewage treatment, cattle breath and landfill sites.

Lichens are simple organisms. Each species of lichen consists of a type of fungus growing with a type of algae. They often grow on tree branches and they are so sensitive to air pollution, particularly to sulphur dioxide, that they are used as **indicator species** for air pollution. In heavily polluted air, no lichens grow on tree branches.

Lichens as indicators of air quality

Crusty lichen   *Foliose lichen*   *Fruticose lichen*   *Lung lichen*

Polluted air ⟶ Exceptionally clean air

WATER POLLUTION

Water pollution can be caused by many things including:

- Untreated sewage entering a river – the sewage provides a food source for microorganisms and so their numbers increase in the water. They use up so much oxygen that larger organisms cannot survive.

- Agricultural **fertilisers** – these may be washed into water from neighbouring fields. They may produce a great increase in the growth of aquatic algae. These eventually die and decay, causing similar effects to those of untreated sewage.

- Acid rain – sulphur dioxide and nitrogen oxides can dissolve in atmospheric moisture and fall as acid rain. This can make the water in rivers and lakes more acidic, preventing some species from surviving. Mussels are used as an indicator species to monitor coastal waters. Mayfly nymphs are used for freshwater.

DEFORESTATION

Deforestation is the removal of trees from the landscape. Large-scale deforestation of tropical rainforests has two main causes:

1 Individuals or small groups of people burn areas of forest to clear space for the growth of crops. Unfortunately, the soil in these areas is poor and soon becomes too infertile for crop growth. This means that the people must move on and clear new areas of forest.

2 Commercial companies are responsible for clearing large areas of forest for activities such as timber production and mining.

Deforestation of hillsides can make the soil unstable. Heavy rainfall can cause landslides because there are no tree roots to hold the soil in place. This can lead to the loss of all vegetation on the lower slopes of hills.

Tropical rainforests are among the ecosystems with the greatest biodiversity. More than half of the world's estimated 10 million species of plants, animals and insects live in these forests. Experts estimate that 137 species of animals, plants and insects are becoming extinct every day because of the deforestation of tropical rainforests.

VIDEO LINK

For more, check out the 'Water Pollution' link at www.brightredbooks.net/N5Biology

DESERTIFICATION

Marginal land that borders the world's deserts has plants that are adapted to survive in dry conditions. These marginal areas act as buffers between the desert and cultivated areas.

In many places, population pressure results in attempts to cultivate marginal land for crops or for grazing animals. Such attempts are very likely to fail because the soil is too poor and because the need to irrigate the crops can disrupt the water table below ground, making the soil barren. This allows the desert to extend into the areas that were once marginal but stable, a process called **desertification**.

ENDANGERED SPECIES

The **evolution** of life on earth has always included the extinction of species. These extinctions may be the result of geological changes, climate changes or the evolution of more successful species.

Today, it is the effects of human activities, such as those mentioned earlier, that are the greatest cause of the extinction of species.

THINGS TO DO AND THINK ABOUT

ONLINE TEST

Take the 'Biodiversity and the distribution of life 2' test at www.brightredbooks.net/N5Biology

There are about 200 species of plants and animals that are recognised as being in danger of extinction in Britain. Scottish Natural Heritage has highlighted 23 of these species in Scotland. Six of these are shown in the photographs.

1 Try to identify the main influences which have led to the endangerment of one of these animal and plant species.

2 Could this have been prevented?

Some of Scotland's endangered species

| Red squirrel | Capercaillie | Scottish wildcat | Great yellow bumble bee | Small cow-wheat | Lesser butterfly orchid |

BIODIVERSITY AND THE DISTRIBUTION OF LIFE 3

ECOLOGICAL SYSTEMS

Ecological systems are studied at various levels: from small ecosystems to large biomes.

Biomes

Biomes are the major ecological regions which are found in different parts of the earth. Each biome has its own characteristic climate and community of plants (flora) and animals (fauna) that are adapted to the conditions.

Classifications of terrestrial biomes include:

- *Arctic and Alpine tundra* – this is the coldest type of biome. It forms the most northerly region of vegetation. Tundra is found south of the Arctic Circle and is based on lichens, mosses and other plants that are able to survive on the frozen soil. Apart from low temperatures, tundra is characterised by low precipitation, a short growing season and low levels of plant nutrients. Alpine regions are found at high altitudes and have a limited number of highly adapted plants. General conditions are similar to those of the tundra.

- *Temperate boreal forest* – this is the great area of coniferous forest that stretches across Canada and northern Europe. It is found south of the tundra. Boreal forests form the largest terrestrial biome. It is characterised by short warm moist summers and long cold dry winters.

- *Temperate deciduous forest* – these broadleaved forests are found south of the boreal forests and also in temperate parts of South America and Australia. The biome is characterised by a more moderate climate, with well-defined seasons and a longer growing season. Much of this biome has disappeared because of human settlement.

- *Temperate grassland* – this is based on perennial grasses and includes the prairies of North America, the pampas of South America, the steppes of Europe and Asia, and the veld of South Africa. These areas have hot summers, cold winters and moderate rainfall. Much of these grasslands are used for agriculture.

- *Mediterranean scrub* – this is found around the Mediterranean Sea and also in North and South America, South Africa and Australia. The vegetation is based on shrubs which are capable of surviving regular dry periods.

- *Desert* – the desert biome is an extremely dry environment which supports a limited range of plants and animals.

- *Tropical grassland* – these areas are found in hot regions which have marked wet and dry seasons. They occur mainly in South America, Africa, India and Australia.

- *Tropical rainforest* – these forests are found in the hot, wet regions of Central and South America, Africa and the islands of south-east Asia. They contain the most varied communities of plants and animals of all biomes. Day length remains close to 12 hours light and 12 hours darkness throughout the year and the only change in seasons is between wet and dry.

In addition to these terrestrial biomes, there are also distinctive aquatic biomes:

- *Freshwater biomes* include ponds and lakes, rivers and streams, and also areas of wetland.

- *Marine biomes* include the oceans, coral reefs and estuaries.

ONLINE TEST

Test yourself on 'Biodiversity and the distribution of life 3' at www.brightredbooks.net/N5Biology

contd

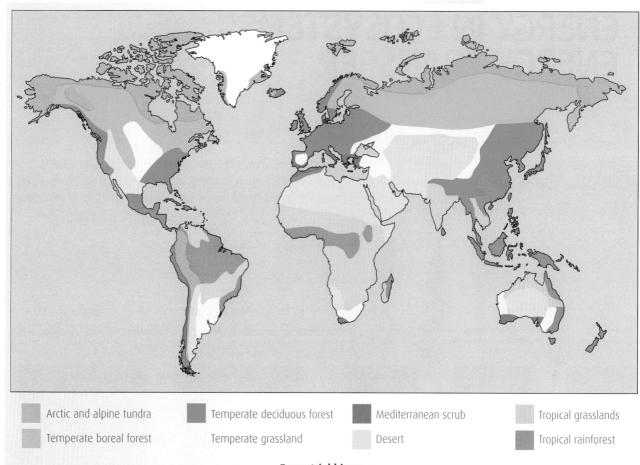

| | Arctic and alpine tundra | | Temperate deciduous forest | | Mediterranean scrub | | Tropical grasslands |
| | Temperate boreal forest | | Temperate grassland | | Desert | | Tropical rainforest |

Terrestrial biomes

Ecosystems

An ecosystem consists of a particular area together with all the organisms which live there. An ecosystem is sometimes described as a **habitat** plus the **community** of organisms which live there. It is characterised by the feeding relationships of the organisms present. It is through these that energy flows through the ecosystem and nutrients are recycled. A full description of an ecosystem would include the various abiotic factors which characterise it.

Niche

A **niche** is the role that an organism plays within its community. A description of a niche would include the range of food sources the organism uses, the range of predators which feed on it, the range of other species it competes with and the habitat it occupies.

For example, the niche of the red fox is that of a predator, active at night and feeding on small mammals, amphibians, insects and fruit. The fox provides blood for blackflies and midges, and is host to numerous diseases. The scraps, or carrion, left behind after a fox's meal provide food for many small scavengers and decomposers. All these are found in the habitat of woodland and meadow.

THINGS TO DO AND THINK ABOUT

Describe the niche of an organism based on a food web. In your description, make sure you account for every arrow pointing to and pointing away from the organism and add any information you have about the habitat.

DON'T FORGET

Decomposers such as bacteria and fungi play an important part in any ecosystem. They are responsible for the breakdown of dead organic matter which allows mineral nutrients to become available for new plant growth.

VIDEO LINK

Check out the clip 'What is an ecosystem?' from www.brightredbooks.net/N5Biology

DON'T FORGET

The niches of different species in a community may overlap, but they are not identical.

ENERGY IN ECOSYSTEMS: ENERGY TRANSFER

FOOD CHAINS

Living organisms obtain the energy they require from their food. Some organisms, namely green plants, make their food by photosynthesis using energy from the Sun. All other organisms obtain their food from the bodies, or the remains, of other organisms.

The transfer of energy between organisms is often represented as a **food chain**.

As shown in the diagram, each stage of a food chain has a name.

A simple food chain

secondary consumers

producer / primary consumer

grass / plant-eating insect / spider / blackbird / fox

- A **producer** is a green plant which makes food by photosynthesis.
- A primary **consumer** is a **herbivore** – an animal which eats plants.
- Secondary consumers are **carnivores** – animals which eat other animals.

The arrows of a food chain represent the direction of energy transfer from organism to organism.

The transfer of energy from one organism to the next is not complete because each organism uses up some of the energy, so there is less energy remaining to be passed to the next stage. Some of the energy obtained by an organism remains in the organism, for example energy is present in new tissues when the organism grows. This will be available to the next stage in the food chain if the organism is eaten. However, energy which is converted to heat or which is used for movement will be lost from the food chain and will be unavailable to the next stage. Some energy will remain in uneaten material such as bones, teeth, fur and feathers. There will also be energy remaining in the undigested material present in faeces. This energy will not be passed to the next stage, although it may be used by decomposers such as bacteria and fungi that are present in the ecosystem.

In total it is estimated that about 90% of the available energy is lost from each stage of a food chain. This means that only 10% of the energy that an organism gains from its food is used for the growth and repair of body tissue.

MORE COMPLEX FEEDING RELATIONSHIPS

In reality, the transfer of energy in an ecosystem is not as simple as it appears in a food chain. This is because most organisms have more than one food source and any one type of organism may be eaten by a range of predators. Therefore, most food chains are interlinked into more complicated systems called food webs.

For example, part of a food web involving the organisms from the food chain is shown below.

A food web

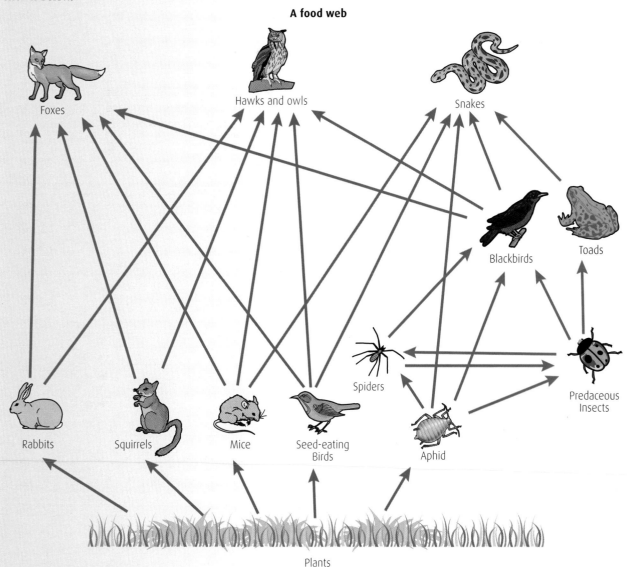

A description of the position that an organism occupies in a food web is very close to a description of its niche.

It is possible to find many individual food chains in a food web such as this.

THINGS TO DO AND THINK ABOUT

1   In the food web, can you find an example of an organism that is part of two individual food chains but that occupies a different relative position in each of them?

2   Food chains rarely have more than four or five stages. Why is this?

ENERGY IN ECOSYSTEMS: PYRAMIDS AND THE NITROGEN CYCLE

PYRAMIDS

Pyramid-shaped diagrams of various sorts are used to represent some of the features of a food chain. Here are some examples.

Pyramid of numbers

The width of each level of a **pyramid of numbers** represents the relative numbers of each organism present in the ecosystem. Therefore, the wider the level, the greater the number of organisms. For example, the diagram represents a typical food chain.

foxes
blackbirds
spiders
plant-eating insects
grass plants

However, some food chains produce irregular shapes when represented by pyramids of numbers.

For example, look at the following food chains and their representative pyramids.

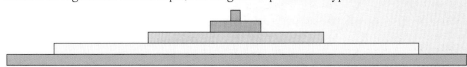

oak tree ⟶ plant-eating insect ⟶ spider ⟶ blackbird ⟶ sparrowhawk

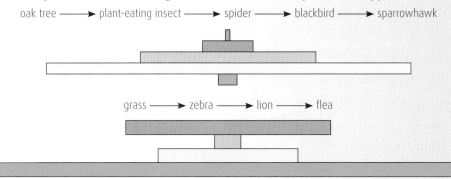

grass ⟶ zebra ⟶ lion ⟶ flea

These irregularities are due to the relative body sizes of some of the organisms. One large producer can support many primary consumers and one large secondary consumer can support many small **parasites** (organisms which live on or in the bodies of other living things).

Pyramid of biomass

Biomass is a measure of the total mass of organisms in an ecosystem. Biomass is measured as the total dry mass in grams of each species present per square metre (g/m^2). Calculating the biomass of each population of organisms in a food chain overcomes the problems caused by the sizes of organisms. Therefore, a normal pyramid shape is achieved. The diagram shows a **pyramid of biomass** for the food chain.

oak tree ⟶ plant-eating insect ⟶ spider ⟶ insect-eating bird ⟶ sparrowhawk

DON'T FORGET

Pyramids of numbers don't always have a true pyramid shape.

However, even this is not an accurate representation of the amounts of energy in a food chain. For example, organisms with a high fat content will have a different energy content compared to other organisms of the same mass but with a lower fat content. Also, plants, such as grasses, which are grazed regularly produce much more biomass than may be apparent. This is because a lot of their biomass is eaten by grazing animals and is quickly replaced by new growth.

contd

Pyramid of energy

The best representation of the organisms present in a food chain is to estimate the amount of energy each species produces per square metre in one year (kJ/m²/year). The energy value is calculated from the dry mass involved.

Here is a **pyramid of energy** for a food chain.

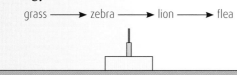

ONLINE TEST

Ready to take the 'Pyramids and the nitrogen cycle' test? Logon and try at www.brightredbooks.net/N5Biology

NITROGEN IN ECOSYSTEMS

Proteins are important substances in all organisms because of their many different functions in cells. Protein molecules are made from smaller amino acid molecules which contain the element nitrogen as part of their structure.

Nitrogen is recycled in ecosystems through food chains and by the action of particular bacteria.

The nitrogen cycle

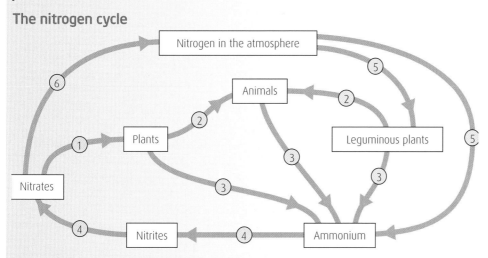

The stages in the **nitrogen cycle** are:

1   Nitrates are absorbed by plants and used to make proteins.

2   Animals obtain protein by eating plants or other animals.

3   Decomposers such as fungi and bacteria break down the remains of plants and animals. Proteins and other nitrogenous waste form ammonium compounds which are released into the soil.

4   **Nitrification** – ammonium compounds are converted into nitrite compounds and then into nitrate compounds by nitrifying bacteria in the soil.

5   **Nitrogen fixation** – atmospheric nitrogen is converted to ammonium compounds by nitrogen-fixing bacteria. Some of these are free-living in the soil. Others are found in **root nodules** of leguminous plants such as peas, beans and clover.

6   **Denitrification** – some nitrates in the soil are used by denitrifying bacteria which release nitrogen gas into the atmosphere.

VIDEO LINK

Watch the clip 'Nitrogen cycle' at www.brightredbooks.net/N5Biology

 THINGS TO DO AND THINK ABOUT

Which of the stages of the nitrogen cycle are dependent on the action of bacteria?

ENERGY IN ECOSYSTEMS: COMPETITION

Competition results when organisms in ecosystems require the same resources for their survival. These resources include food, water, light and territory. Competition does not mean that individuals fight over the resource, but it does mean that some organisms receive less of the resource than others. These individuals have a lower chance of survival.

INTERSPECIFIC COMPETITION

Interspecific competition occurs when individuals of different species in an ecosystem require similar resources. Whenever this happens, one species will prove to be a stronger competitor than the other. This results in the population of the weaker species declining in the ecosystem and perhaps being eliminated from it.

The distribution of red squirrels and grey squirrels 1998

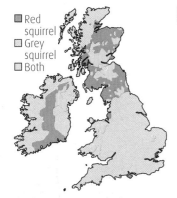

☐ Red squirrel
☐ Grey squirrel
☐ Both

Red squirrel   **Grey squirrel**

EXAMPLE 1

Red squirrels and grey squirrels

Red squirrels are the native squirrel species in Britain. Grey squirrels were introduced into Britain from North America over a period of years from 1876 as a novelty species. Both species can live in mixed woodlands which contain broad-leaved and coniferous trees. However, grey squirrels are bigger and more robust than red squirrels.

They are stronger competitors and populations of red squirrels are eliminated when both species are present in such habitats.

In coniferous woodlands, grey squirrels are not as well adapted as red squirrels because they cannot survive on a diet of pine seeds. This means that red squirrels can survive in some areas where pine and spruce trees form the predominant vegetation.

The overall reduction in the areas of woodland in Britain and the tendency for replacing coniferous woodlands with broadleaved tree species has contributed to the decline of red squirrels in Britain.

ONLINE

Discover more about the battle between red and grey squirrels online at www.brightredbooks.net/N5Biology

EXAMPLE 2

Brown trout and rainbow trout

Brown trout are a native freshwater fish. Rainbow trout are a different species, introduced from the USA for angling and as a food.

Brown trout

Rainbow trout

ONLINE TEST

To see how much you know about competition in ecosystems, test yourself at www.brightredbooks.net/N5Biology

Both species lay eggs in hollows, or redds, scraped in the gravel of a river bed. Research has shown that when both species use the same areas of a river bed for redding, the eggs of the brown trout suffer a greater mortality rate than those of the rainbow trout. This means that the population of brown trout declines in rivers where both species are present.

INTRASPECIFIC COMPETITION

Intraspecific competition occurs between members of the same species. It can be very intense because the requirements of all the individuals involved are identical. Competitive success is based on variations between the individuals. It ensures that the fittest and best adapted have the greatest chance of surviving and reproducing.

EXAMPLE 1

Territorial behaviour in robins

Robins are very territorial birds. Each male robin defends his territory against other robins to ensure that he controls an area with sufficient food for himself and his offspring. The red breast is a warning to other robins to stay out of the defended territory.

Posturing and singing are usually enough to deter other robins and to prevent actual fighting. However, if these warnings are ignored, then a robin will attack an intruder in order to prevent a competitor from obtaining the resources available in the territory.

EXAMPLE 2

Grasshoppers competing for food supply

Grasshoppers eat the leaves of plants. They do not challenge each other for the food but simply compete by eating. By doing so, they reduce the food available to their competitors.

EXAMPLE 3

Trees growing close together compete for water, light, nutrients and space

Competition for light encourages trees to grow tall. A single tree may not grow as tall as trees of the same species which are growing close together, but it will have more resources and be wider and heavier than a tree from a group.

DON'T FORGET

Competition can occur between different species or between individuals of the same species – whenever two organisms require the use of the same resources there will be competition for that resource.

THINGS TO DO AND THINK ABOUT

The diagram shows the set up for an investigation into competition between radish seedlings.

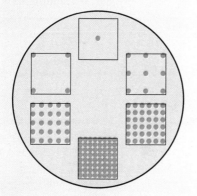

Petri dish with wet filter paper on the bottom

1 cm² areas containing different numbers of radish seeds evenly spaced out

1 By using one dish for all the samples, what factors are being kept the same?

2 How can you measure the effect of increasing competition on the growth of the seedlings?

3 Is the average height of the seedlings in each sample a suitable measure?

4 What would be a better measure of seedling growth?

5 How could the results be made more reliable?

SAMPLING TECHNIQUES AND MEASUREMENT OF BIOTIC FACTORS 1

SAMPLING PLANTS

Quantitative sampling enables estimates to be made of the population sizes of the organisms in a habitat. Different techniques are available to suit different circumstances. In all cases, it is important that the samples are representative of the whole area and that enough samples are taken to make sure that the results are reliable.

This is usually achieved by selecting the sample sites randomly, so that the results are not influenced by any preconceived ideas of the investigator. The number of samples taken should be large enough to ensure that the effects of any extreme or atypical results are reduced when an average value is calculated.

Plants do not move and this makes sampling them easier.

Quadrats

A **quadrat** is a square frame, usually measuring 0·5 metre × 0·5 metre, giving it an area of 0·25 m².

If you wanted to compare the distribution of daisies on two different lawns, you could count every single daisy but this would be very time consuming. Instead, sample sites are chosen at random and a quadrat is placed at each site. The number of daisies in each quadrat is counted and an average is calculated. From this, the total number of daisies in the lawn can be estimated.

Quadrats can also be used to measure the proportion of the ground that is covered by plants which are too difficult to count individually, for example grasses and mosses.

To do this, the quadrat is divided into a grid of smaller squares using string. When the quadrat is positioned at the sample site, the number of small squares containing the plant is used as an estimate of the abundance of the plant in terms of the percentage ground cover.

The diagram shows a quadrat positioned on part of a lawn which contains patches of moss.

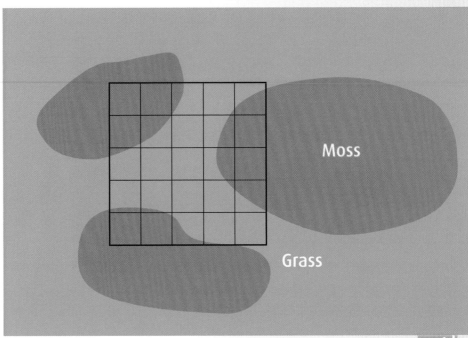

contd

Moss is present in 20 of the 25 squares of the quadrat. Some of these squares are completely filled with moss and some have hardly any. When using a quadrat to estimate ground cover, only the squares that are at least half-filled are counted.

In this case, 9 of the 25 small squares of the quadrat are at least half-filled with moss. This equals 36%. If this pattern was found to be the average of several sample sites, it could be concluded that 36% of the lawn was covered in moss.

Transects

Transects involve placing quadrats at regular intervals along a line. The results of samples can be used to study the effect of changes in an abiotic factor on the distribution of plants.

For example, a **transect** may be positioned down a slope to investigate the effect of increasing soil moisture from the top to the bottom of the slope. Another example could be to position the transect from a shaded area into open ground to investigate the effect of increasing light intensity. Read more about abiotic factors which affect ecosystems on page 91.

 THINGS TO DO AND THINK ABOUT

The diagrams represent two lawns. The sites of quadrats are shown, together with the number of daisies found in each of them. Each quadrat is 0·25 m².

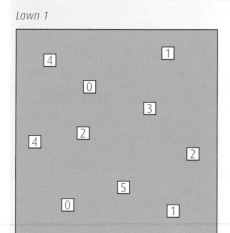

Lawn 1

Lawn 2

Lawn 1

Total number of daisies in quadrats

$= 4 + 1 + 0 + 2 + 3 + 4 + 2 + 0 + 5 + 1 = 22$

Average number of daisies in quadrats

$= 22 \div 10$

$= 2\cdot2$ per 0·25 m² = 8·8 per m²

Estimated total in Lawn 1 = 8·8 × 50 × 50 = 22 000

1 Estimate the total number of daisies in Lawn 2.

2 Which lawn contains the most daisies?

3 Which lawn has the greater density of daisies (number per unit area)?

DON'T FORGET

The same precautions must still be taken to ensure that the samples are representative and reliable. There often simply isn't time to count every plant in the area being investigated, but it is important to take as many samples as possible to ensure unrepresentative results are averaged out.

ONLINE

Find out more about plant sampling techniques online at www.brightredbooks.net/N5Biology

ONLINE TEST

To see how much you know about sampling plants, test yourself at www.brightredbooks.net/N5Biology

SAMPLING TECHNIQUES AND MEASUREMENT OF BIOTIC FACTORS 2

SAMPLING ANIMALS

Animals which do not move quickly, such as limpets on rocks at the seashore, may be sampled using a quadrat. For animals which move about, a method of trapping them is needed in order to take a sample.

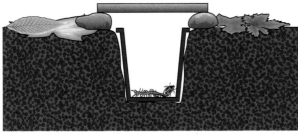

A pitfall trap

Pitfall trap

The **pitfall trap** is the most common method used to trap small invertebrates. It consists of a container buried level with the soil surface and protected with a suitable cover. It is left for some time and then examined to see what animals have fallen in.

Some precautions must be taken when using pitfall traps if they are to give usable results:

- The rim must be level with the soil surface to enable animals to fall in.
- The trap must be covered to stop rain getting in and to prevent birds eating any trapped animals.
- There must be a gap between the cover and the soil to allow animals to reach the trap.
- The container should have small holes in the base to allow any rain water to drain away.
- The trap must be checked frequently to collect results before some of the trapped animals eat others.
- A sufficient number of traps must be set to ensure representative and reliable results.

An estimate of the population size for any of the trapped species can be made using a capture and recapture technique. This involves the following procedure:

1 Capture a sample of individuals of the species being studied and count them.

2 Mark each individual in some way, for example with a spot of waterproof ink on their backs.

3 Release them and re-set the traps to capture a second sample.

4 Count the total number of individuals in the second sample and also count how many of them were part of the first sample.

5 The estimated total population of the species is calculated as:

$$\frac{\text{number caught in first sample} \times \text{number caught in second sample}}{\text{number of marked individuals in second sample}}$$

Tullgren funnel

This is used for sampling organisms in soil or in leaf litter. It consists of a funnel fitted with a mesh platform. The soil or leaf litter sample is placed on the mesh and a lamp is positioned above the sample. The small animals move away from the heat and light, falling into the container.

Tree beating

This is used to sample organisms that rest or feed in the branches and foliage of trees. As the branches are shaken, the organisms fall and are collected on a sheet.

VIDEO LINK

See how to set up a pitfall trap correctly at www.brightredbooks.net/N5Biology

DON'T FORGET

When sampling animals, it is vital to check your traps regularly so that none of the animals in your sample are eaten by others, which may be predators.

ONLINE TEST

How well do you know your sampling and measurement techniques for biotic factors? Check at www.brightredbooks.net/N5Biology

IDENTIFYING ORGANISMS

You may want to identify animals or plants that have been found in a sample. This is normally carried out using a **paired-statement key**.

This key consists of a set of paired statements about features of organisms likely to be present in the habitat. The pairs of statements are organised in a sequence so that when the features of an unknown organism are compared with the statements, they lead the scientist through the key until the organism is identified.

The photographs show some common invertebrates found in leaf litter. Note that the photographs *do not* show the organisms to the same scale.

The key can be used to identify them.

Look at photograph A and start at the beginning of the key. As you compare the features of the animal with the statements, you will be led from statement 1 to 2 to 3 to 4 to 7 to 8 and finally to the name Spider.

Key

Number	Paired statements	Organism name or further instruction
1	Shell present	Snail
	Shell not present	Go to 2
2	Body without segments	Slug
	Body with segments	Go to 3
3	Legs not present	Earthworm
	Legs present	Go to 4
4	Three pairs of legs	Go to 5
	More than three pairs of legs	Go to 7
5	Wings absent	Ant
	Wings present	Go to 6
6	Short wing covers and exposed abdomen	Devil's Coach Horse Beetle
	Long wing covers and covered abdomen	Ground Beetle
7	Four pairs of legs	Go to 8
	More than four pairs of legs	Go to 9
8	Body divided into two parts	Spider
	Body not divided into two parts	Harvestman
9	Body with fewer than 15 segments	Woodlouse
	Body with more than 15 segments	Go to 10
10	One pair of legs per segment	Centipede
	Two pairs of legs per segment	Millipede

 ## THINGS TO DO AND THINK ABOUT

Use the key above to identify all the other invertebrates shown in the photographs.

SAMPLING TECHNIQUES AND MEASUREMENT OF ABIOTIC FACTORS

Abiotic factors are the physical factors which characterise a habitat. The measurement of abiotic factors is important in understanding the distribution of organisms in the habitat.

Just as with the sampling of organisms, the measurement of abiotic factors must be representative and reliable. This means that care must be taken to avoid errors with the measurements and that the measurements must be repeated, so that average values can be calculated. This reduces the effect of any extreme or atypical measurements.

TEMPERATURE

Measurements are made in degrees Celsius (°C) using a thermometer or a temperature probe attached to a data recorder.

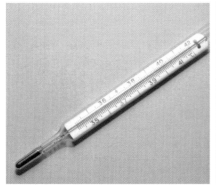
Thermometer

Soil thermometer

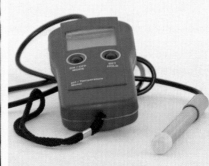
Data recorder and temperature probe

Whichever method you are using to record temperature, it is important to take the following precautions:

- Make sure the detecting part of the instrument is surrounded by the material being measured, whether it is water, air or soil.

- Avoid touching the detecting part of the instrument with your hand so that the results are not affected by your body heat.

- Allow the instrument to stabilise before you read the temperature.

LIGHT

Several different properties of light may be measured. Normally, it is the amount of light per unit of area, or light intensity, which is of interest. This is measured in lux (lx) using a light meter, which may be connected to a data recorder or can be a stand-alone instrument. Often light-measuring instruments are calibrated with arbitrary units of measurement.

When measuring light intensity, it is important to observe the following precautions:

- Make sure the detector is not dirty.

- Angle the detector so it is facing towards the source of light.

- Avoid shading the detector with your body or any other object.

DON'T FORGET

To get accurate readings every time, ensure you do not alter the results by touching the thermometer bulb or blocking the light meter!

pH

pH is a measure of acidity or alkalinity. The pH scale goes from 0 to 14; pH 7 is described as neutral – that is neither acidic nor alkaline. Strong acids and alkalis have values close to the extreme ends of the scale. Weak acids and alkalis have values close to the middle of the scale.

The pH of soil water is an important factor in determining which plants are able to survive in a habitat. The pH of waterways has been discussed earlier in this topic, on page 91.

pH can be measured using indicator solutions which change colour at different pH values. For more accurate measurements a pH meter is used. This may be in the form of a probe attached to a data recorder or a stand-alone unit. Care must be taken to:

- ensure good contact between the probe and the material to be measured

- clean the probe between each measurement to make sure traces from a previous measurement do not affect the reading.

SOIL MOISTURE

This is another important factor which influences the distribution of plants. It is measured using a moisture meter. The format and precautions in the use of moisture meters are the same as for pH meters.

Some soil monitors combine several functions into a single unit.

A soil monitor combining light, soil pH and soil moisture meters.

VIDEO LINK

Check out the video about water sampling to see how biologists use these methods of measurement at www.brightredbooks.net/N5Biology

ONLINE TEST

Test how well you know your sampling and measurement techniques for abiotic factors at www.brightredbooks.net/N5Biology

THINGS TO DO AND THINK ABOUT

The diagram shows the positions of 10 quadrats placed 1 metre apart along a transect. The transect runs from the bottom of a tree into open ground.

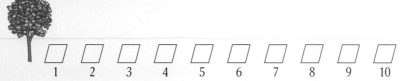

The table shows the number of daisy plants found in each quadrat, together with the values of some abiotic factors.

Quadrat	Number of daisies	Soil pH	Soil temperature (°C)	Soil moisture (units)	Light intensity (units)
1	0	6·5	14	4	8
2	1	6·4	15	6	8
3	1	6·8	14	8	9
4	3	6·7	15	12	10
5	4	6·5	16	9	13
6	6	6·4	15	7	15
7	9	6·7	15	11	16
8	10	6·6	15	11	16
9	9	6·5	14	10	18
10	10	6·7	15	8	18

1 Which of the abiotic factors is having the greatest influence on the distribution of the daisies?

2 Can you explain your answer?

ADAPTATION, NATURAL SELECTION AND THE EVOLUTION OF SPECIES 1

MUTATION OF GENETIC INFORMATION

The characteristics of organisms are controlled by the genes located on chromosomes. The main component of a chromosome is a molecule of DNA, arranged as a double helix. Each chromosome contains many genes. Each gene consists of a length of the DNA which has the base sequence code for the synthesis of one polypeptide. Each gene may exist in a number of different forms, called **alleles**.

Body cells are diploid; that is they contain two complete sets of chromosomes. This means that there are two alleles present for each characteristic.

Gametes are haploid and contain only one complete set of chromosomes. This means that they carry only one allele for each characteristic.

Changes to genetic information are called **mutations**. They occur as the result of random errors during cell divisions.

Mutations can occur during the division of body cells. These may have adverse effects, such as the development of cancers, but they have no evolutionary significance because they cannot be inherited.

Mutations which occur during the production of gametes can be inherited, if such a gamete is involved in fertilisation. In this case, the mutation forms part of the genotype of the new individual and may be passed on to their offspring.

Some mutations are the result of damage to the structure of chromosomes, leading to the loss of genes or to the loss of gene function. Other mutations result from errors in the DNA base-sequence copying process. These mutations change the genetic information and are the only way in which new genetic information can arise. In other words, they are the only source of new alleles that can alter the characteristics of a species. The ability of a species to adapt and to evolve depends on changes to the genetic information.

ONLINE

To find out more about how DNA mutation works, visit www.brightredbooks.net/N5Biology

EFFECTS OF MUTATION

Mutations affect the genetic information present in the gametes of an organism.

Disadvantageous mutations

The altered genetic information gives rise to a protein that is unlikely to function normally. The individual organism which inherits this information may suffer because of this. Such mutations are described as disadvantageous.

> **EXAMPLE:**
>
> An example is a mutation of the gene which codes for the production of a blood-clotting protein. Lack of this protein causes haemophilia, a disorder that reduces the ability of the blood to clot. It is estimated that 33% of cases of haemophilia are the result of spontaneous mutation. The remaining cases are the result of inheriting the defective allele.

Neutral mutations

Some mutations cause no adverse consequences and are described as neutral. For example, some different DNA base sequences code for the same amino acid and so some mutations which alter the DNA code have no effect on the resulting proteins.

VIDEO LINK

Go online and watch the video to learn more about genetic mutation at www.brightredbooks.net/N5Biology

contd

Advantageous mutations

In some very rare instances, a mutation may cause a genetic change which has a beneficial effect. In this case, the mutation is described as advantageous.

> **EXAMPLE:**
>
> An example of this is a mutation of a gene which codes for a protein that helps to prevent accumulation of cholesterol in arteries. The resulting protein is even better than the normal protein at carrying out this function. People possessing this mutation have a reduced risk of heart disease compared to the rest of the population. About 3·5% of people in a village in northern Italy possess this gene. It can be traced back to a mutation in one man who lived there in the eighteenth century and who passed it on to his offspring.

CAUSES OF MUTATION

Mutations are random. They happen spontaneously and cannot be predicted. However, it is known that certain environmental factors can increase the rate at which mutations occur. This is because they increase the chance of errors during the formation of gametes.

Such environmental factors are called **mutagens** and they include various forms of radiation, for example ultraviolet light, X-rays and gamma radiation. Some chemicals are also mutagens, for example asbestos fibres, benzene, mustard gas and tobacco smoke.

ONLINE TEST

Test your knowledge of mutation and its causes at www.brightredbooks.net/N5Biology

DON'T FORGET

Remember a mutation is a change to the genetic information in an organism. It is not the organism itself!

THINGS TO DO AND THINK ABOUT

This type of apron has a lead lining. It is used by staff who operate X-ray machines.

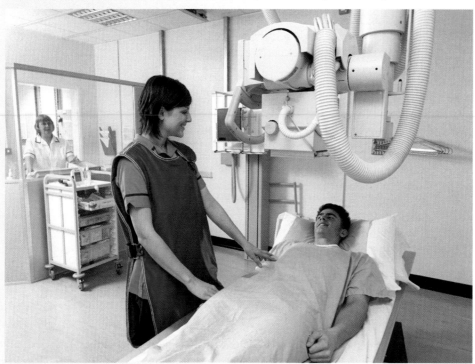

X-ray apron

1 Why are such precautions necessary?

2 Why is it especially important that such clothing protects the reproductive organs?

ADAPTATION, NATURAL SELECTION AND THE EVOLUTION OF SPECIES 2

ADAPTATION AND VARIATION

An **adaptation** is an inherited characteristic that makes an organism well suited to its environment, enabling it to survive. Adaptations are the result of variations which appear in a population of organisms due to random advantageous mutations. Such variations may allow a species to adapt to changing environmental conditions, or to become better adapted to the existing conditions.

EXAMPLES OF ADVANTAGEOUS ADAPTATION

Kangaroo rats are extremely well adapted to desert living

Examples of parallel adaptation

Angrecum orchid and Madagascan hawk moth

EXAMPLE 1   Kangaroo rats

These are desert mammals that are able to survive in regions of high temperatures and low water availability. They show many adaptations, including: high levels of a hormone that promotes reabsorption of water from the kidneys back into the blood; remaining in cool humid burrows during the day; coming out to feed at night; producing very dry faeces; having no sweat glands.

EXAMPLE 2   Angrecum orchid and Madagascan hawk moths

The flowers of this orchid have nectaries that are 30 cm long. The proboscis (feeding tube) of the moth is equally long. The moth is the only insect able to reach the nectar and so it is the only insect capable of pollinating the flowers.

Both species benefit from this relationship. The orchid is certain to have its flowers pollinated because it is the only source of food for the moth. The moths have no competition from other species for the nectar.

This is an example of adaptations developing in two species in parallel. The result is that the two species become dependent on each other.

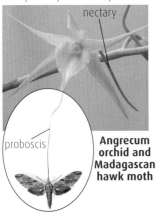

Swollen-thorn acacia and acacia ants

EXAMPLE 3   Swollen-thorn acacia and acacia ants

Acacia trees possess very sharp thorns and poisonous leaves which help to protect them from many grazing animals and insect pests. The swollen-thorn acacia, however, is different. Its thorns are larger and hollow, and its leaves are not poisonous. The thorns are used by one species of ant as nesting sites. The ants also feed on nectar from the flowers of the tree. In addition, the tree produces parcels of food material on their leaves which the ants collect and feed to their young. These parcels have no other function.

In return for shelter and food, the ants protect the acacia. If any animal begins grazing on the tree or any insect begins eating its leaves, the ants swarm out of their nests and attack the offender. The ants will even kill any other plants, such as vines, which try to grow up the acacia.

This is another example of adaptations developing in parallel in two species in such a way that they become dependent on each other.

The bee orchid flower

EXAMPLE 4   Bee orchid

The flowers of this plant have become adapted in such a way that they mimic a female bee. This attracts male bees to the flowers in an attempt to mate. In doing so, the bees act as pollinators for the orchid.

contd

These examples demonstrate that adaptation is a continuous process for all species. If a species does not show continuous adaptation, it will fail to survive because it will eventually be out-competed by another species.

This is sometimes referred to as the Red Queen model of evolutionary change. It is a reference to the Red Queen in Lewis Carroll's book *Through The Looking Glass* in which the Red Queen states,

'… here it takes all the running you can do just to remain in the same place.'

DON'T FORGET

Adaptation can occur in parallel between two species or singularly in one species and is the result of random mutations.

EXAMPLES OF ADAPTATIONS WHICH CAUSE PROBLEMS

Although adaptation is largely advantageous to the survival of species, sometimes it can cause problems. Here are two examples.

ONLINE TEST

For a test on adaptation, visit www.brightredbooks.net/N5Biology

> **EXAMPLE 1**   Over-prescription of antibiotics
>
> Antibiotics are powerful tools in combating diseases caused by bacterial infections. They kill disease-causing bacteria. Unfortunately, bacteria have the ability to produce variants, some of which may be resistant to the antibiotic that is being used against them. This resistance can be passed on when the bacteria reproduce. Even if just a few bacteria survive the antibiotic treatment, they can quickly produce a population of offspring that are all resistant. This means that an alternative antibiotic, or a stronger dose of the original antibiotic, would be needed in future treatments. Continued variation in the bacteria eventually may create resistance to the new or stronger antibiotic.
>
> The over-prescription of antibiotics for the treatment of minor infections has been one of the reasons for the development of resistant strains of bacteria. This process has led to some infections being very difficult to treat.
>
> For example, MRSA (methicillin-resistant *Staphylococcus aureus*) and C. diff. (*Clostridium difficile*) are bacteria which cause great problems in some hospitals because of their resistance to normal antibiotics and because of the danger they pose to patients in a weakened condition.

ONLINE

To learn more about the over-prescription of antibiotics and the problems it can cause, read the NHS article on the subject at www.brightredbooks.net/N5Biology

> **EXAMPLE 2**   Pests of GM crops
>
> Genetic modification has been used to give some crops in-built protection against serious pests by inserting genes which give the plants the ability to produce toxins. For example, some varieties of cotton have been modified to make them resistant to the caterpillars of the bollworm moth. Similarly, some varieties of maize have been modified to make them resistant to the caterpillars of the European corn borer moth. We call these **GM organisms**.
>
> In both cases, it is the caterpillars of the moths which cause the damage to the crops and, in both cases, adaptations arise which give the caterpillars resistance to the toxins produced by the crop plants. Potentially, this could lead to problems of widespread resistance in the moths. To reduce the risk of this happening, the GM crops are grown alongside non-GM varieties of the crop. This reduces the overall damage caused by the moths, while not increasing the chance that **natural selection** will produce populations of moths that are all resistant to the plant toxins.

THINGS TO DO AND THINK ABOUT

1   For each of the adaptations of the kangaroo rat described in Example 1, decide whether it is a behavioural or a physiological adaptation and say how it contributes to the survival of the animal.

2   How does the Lewis Carroll quote of the Red Queen illustrate the idea of the need for constant adaptation by a species?

3   What are the potential benefits and potential problems which can result from the use of genetic modification of organisms in the production of foods?

ADAPTATION, NATURAL SELECTION AND THE EVOLUTION OF SPECIES 3

NATURAL SELECTION AND SPECIATION

Natural selection

Natural selection is sometimes referred to as **'the survival of the fittest'**. It is the result of two factors acting together.

- In normal conditions, every species produces more offspring than the environment can support. This produces intraspecific competition between the individuals of a species.

- Variations occur naturally in a species. This means that some individuals will be better adapted to their environment than others. These individuals have a greater chance of surviving, reproducing and passing on the genetic information which gave them the beneficial variations.

In this way, the environment, or nature, selects individuals who possess beneficial variations. These individuals survive better than individuals who do not possess the variations. In the species as a whole, the genes which produce the beneficial variations persist and increase in the population. Genes that produce less beneficial or disadvantageous variations become less frequent in the population.

Speciation

A species is normally defined as a group of individuals which can interbreed to produce fertile offspring.

Speciation is the process by which new species come into existence and by which the number of species increases. Speciation depends on evolutionary change through the process of natural selection, as described earlier. Speciation begins with populations of individuals must become isolated from other populations of the same species.

Variations still occur within separated populations, but the process of natural selection will be different in each. This is because the environmental conditions experienced by each population are different. Natural selection, therefore, favours different variations in each population. Given enough time, isolated populations will become so different that they will be unable to interbreed, even if the separated populations were able to merge together. At this point, the separated populations are considered to be different species.

Here are some examples of speciation.

 **EXAMPLE 1**   Galapagos finches

The Galapagos Islands are volcanic islands in the Pacific Ocean. In the years following their formation they were gradually colonised by plants and animals which arrived there by chance and which became isolated from the mainland populations.

Included in these arrivals were members of a species of finch from the mainland of South America. Through the mechanism of variation and natural selection, this single species of finch has evolved into a range of different species which utilise different food sources. In this way, they occupy different ecological niches. This was not possible on the mainland because the equivalent niches were already occupied by other species. Niches are covered on page 95.

Niches are covered on page 95.

The Galapagos finches evolved from a single species from mainland South America

contd

EXAMPLE 2   Arctic char

The Arctic char is a species of fish related to salmon. Like salmon, they breed in freshwater and migrate to the sea as young fish. They return to rivers to breed when they are mature.

During the last ice age, populations of these fish became trapped in some deep freshwater lochs in Scotland. Here they became isolated populations and have evolved into a true freshwater species.

They are a relatively rare species in Scotland but attempts are being made to farm them for food, in the same way as salmon are farmed.

The Arctic char

EXAMPLE 3   Arran whitebeam

The Arran whitebeam is a species of tree found only on the Scottish island of Arran. It is thought to be a hybrid of two related tree species. It has become established in an ecological niche which the two parent species are unable to occupy successfully. It is found in only a few isolated sites on the island and is considered to be in danger of extinction.

The Arran whitebeam

EXAMPLE 4   St Kilda wren

St Kilda is a remote Scottish island which was inhabited until 1930, when the remaining residents were evacuated to mainland Scotland.

It has a population of wrens that is a different sub-species to the mainland population of wrens. The St Kilda wren is larger, heavier, paler in colour, has longer wings and a stouter bill. Given enough time, this isolated population will evolve into a separate species.

ONLINE

Find out more about the wildlife of St. Kilda by watching the clip at www.brightredbooks.net/N5Biology

St Kilda wren

Mainland wren

ONLINE TEST

To see how much you've learned about natural selection and speciation, test yourself at www.brightredbooks.net/N5Biology

THINGS TO DO AND THINK ABOUT

1   For each of the Examples 1–4 decide what barrier caused the isolation of one population from other populations of the same species.

2   What other factors could result in isolation of one population from another?

HUMAN IMPACT ON THE ENVIRONMENT 1

FOOD PRODUCTION

The increasing human population

For most of the time that humans have existed on Earth (perhaps as long as 50 000 years), the total population size has remained relatively small. This began to change in the 1800s when industrialisation and changes in agriculture led to increases in food production and wealth.

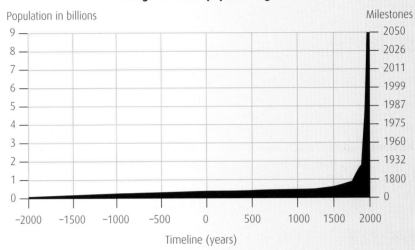

Changes in world population growth

Population in billions

Milestones: 2050, 2026, 2011, 1999, 1987, 1975, 1960, 1932, 1800, 0

Timeline (years)

DON'T FORGET ✚

An increase in food production is necessary to support the world's increasing human population. This inevitably has effects on the Earth's ecosystems and on other species of animals and plants.

Notice that the total population did not reach 1 billion until about 1800. It then took only another 132 years to reach 2 billion, then another 28 years to reach 3 billion, 15 more years to reach 4 billion, 12 years to reach 5 billion and 12 more to reach 6 billion. At the present time, there are more than 7 billion humans alive.

It is possible to produce enough food to feed all of the Earth's population but problems of distribution, conflicts, political disputes and adverse weather conditions mean that widespread starvation still occurs in some parts of the world.

METHODS OF INCREASING FOOD PRODUCTION

The dramatic increase in the human population has been possible because of increases in food production. This has been due to a number of factors:

- Increased mechanisation – this has led to more intensive farming, which gives an increase in production using fewer workers.

- **Monoculture** – this is the growing of a single crop on a large scale. Fewer types of resources are needed, such as the machinery for soil preparation, planting, harvesting, storage and transport. Monoculture encourages specific pests because of the abundance of a particular crop.

- **Pesticides** – crops can be badly affected by a range of pests. These include insects which feed on the crop plants, weeds which compete for resources needed by the crop plants and fungi and viruses which cause diseases in the crop plants. Pesticides are chemicals which are used to prevent loss of crops by killing the pests.

- Genetically modified (GM) crops – it is now possible to insert specific genes into varieties of crop plants to give them desirable characteristics, such as increased

contd

growth rates, resistance to pests and diseases, and increased content of specific nutrients. The use of GM food is subject to legal approval and this varies from country to country. Early use of GM crops was in the production of vegetable oil used for cooking and margarine manufacture, and in the production of sugar and corn. The use of GM crops is expected to increase as time goes on.

- Fertilisers – planting and harvesting crops results in the continual removal of nutrients from the soil. When crops are harvested, these nutrients are not replaced by the natural processes of death and decay. The application of manure has long been used to replace nutrients in the soil, but in modern agriculture artificial fertilisers are used as the main method of replacing important minerals.

The table shows the importance of two minerals to plants.

Mineral element	Importance	Deficiency symptoms
Nitrogen	Nitrogen is present in protein, nucleic acids, ATP, chlorophyll and other important compounds.	Very stunted growth Yellow leaves (rather than green) Leaf bases turn red
Magnesium	Magnesium is part of the structure of chlorophyll molecules.	Poor growth Yellow leaves (rather than green)

PROBLEMS ASSOCIATED WITH INTENSIVE FARMING

The methods used to produce food on a large scale create a number of problems which can affect the environment:

- Fertilisers – in some circumstances fertilisers are washed out of the soil and into local waterways, such as rivers and lochs. This is especially so if an excess of fertiliser has been used. The fertiliser can cause excessive growth of aquatic algae, called an **algal bloom**. The algae eventually die and bacterial concentrations in the water increase as they feed on and decompose the dead algae. The bacteria use dissolved oxygen from the water and the decreased oxygen availability can lead to the death of other organisms, such as fish and aquatic invertebrates.

- Pesticides – the chemicals used to control the pests of crops are, by definition, toxic. In the past, some of these chemicals were found to be persistent. This means that once they enter the tissues of an organism, they remain and are not removed.
The amount of such a chemical may be small in the body of an individual pest organism, but if a larger predator species eats several of the pests the chemical will accumulate in the body of the predator. This effect can happen at each stage of food chains, multiplying the amount of chemical present (**bioaccumulation**). The result is that toxic quantities can be built up in the bodies of larger predators. Populations of many birds of prey declined because of the use of persistent pesticides. The birds produced eggs with thin shells that failed to develop and hatch. One such chemical is DDT. This used on a large scale as an insecticide in many parts of the world. Its use as an agricultural pesticide is now banned throughout the world but, controversially, it is still used in some countries to control insect pests which carry diseases such as malaria. Despite being banned in the USA in 1972, DDT was found in almost all human blood samples tested there in 2005. DDT was not banned in Britain until 1984.

ONLINE TEST

Check how much you know about intensive food production at www. brightredbooks.net/ N5Biology

ONLINE

Find out more about the effects of intense farming online at www. brightredbooks.net/ N5Biology

THINGS TO DO AND THINK ABOUT

DDT has been found to be present today in human milk and in the tissues of ocean fish. How can this be explained?

HUMAN IMPACT ON THE ENVIRONMENT 2

THE CONSEQUENCES OF PEST CONTROL

The increased use of pesticides causes many environmental problems which must be monitored. Alternative methods of dealing with pests may be available, but these can cause other problems.

INDICATOR SPECIES

We have already discussed the importance of lichens as indicators of air pollution (page 92). Other organisms also act as important indicators, their presence or absence giving information about the levels of pollution in a habitat.

EXAMPLE 1   Nymphs of mayflies and stoneflies

These are the juvenile forms of flying insects. They spend several years in freshwater rivers and streams before emerging as flying adults. They can only survive in unpolluted water which has a high dissolved oxygen concentration and so they are used as indicators of little or no pollution.

Mayfly nymph

Stonefly nymph

EXAMPLE 2   Tubifex worms and rat-tailed maggots

Tubifex worms are small segmented worms, sometimes known as sludge worms. Rat-tailed maggots are the larval stages of drone flies. They have long breathing tubes through which they can breathe air. Both species can survive in polluted, oxygen-deficient water and they are used as indicators of these conditions.

Tubifex worms

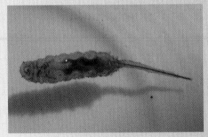

Rat-tailed maggot

ONLINE TEST ✓

Test how much you know about indicator species at www.brightredbooks.net/N5Biology

BIOLOGICAL CONTROL

Biological control is the use of natural predators and diseases to control pest organisms as an alternative to the use of toxic chemicals.

contd

Myxomatosis

Myxomatosis is a disease-causing virus which is used to control rabbit populations that have reached problem levels.

In 1950, the virus was introduced into the rabbit population in Australia. In two years rabbit numbers decreased from 600 million to 100 million. In 1955, myxomatosis killed 95% of rabbits in Britain.

Rabbit affected by myxomatosis

Rabbits which survive the disease are resistant and so numbers do recover. However, not all the offspring of these rabbits are resistant, so the disease is still present in rabbit populations today and affected animals can still be found.

Ladybirds

Both the larval stage of ladybirds and the adults are voracious predators of aphids. Aphids can cause great damage to plants by their feeding and by the transmission of diseases. Ladybirds can be raised in large numbers and released onto crop plants where they can be effective in reducing the number of aphids.

Ladybird eating an aphid

Cactus moth (Cactoblastis) caterpillars

These caterpillars feed on cactus plants. In South America, the moths have been introduced into areas outside of their natural habitat in order to prevent the spread of cactus plants into areas needed for agriculture. In some areas, they have been so successful that steps have been taken to kill the moths in order to prevent complete destruction of the cacti. This demonstrates the problems that can occur when a species is introduced into a different environment where there may be no natural predators.

Cactoblastis caterpillars feeding on a cactus

GENETICALLY MODIFIED CROPS

The use of GM crops has already been mentioned in relation to increasing food production (page 114). The insertion of specific genes which increase crop yields by giving resistance to pests and diseases or by enabling faster growth of the crops may help in the production of more food without causing some of the problems associated with the use of chemicals. However, use of GM crops could result in problems similar to those associated with the overuse of antibiotics. That is, variation and natural selection may result in pest species becoming resistant to the built-in deterrents of GM crops, making them more difficult to control.

 **DON'T FORGET**

Often, in the attempt to rid ourselves of one problem affecting ecosystems we introduce a new and more complicated issue!

 THINGS TO DO AND THINK ABOUT

Introduced species may have an adverse effect on native species by out-competing them or by becoming a predator of them. Sometimes another predatory species may be introduced as a biological control for the introduced species.

Suggest how this measure may:

1   increase biodiversity in the area

2   decrease biodiversity in the area.

UNIT 1 – CELL BIOLOGY

Active site
The area on the surface of an enzyme molecule where substrate molecules become attached and undergo a chemical reaction.

Active transport
The movement of a substance across a cell membrane from a low concentration to a high concentration. This requires the expenditure of energy by the cell.

Aerobic respiration
The release of energy from foods such as glucose using oxygen; also produces water and carbon dioxide.

Amino acid
The building blocks of proteins.

Antibody
A y-shaped protein which targets and neutralises foreign objects such as bacteria and viruses in the body. Different antibodies are specific for different foreign proteins.

Aseptic technique
A procedure carried out using precautions which ensure sterile conditions. Such procedures are used when working with cell cultures and in hospital operations.

ATP
Adenosine triphosphate – an important chemical involved in the management of chemical energy in cells.

Base pairs
The bonding of complementary bases in DNA and RNA which contribute to the double helix structure of DNA, the replication of chromosomes prior to cell division and to the synthesis of proteins in cells.

Callus
A mass of unspecialised plant cells grown from samples of plant tissue cultured artificially. Such a callus may be induced to develop into a whole plant.

Carbon fixation
A stage of photosynthesis which does not require light and in which carbon dioxide is combined with hydrogen to form carbohydrate.

Catalyst
A substance which speeds up a chemical reaction but which is left unaltered after the reaction.

Cell
The smallest living structure. Cells are the building blocks of multicellular organisms and they also exist as independent unicellular organisms.

Cell culture
The growth of cells in artificial conditions and in isolation from their original source.

Cell equator
The area at the middle of a cell where chromosomes become aligned during cell division.

Cell membrane
The membrane which separates the interior of a cell from the outside environment. It consists of a double layer of lipid molecules with associated proteins and is responsible for controlling the movement of substances into and out of the cell.

Cell wall
The structural part of a plant cell found outside of the cell membrane and which holds the cell in place with its neighbours. It is formed mainly of cellulose and gives support to plant tissues. Cell walls of fungi and bacteria have a different structure.

Cellulose
A structural carbohydrate which forms the major component of plant cell walls.

Chlorophyll
A green pigment found in the chloroplasts of green plants. It is responsible for the absorption of light during the first stage of photosynthesis.

Chloroplast
A membranous organelle present in the cytoplasm of cells in the green areas of plants. Several chloroplasts can be present in a single cell. These contain the pigment chlorophyll and are the sites of photosynthesis.

Chromatid
One of a pair of identical DNA strands which together form a chromosome.

Chromosome
An organised structure composed of dna and associated proteins, present in the nucleus of a cell. The dna contains the genetic information of the organism which controls the development and activities of the cell. The number of chromosomes present varies from species to species.

Concentration gradient
The difference in the concentration of a dissolved substance between two areas, often the inside and outside of a cell.

Cytoplasm
A gel-like substance inside a cell and surrounded by the cell membrane. The cytoplasm contains the cell organelles and is the location of the chemical reactions of the cell.

Degradation
A chemical reaction in which a larger substrate molecule is broken down into smaller product molecules.

Denaturation
Changes to the shape and structure of an enzyme molecule which stop it functioning. Denaturation is usually the result of high temperatures or extremes of pH.

Diffusion

The movement of gaseous or dissolved particles from an area of higher concentration to one of lower concentration. It is essentially a spreading of atoms or molecules and results from their natural movement. It can cause the movement of substances into or out of cells without any energy expenditure by the cell.

Diploid number

This is the number of chromosomes present in the body cells of an organism. It refers to the two sets of chromosomes inherited by the organism, one set from each parent.

DNA

Deoxyribonucleic acid – the chemical which forms the structure of chromosomes and which contains the genetic information of the organism.

Double helix

The shape of the DNA molecule in a chromosome. It refers to the two parallel strands of the molecule which are held together by bonds between complementary base pairs.

Electron microscope

A type of microscope which uses beams of electrons instead of light rays to produce images. Electron microscopes have enabled the ultrastructure of cells to be studied.

Enzyme

A protein catalyst produced by a cell. Enzymes are responsible for all the chemical reactions which take place in cells. Each enzyme is specific to one type of substrate and for one type of chemical reaction.

Ethanol

A substance produced from pyruvate during the process of fermentation in yeast.

Fermentation pathway

The chemical pathway which occurs during respiration in the absence of oxygen. It involves the conversion of glucose to pyruvate, and then to lactic acid, or to ethanol and carbon dioxide.

Fermenter

A container in which the conditions can be controlled and made ideal for the growth of microorganisms.

Flaccid

The state of a plant cell which contains less than the maximum amount of water it can hold. The cell contents do not push against the cell wall. A tissue in which the cells are flaccid will be soft and limp. In extreme circumstances, the cells may become plasmolysed.

Fluid mosaic model

The term used to describe the structure of cell membranes as a fluid double layer of lipid molecules with associated protein molecules.

Gene

A region of a chromosome which contains the genetic information for the production of a particular protein. A gene is often responsible for a particular inherited characteristic of an organism.

Genetic code

The sequence of bases on a DNA molecule which controls the sequence of amino acids in the synthesis of a protein.

Genetic engineering

The artificial transfer of genetic information (genes) from one cell to another, often of a different species.

Genetically modified organism

An organism which has had new genetic information inserted into its cells. This gives the organism new characteristics.

Glycolysis

The first stage of respiration in which glucose molecules are broken down into pyruvate molecules. Glycolysis takes place whether oxygen is present or absent.

Hormone

A chemical which is released in one part of the body, transported in the blood and affects cells in other parts of the body. They help control development and coordination. Some, but not all, hormones are proteins.

Lactic acid

A substance produced from pyruvate during the process of fermentation in bacteria and animal cells.

Light reaction (photolysis)

The first stage of photosynthesis involving the absorption of light by chlorophyll and the production of ATP and hydrogen, needed for carbon fixation.

Limiting factor

An essential factor required by a process and which limits the rate of that process because it has limited availability. If several factors are required, normally only one of them will be limiting the process at any given time.

Lipid

A type of fat molecule found in cell membranes.

Lock and key hypothesis

The description of the mechanism of enzyme action in which the shape of the enzyme's active site must match the shape of the substrate molecule for a reaction to take place.

Mitochondrion

A membranous organelle found in the cytoplasm of cells. Many mitochondria may be present in a cell. They are the sites of the aerobic stages of respiration.

GLOSSARY

Mitosis
The process of division of a cell nucleus prior to the division of the cell into two daughter cells. Mitosis involves the separation of replicated chromosomes into two identical diploid sets so that the daughter cells are both genetically identical to the parent cell.

Nucleus
The cell organelle which contains the chromosomes of the cell. It is surrounded by a membrane which separates the chromosomes from the cell cytoplasm.

Optimum conditions
The values of factors such as temperature, pH and substrate concentration at which an enzyme-controlled reaction takes place at its maximum rate.

Organelle
A small structure found in the cytoplasm of a cell and which has a particular function. There are several types of organelles present in most cells.

Osmosis
The movement of water molecules from an area of high water concentration to an area of lower water concentration through a selectively permeable membrane. Osmosis is a particular example of diffusion and does not require energy expenditure by a cell.

Palisade mesophyll
A layer of cells close to the surface of a leaf. The cells contain numerous chloroplasts and carry out most of the photosynthesis for the plant.

Passive transport
The movement of substances into or out of a cell without the need for energy expenditure by the cell. Diffusion and osmosis are the most common examples of passive transport.

Photosynthesis
The process by which green plants produce food. It involves the production of sugar from the raw materials carbon dioxide and water using light energy. Oxygen is also produced as a by-product.

Plasmid
A small circular molecule of DNA found in bacteria, separate from the chromosomal DNA. Plasmids can be transferred between bacterial cells, allowing the transfer of genetic information. This ability is used in genetic engineering.

Plasmolysed
The condition of a plant cell which has lost water by osmosis to the extent that its vacuole and cytoplasm have shrunk away from the cell wall.

Product
The chemical(s) which are formed at the end of a chemical reaction, including a reaction controlled by an enzyme.

Pyruvate
The end product of glycolysis.

Respiration
The process by which a cell releases energy from food molecules. In aerobic conditions, glucose is broken down into carbon dioxide and water. This is more efficient than the partial breakdown achieved in conditions which lack oxygen.

Ribosome
A small organelle which acts as the site of protein synthesis in a cell. Ribosomes are very numerous.

RNA
Ribonucleic acid – a nucleic acid similar to DNA but with some structural differences and with smaller molecules. Messenger RNA (mRNA) is involved in protein synthesis, carrying a copy of the genetic code from DNA to the ribosomes.

Selectively permeable
The property of cell membranes which allows small soluble molecules to pass through but which prevents larger molecules from doing so.

Specificity
The ability of an enzyme molecule to catalyse only one type of chemical reaction. It is due to the need for the shape of the enzyme active site to match the shape of the substrate molecule(s).

Spindle fibres
Microscopic fibres produced in a cell during cell division and which control the separation of chromatids between the daughter cells.

Spongy mesophyll
A layer of loosely packed cells below the palisade mesophyll cells in a leaf. The spongy mesophyll cells carry out photosynthesis but they are also important because air spaces between the cells allow absorption of the carbon dioxide needed for photosynthesis.

Starch
An insoluble carbohydrate. Its large molecules consist of chains of glucose molecules. It is used as a storage material by plants.

Structural protein
These are fibrous proteins such as keratin which forms the hair, nails, claws, skin and feathers of animals. Other structural proteins are found in muscle tissue, tendons and ligaments.

Substrate
The substance(s) which binds to an enzyme and which then undergoes a chemical reaction.

Synthesis
A chemical reaction in which smaller substrate molecules react to form a larger product molecule.

Turgid

The state of a plant cell which contains the maximum amount of water it can hold. The cell contents are swollen and push against the cell wall. A tissue in which the cells are turgid will be firm and so turgidity contributes to the support of a plant.

Vacuole

A membrane-bound sac containing a watery solution and found in the cytoplasm of plant cells. The vacuole contributes to the state of turgidity of the cell.

Vector

A vehicle used to transfer genetic material such as a gene from one organism to another.

Virus

A small particulate structure which can replicate only inside the cells of living organisms. A virus consists of a protein coat and a strand of DNA or RNA which controls the metabolism of the host cell, causing it to produce more virus particles.

UNIT 2 - MULTICELLULAR ORGANISMS

Allele

One of a number of alternative forms of the same gene. Diploid cells contain two alleles for each gene, one in each of the two sets of chromosomes. Haploid gametes contain only one allele for each gene.

Alveolus

A microscopic, thin-walled air sac found at the end of the bronchioles in the lungs. The alveoli form the gas-exchange surfaces between the blood and the air.

Aorta

The largest artery in the body. The aorta carries oxygenated blood from the left ventricle and branches from the aorta pass blood to all areas of the body.

Artery

A blood vessel with thick, muscular walls which carries high pressure blood away from the heart to other parts of the body.

Atrium

A receiving chamber of the heart. The left atrium receives blood from the lungs and the right atrium receives blood from other parts of the body. Blood passes from the atria into their associated ventricles.

Blood

A liquid tissue, consisting mainly of plasma and blood cells, which transports materials around the body. Plasma is a watery fluid containing dissolved substances. Red blood cells transport oxygen and white blood cells help protect the body against infection.

Bronchiole

A small air tube of the lungs. Bronchioles branch into smaller and smaller tubes which end at clusters of alveoli.

Bronchus

One of the two large air tubes of the breathing system. The bronchi are branches of the trachea. One bronchus leads to each lung.

Capillary

A microscopic blood vessel. The capillaries are the sites of exchange of substances between the blood and the body cells. Blood passes from small arteries into the capillaries and then into small veins.

Cartilage

A tough protective material of the body. Rings of cartilage strengthen the main air tubes of the lungs, preventing them from closing over when bending.

Central nervous system

The central nervous system (CNS) consists of the brain and the spinal cord. These areas receive sensory information, process it and initiate any necessary responses to it.

Cerebellum

The area of the brain which coordinates information about movement and position, and contributes to the fine control of muscles involved in maintaining balance.

Cerebrum

The area of the brain which controls voluntary muscular movement and is the centre for functions such as memory, learning and decision-making.

Cilia

Small hair-like structures that are part of cells and which line the air tubes of the breathing system. They move with a sweeping action which shifts mucus and any trapped material away from the lungs and towards the throat.

Companion cell

A small cell which lies alongside a sieve tube cell of the phloem. Sieve tube cells do not have a nucleus and the companion cells control their activities.

Coronary artery

A branch of the aorta which carries blood to the muscle cells of the heart walls, supplying them with nutrients and oxygen.

Diabetes

A disease which results in a high blood sugar level. Type 1 diabetes is caused by the failure of the pancreas to produce the hormone insulin. It is controlled with insulin injections. Type 2 diabetes is caused by the failure of the body to respond to insulin. It can be controlled with other medications and diet.

Diploid

This refers to a cell with the diploid number of chromosomes – in other words, the full chromosome complement of two sets. One set of chromosomes is inherited from the female parent and one set is inherited from the male parent. The diploid number is usually referred to as 2n, where n = the number of chromosomes in a single set.

Dominant

This refers to an allele which shows its effect when present together with a different allele of the same gene.

Endocrine gland

A gland which produces a hormone and secretes it into the blood for transport around the body.

Endocrine system

The system of hormonal control in the body.

Epidermis

The outermost layer of cells of an organism. It acts as a barrier, protecting other cells.

Fertilisation

The fusion of the nucleus of a male gamete with the nucleus of a female gamete. Each gamete is haploid (contains one set of chromosomes) and the resulting zygote is diploid (contains two sets of chromosomes).

Gamete

A sex cell which takes part in fertilisation. Gametes are normally referred to as male or female. Male gametes are called sperm cells in animals and pollen cells in plants. They are called egg cells or ova in animals and ovule cells in plants.

Gene

A unit of genetic information which controls a characteristic of an organism.

Genotype

The genetic information contained in a cell with respect to a particular characteristic. The genotype is usually shown as the abbreviations of the two alleles involved.

Glucagon

A hormone, produced by the pancreas, which causes the conversion of glycogen to glucose by the liver. It has the opposite effect to insulin and is part of the mechanism which controls the blood sugar level.

Glycogen

An insoluble carbohydrate consisting of chains of glucose molecules. It is used as a storage chemical in animals, particularly in the liver.

Guard cell

A cell which helps to form a stoma. Two curved guard cells create a pore (the stoma) between them. Changes in the shape of the guard cells cause the opening and closing of the stoma (plural, stomata).

Haemoglobin

A protein which contains an atom of iron and which is found in red blood cells. Haemoglobin combines with oxygen molecules for transportation around the body.

Haploid

This refers to a cell with the haploid number of chromosomes – in other words, only a single set of chromosomes. Such cells are gametes which are intended to join with another gamete at fertilisation, restoring the diploid chromosome number. The haploid number is usually referred to as n, where n = the number of chromosomes in a single set.

Heart

The organ which pumps blood around the body. In mammals it consists of four chambers: two atria which receive blood and two ventricles which pump blood.

Heterozygous

An organism which contains two different alleles for a particular characteristic.

Homozygous

An organism which contains two of the same alleles for a characteristic. It does not matter whether the alleles are both dominant or both recessive.

Hormone

A chemical which is produced by an endocrine gland, released into the blood and causes a response at some other part of the body. Hormones are involved in the development of the body and in regulating some metabolic processes. Plants also produce hormone-like substances.

Insulin

A hormone, produced by the pancreas, which causes the conversion of glucose to glycogen by the liver and the uptake of glucose from the blood by other body cells. It has the opposite effect to glucagon and is part of the mechanism which controls blood sugar level.

Lacteal

A small vessel in the villus which absorbs the products of fat digestion.

Lignin

A substance which is deposited in the walls of xylem cells. It strengthens the cells for their role in water transport in plants. It also forms the woody supporting tissue of plants that live for many years.

Liver

A organ of the body which has many functions including the storage of glycogen, the breakdown of old red blood cells, the production of hormones, detoxification of harmful substances such as alcohol and the production of bile, which aids digestion.

Medulla

The area of the brain which controls processes such as heart rate and breathing rate.

Meristem

Plant tissue consisting of undifferentiated cells which divide to produce the new cells needed for growth. Meristems are located in particular areas of plants, meaning that plant growth is localised.

Mesophyll

The inner photosynthetic tissue of plant leaves. There are two types, palisade mesophyll and spongy mesophyll.

Palisade mesophyll is a layer of cells close to the surface of a leaf. The cells contain numerous chloroplasts and carry out most of the photosynthesis for the plant.

Spongy mesophyll is a layer of loosely packed cells below the palisade mesophyll cells in a leaf. The spongy mesophyll cells carry out photosynthesis but they are also important because air spaces between the cells allow absorption of the carbon dioxide needed for photosynthesis.

Mitosis

Division of the nucleus during cell division. It ensures that the two daughter cells produced have the same chromosome complement as that of the parent cell.

Mucus

A slippery substance produced by mucus glands. It lubricates food for swallowing and traps foreign particles in the air passages of the breathing system.

Neuron

A nerve cell. There are different types of neurons. Sensory neurons carry impulses from sensory receptors to the CNS. Motor neurons carry impulses from the CNS to muscles or glands. Relay neurons transfer impulses within the CNS.

Organ

This is a part of the body, such as the heart, stomach or brain, which has a particular function. An organ consists of a number of different types of tissue which contribute to the overall function.

Oxyhaemoglobin

The form of haemoglobin when it has combined with oxygen.

Pancreas

The organ which produces the hormones insulin and glucagon. It also produces a range of digestive enzymes.

Peristalsis

Muscular movements which push food along the alimentary canal by means of wave-like contractions of the circular muscles.

Phenotype

The characteristics possessed by an organism which result from the inherited information of its genotype, although these features may be altered by environmental effects. Phenotype may be used for individual characteristics.

Phloem

Plant tissue responsible for the transport of dissolved sugar around the plant. It consists of elongated cells which form sieve tubes and associated companion cells.

Polygenic

The inheritance of a characteristic which is controlled by two or more genes. This produces greater variation of that characteristic and is part of the reason for the continuous variation shown by some characteristics.

Pulmonary artery

An artery which carries blood from the right ventricle to the lungs.

Pulmonary vein

A vein which carries blood from the lungs to the right atrium.

GLOSSARY

Recessive
This refers to an allele which does not show its effect when present together with a different allele of the same gene.

Red blood cell
A cell carried by the blood which is responsible for the transport of oxygen. Red blood cells are very numerous and are characterised by their biconcave shape and lack of a nucleus.

Reflex action
An automatic, involuntary response to a stimulus. Reflex actions are protective or they help maintain body processes. Protective examples are coughing, sneezing and the withdrawal from hot objects. Examples which maintain body processes are the production of saliva and the control of breathing rate.

Reflex arc
A nervous pathway which controls a reflex action. It does not require a conscious input from the brain, allowing the response to take place almost instantly.

Root hair
An extension of a plant root hair cell which provides an enlarged surface area for the uptake of water and minerals from the soil.

Sensory receptor
A cell which produces a nerve impulse in response to a stimulus. Such cells may form part of a specialised sense organ.

Stem cell
An undifferentiated animal cell which has the ability to divide by mitosis to produce more similar cells and which can develop into one of a number of specialised cell types.

Stimulus
Something which causes a response. In the body, a stimulus is detected by a sensory receptor.

Stoma
A pore in the epidermis usually on the bottom surface of a leaf. Stomata are very numerous and each is formed by two curved guard cells which can open and close the pore.

Synapse
The gap between two neurons. The nerve signal is carried across a synapse by a chemical transmitter that is produced at the end of one neuron and detected by the other neuron.

Tissue
A group of similar cells which are adapted to perform the same function. Tissues of different types may be associated together in a particular organ.

Trachea
The main air tube of the breathing system. The trachea passes down from the throat into the chest, where it branches into two bronchi. One bronchus goes into each lung.

Transpiration
The loss of water from the leaves of a plant. Water evaporates from the surfaces of the spongy mesophyll into the air spaces of the leaf. It then diffuses through the stomata into the outside air.

Valve
A structure found in the heart and in veins which prevents the backflow of blood.

Variation - continuous
Differences in a characteristic which show a continuous range of possibilities between a minimum value and a maximum value. Such variations, for example mass and height, are normally the result of polygenic inheritance.

Variation - discrete
Differences in a characteristic which show a limited range of distinct possibilities. Such variations, for example blood group and tongue rolling ability, are normally the result of single gene inheritance.

Vein
A blood vessel which carries low pressure blood towards the heart from other parts of the body.

Vena cava
The largest vein in the body. The vena cava carries deoxygenated blood from various parts of the body to the right atrium.

Ventricle
A pumping chamber of the heart. The right ventricle pumps blood to the lungs and the left ventricle pumps blood to other parts of the body. Blood passes into the ventricles from their associated atria.

Villus
A small projection on the inner lining of the small intestine. Villi increase the surface area to increase the rate of absorption of digested food.

Xylem
Plant tissue responsible for the transport of water and dissolved minerals from the roots to other parts of the plant. It is made from elongated dead cells which form continuous hollow tubes that are strengthened with lignin.

Zygote
The cell produced by the fertilisation of one gamete by another. The zygote is the first cell of a new individual. It has a diploid chromosome complement which is maintained in all subsequent body cells by mitosis.

UNIT 3 - LIFE ON EARTH

Abiotic factor
A non-living chemical or physical factor in the environment which has an effect on the ecosystem. Chemical factors include industrial waste, pH and fertiliser run-off. Physical factors include light, temperature and humidity.

Adaptation
A characteristic of an organism or species that has developed by evolution and which aids its survival. It could also mean the process of adapting.

Algal bloom
The rapid growth in the population of aquatic algae in ponds and lakes caused by an increase in the concentration of inorganic nutrients. These could be due to fertiliser run-off or industrial waste entering water courses. The subsequent death and decomposition of the algae can lead to a reduction in the oxygen concentration of the water and the death of fish and other animals.

Allele
One of a number of alternative forms of the same gene. Diploid cells contain two alleles for each gene, one in each of the two sets of chromosomes. Haploid gametes contain only one allele for each gene.

Bioaccumulation
The build-up of toxic substances in the tissues of an organism because the substance is persistent. This means that the rate at which the substance is broken down or excreted by the organism is slower that the rate it absorbs it from its food or its environment.

Biodiversity
The range of different species present. Biodiversity is normally considered within an ecosystem but it can be considered at other levels, for example within a biome or over the whole planet. Biodiversity may consider the variations that exist within a single species.

Biological control
The use of living organisms to control pests. The control organism may act as a predator or it may cause a disease of the pest organism.

Biome
A biome is a major region of the earth. Each biome is characterised by a distinctive community of plants and animals that are adapted to the climatic and geographic conditions existing in the biome.

Biotic factor
A biological factor, one which involves a living organism, in the environment which has an effect on the ecosystem. Biological factors include food sources, predation and disease.

Carnivore
An animal which gets its energy by eating other animals.

Community
The populations of all the different species present in an ecosystem.

Competition - interspecific
Competition for a resource which occurs between individuals of different species.

Competition - intraspecific
Competition for a resource which occurs between individuals of the same species. This type of competition can be the most severe because the requirements of the individuals involved are identical.

Consumer
An organism which gets its energy by feeding on other organisms or their waste.

Decomposer
An organism which is involved in the breakdown of dead organic material and organic waste. This process is important because nutrients are released into the soil and become available for new plant growth. Bacteria and fungi are the main groups of decomposers.

Deforestation
The large-scale removal of trees from an area. This may be to gain the timber or to clear land for agriculture. The effect can be to make the soil vulnerable to erosion.

Denitrification
A stage in the nitrogen cycle carried out by denitrifying bacteria in soil in which nitrates are converted into nitrogen gas.

Desertification
A process in which arid land becomes desert. It may be the result of climate change. It may also be caused by attempting to cultivate unsuitable land which borders an area of desert. If this attempt fails it can allow the area of desert to spread.

Ecosystem
An ecological system consisting of a habitat together with its community of organisms. The organisms are interlinked through food webs; energy and nutrients are transferred through these.

Evolution
The change in the inherited characteristics of organisms from generation to generation. Evolution leads to the gradual change in the characteristics of a species and also to the divergence of populations into new species.

Fertiliser

Material that is added to soil in order to increase the supply of nutrients to plants. Fertiliser can be organic, for example manure. It can also be inorganic, for example compounds of nitrogen, phosphorus and potassium. Excess inorganic fertiliser may be washed into rivers and streams, and cause problems of pollution.

Food chain

A linear sequence of organisms showing the feeding relationships between them. A food chain always starts with a producer (green plant) and ends with a top predator that is not eaten by anything else. Each link in the food chain represents the transfer of energy and nutrients from one species to the next. Food chains are normally parts of much more complex food webs.

Genetically modified (GM) organism

An organism which has had new genetic information inserted into its cells. This gives the organism new characteristics.

Habitat

An ecological or environmental area in which a population of organisms live.

Herbivore

An animal which gets its energy by eating plants.

Indicator species

A species of organisms whose populations are easily affected by changes in environmental conditions. Monitoring the populations of such species can indicate changes in, for example, levels of pollution or climate change.

Monoculture

The large-scale cultivation of a single crop. This has economic benefits because large yields can be obtained with minimal labour and range of equipment. It can cause problems of soil depletion and the encouragement of pests and diseases.

Mutagen

A mutagenic agent – something that can increase the chance of a mutation taking place. Examples of mutagens are various forms of radiation, such as x-rays, gamma rays and ultraviolet radiation. Some chemicals are mutagenic because they can react with DNA.

Mutation

A change to the genetic information of an organism. This may be a change to the number or structure of the chromosomes, or a change to the DNA base sequence of a chromosome. Mutations normally occur as mistakes during cell division. Mutations during the formation of gametes are of greater significance because these mistakes may become part of the genetic information of a new individual.

Natural selection

The process by which variations may increase or decrease in frequency in a species because the variations affect the chance of survival of individuals which possess them. Individuals with advantageous variations are selected by the natural environment to survive and reproduce. In doing so, the advantageous variations increase within the species and disadvantageous variations decrease.

Niche

This is the role of a species within its ecosystem. The niches of different species may overlap but they are not identical. A description of a niche would include the food and other resources used by the species, its predators and the habitat it occupies.

Nitrification

A stage in the nitrogen cycle carried out by nitrifying bacteria in soil in which ammonium compounds, produced by decomposition, are converted to nitrites and then to nitrates, which can be absorbed by plants.

Nitrogen cycle

The cyclic series of processes by which nitrogen is circulated between the atmosphere, plants, animals, bacteria and soil.

Nitrogen fixation

A stage in the nitrogen cycle carried out by nitrogen-fixing bacteria in soil and in the root nodules of some plants. Nitrogen fixation involves the conversion of atmospheric nitrogen to ammonium compounds, which are converted to nitrites, which can be used by plants.

Paired-statement key

An identification tool in which a series of pairs of contrasting statements are applied to an unknown organism. Only one of the statements will be true for the organism and this will the lead to the next pair of statements. Each step reduces the number of possibilities for the organism until only one possibility is left and the organism is identified.

Parasitism

A relationship between organisms (usually of different species) in which one organism, the parasite, benefits at the expense of the other organism, the host.

Pesticide

A chemical used to kill pests. Pesticides may be specific to particular types of pests. Herbicides are used to kill unwanted plants, insecticides are used to kill insects and fungicides are used to kill fungi.

Pitfall trap

A sampling technique used to catch ground-living invertebrates.

Pollution

Something which contaminates the natural environment and which has an adverse effect.

Population

All the members of a single species in a given area.

Producer

Green plants which make their food by photosynthesis. They are the first organisms in a food chain.

Pyramid of biomass

A representation of the total biomass present at each stage of a food chain. It should include all the organisms of all species at each level of a food web; that is, all the producers, all the primary consumers and so on. Pyramids of biomass usually have a pyramidal shape but they can be distorted by large seasonal changes in biomass.

Pyramid of energy

A representation of the total energy turnover at each stage of a food chain. It gives a truer picture than pyramids of numbers or biomass because it is scaled to equivalent units of area and time for each level of the pyramid.

Pyramid of numbers

A representation of the total numbers of organisms present at each stage of a food chain. The pyramidal shape is often distorted because of large differences in the size of individual organisms at different levels.

Quadrat

A sampling tool consisting of a square frame with a standard area, used to count the numbers of stationary organisms.

Root nodule

A swelling on the roots of leguminous plants such as peas, beans and clover. The swellings contain nitrogen-fixing bacteria which enable these plants to gain additional nitrates.

Speciation

This is the origin of new species through the process of evolution. Speciation normally involves some sort of isolation of members of a species into separate sub-populations which are unable to interbreed. Continued evolution then takes place along different paths for the separated groups. Given enough time the separated sub-populations will be so different that they are considered to be different species.

Species

A group of interbreeding organisms whose offspring are fertile.

Survival of the fittest

A common interpretation of the term 'natural selection'.

Transect

A sampling technique which involves taking samples at regular intervals along a straight line. It can be used when studying the effect of changes in a variable from one area to another, for example the effect of changes in light intensity between a shaded area and an exposed area.